MURALS

WRITTEN BY
William Kelly

WITH CONTRIBUTIONS FROM
Tom Kelly
Kevin Hasson

DOCUMENTED BY
Paul Kelly

the bogside artists

ISBN 0-9541232-0-4

First published in 2001 by
The Bogside Artists
51 Stanley's Walk
Bogside, Derry
Northern Ireland
BT48 9HH
T: (028) 7128 4123
http://cain.ulst.ac.uk/bogsideartists

Guildhall Press
Unit 4, Ráth Mór Centre
Bligh's Lane
Derry, Northern Ireland
BT48 0LZ
T: (028) 7136 4413
www.ghpress.com

This book has received support from the Cultural Diversity Programme of the Community Relations Council, which aims to encourage acceptance and understanding of cultural diversity. The views expressed do not necessarily reflect those of the NI Community Relations Council.

We would also like to thank Derry City Council's Recreation and Leisure Department for supporting this publication.

WITH THANKS

The first people to be thanked are the ordinary people of the Bogside who chipped in their pennies to enable us to make the murals. Others who deserve to be mentioned are as follows: in Philadelphia, James Klingler and Molly Doherty have both to be congratulated in putting on the shows at the John Moore Gallery and at Villanova University itself; it was a resounding success in both venues. In Australia, Judith Carroll took the reins and staged the work at the UCCA, Sydney (twice), where she teaches, and also at the Sydney University. Judith is a remarkable woman by any standards. Her tireless industry on behalf of her students, her erudition, humanity and warmth demonstrate the very best there is in any of us. Her efforts on our behalf, then and subsequently, are not to be forgotten. Professor Peter Sheehan's heartfelt address at the first opening and Murdach Dynan's at the second were also memorable. Dr Dynan brought the work to the UCCA, Brisbane, and later introduced it to the Irish Association at Brisbane.

The Association is one of the largest in Australia and boasts a membership of almost 10,000. Dr Farrell also spoke there. In fact, without the help of Dr Lindsay Farrell, the Brisbane venture would not have been half as successful as it turned out to be. Dr Farrell, who teaches art at the UCCA, Brisbane, is an accomplished artist in his own right and, in his spare time, the perfect host. (His father, a sculptor, has done some wonderful work for the city of Brisbane.) Also in Australia, a special thanks to William's daughter, Claire, and to his son, Paul, who took charge of photographing and documenting the work in stills and video. Artist and teacher at Ballarat, Steve Davidson: film-maker and teacher, Tony Redmond of Melbourne, who has made a fascinating film on the theatre in Northern Ireland featuring Derry and Belfast playwrights; artists and teachers Greg Bell and Gary Mitchell at Newcastle and the curators of the galleries at Mildura, Onkaparinga, the Red House, Pica, the Irish Centre, Manhattan, as well as the department administrators of the various colleges and TAFEs we have talked at are all to be commended. We apologise for omitting the names of many other individuals who have been of enormous help to us.

Back at base, we extend our thanks to Maureen Hetherington, Bernard Devine and, of course, Eamonn Deane. Frankly, without Eamonn's consistent support and encouragement, the Bogside Artists would have despairingly chucked their paintbrushes into the bin a long time ago. Others who must be mentioned are: Mitchel McLaughlin, Damian Gorman, Pat Ramsay, Cathal Crumley, Mary Crumley, the NI Housing Executive, the McGavigan family, Raymond McCartney, Paddy Coyle, Evelyn Valley, John Kelly and Michael McKinney (Bloody Sunday Justice Campaign), Wellspring Christian Community, Derry City Council, Guildhall Press, John Moore, Charlie McManus (NYPD), Dave Burke, Jack Meehan, John Maguire, Joe McNabb, Barry and Paul Hasson, Brendan McClintock, Patricia and Gerry and all the other staff at the Central Library, Seán Doran, the *Irish News*, the *Derry Journal*, John McFadyen, Julie Pritchard and Maire Liberace, Thomas Doherty, Dermot O'Donnell, Daniel McDaid, Charlie McConnellogue, Mickey Walker, Frankie McMenamin, Hugh Gallagher, Stephen Latimer, Paul Kelly, Barney McMonagle, Eamon Melaugh, Dr Martin Melaugh (http://cain.ulst.ac.uk), City Paint and the Wilkinson family from Sydney. A special thanks to the distinguished people who wrote their commentaries for us. A particular thanks goes to the Pat Finucane Centre who have been of great assistance to us. And a special thanks also, to Seán Loughrey, who worked with us on *The Petrol Bomber* and the *Bloody Sunday* murals, as did Alan McCormick. Likely as not, we have left a few out. If so, we extend an apology to those omitted. To thank all the people who ought to be thanked would require an entire book by itself.

Brian Friel
Internationally renowned playwright and author

The work of the Bogside Artists is celebrated locally and internationally, but it is their reputation that is important both to the artists and to their locality.

The work is remarkable in that it is simultaneously a vibrant response to events still vivid in the psyche of the community and, even as it testifies, it transcends those immediate passions and proposes an historian's distance and objectivity. The work says: You know the people in these pictures because they are your neighbours and your allies and you know what they endured; but have you thought about them in this way – as a people caught up in a chaos of tumultuous events and at the same time taking control of those events and shaping a new destiny? Because we, the Bogside Artists, believe that that is what has happened. That is what we are talking about.

This dual vision is made insistent by the theatricality of the events depicted, by the almost surrealism of the painting technique, by the political awareness that animates every event depicted, and, of course, by the very scale of the work and its dominant location in the centre of communities.

This is work of conscious ostentation, of deliberate defiance. It is work that Diego Rivera would have approved of. But it has delicacy too. Every mural explains – but it also embraces. Every mural instructs – but at the same time each has the intimacy and the consolations of a family photograph.

These murals tell the city about itself, what happened to it over the past seventy years and what futures may be available to it. I suspect the Bogside Artists have a lot of excitement squaring up each new virgin gable and a lot of fun endowing it with eloquence.

They are important people.
I wish them well.

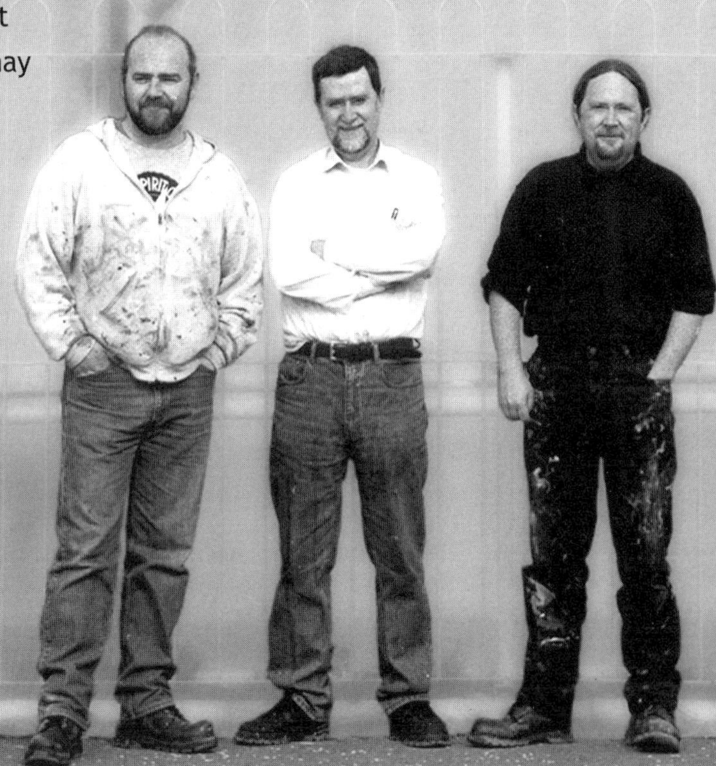

CONTENTS

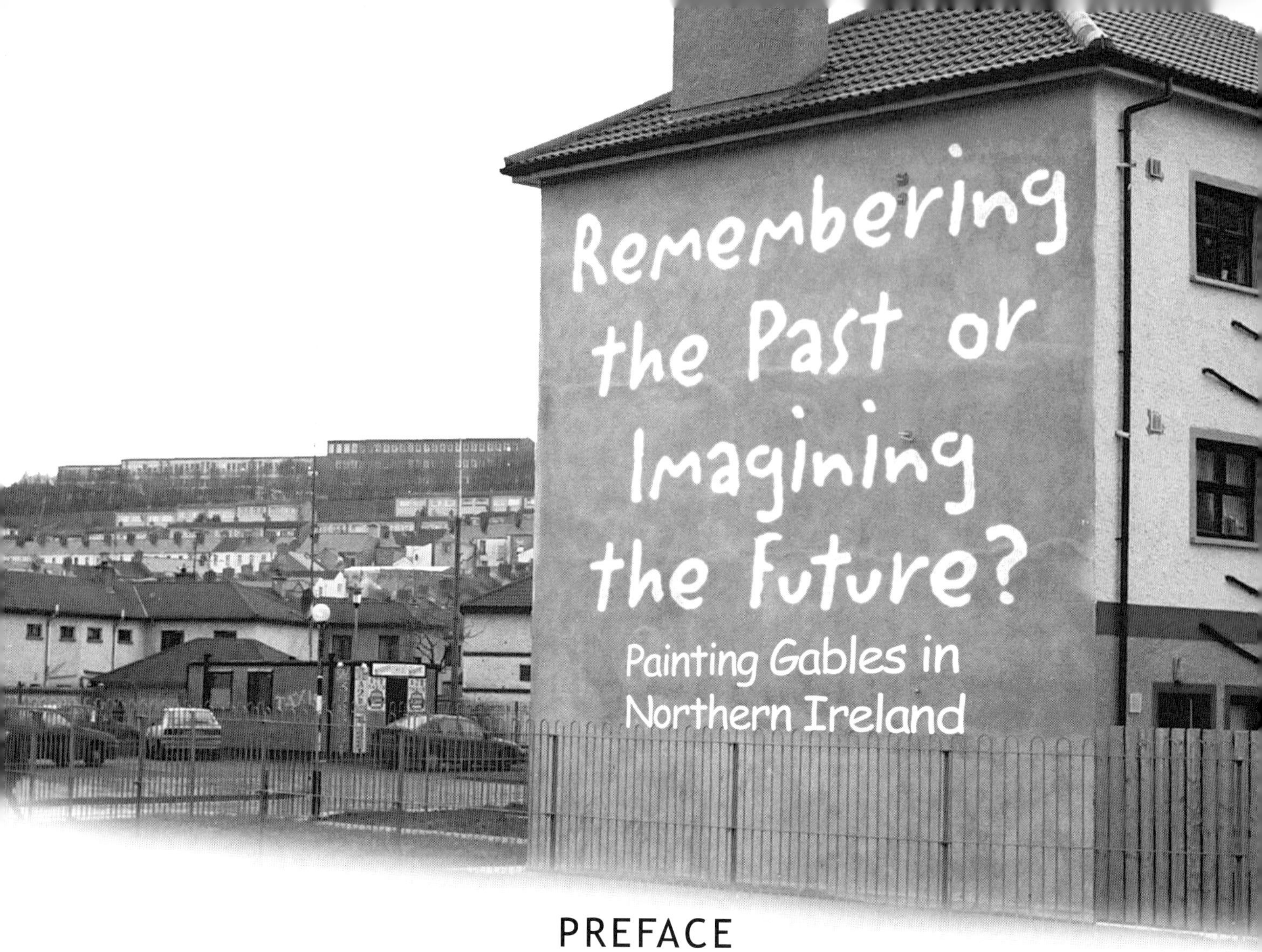

PREFACE

Dr Neil Jarman,
Deputy Director, Institute for Conflict Research, Belfast

Over the past twenty years mural painting has developed into one of the most dynamic means of cultural and symbolic expression in the North of Ireland. On any journey through the working-class estates of Belfast or Derry, whether physical, televisual or virtual, one is bombarded by an often-elaborate variety of visual statements. In recent years, these images have become increasingly complex and extensive in their design and professional in their execution. Nowadays scaffolding is often erected in front of the walls which are to be transformed, the surface is sometimes rendered to provide a better surface and the painters spend days, or even weeks, working to cover a wall with symbols, icons and images. We have come a long way from the early days of the *Troubles,* when two men were sentenced to six months imprisonment for painting a tricolour at Annadale Street, or from 1980, when a sixteen-year-old youth was shot dead by a policeman while painting Republican slogans because the police officer claimed he thought the paintbrush was a gun. Nowadays, mural painting is largely acknowledged as an established, if not entirely legitimate, political practice for all sections of the community.

Visual displays have been a feature of popular culture and commemorations in Ireland since at least the eighteenth century. Since the early years of the nineteenth century, much of the public visual culture in the North of Ireland has been associated with the Protestant community. Each year, an elaborate display of flags, flowers and bunting were hung from houses and across streets for the July commemorations of the Boyne, while vibrant and colourful banners were carried as part of the parades. Each year, wooden, metal or floral arches were installed in the centre of many towns and villages and in staunchly Protestant residential areas. The displays were highly formalised and showed little variation in their symbolic content from year to year or from place to place. Each area was content to affirm its loyalty to the memory of King William III and celebrate the victory at the Boyne. Such displays served to mark out those towns, villages and streets that were loyal and Protestant.

These displays for the Twelfth of July marked the beginnings of a visible sectarianisation of place. But they were short lived. Most lasted for no more than a few days and then the streets and buildings returned to their everyday appearance with no overt demonstration of collective identity. However, the introduction of mural paintings in the early part of the twentieth century changed this. The availability of new industrial paints was one factor that facilitated the production of images of King William III and other Orange symbols on the gable walls of terraces of working-class Belfast. They were yet another means of asserting the Protestant people's sense of British identity that flowered during an extended period of political crisis. In the later stages of the Home Rule campaign, and, following partition in 1921, in the period of consolidation of the Northern Irish state, mural paintings were used to complement and extend the existing forms of Orange displays. Mural painting was quickly recognised as an established feature of Protestant popular culture and helped to define the political and cultural parameters of the Northern Ireland state. New murals, arches and other displays were ritually unveiled by politicians in Protestant areas each July, but, at the same time, the law and the police were utilised to ensure that the Nationalist population did not develop a similar tradition within a British Northern Ireland.

Although an area was readily acknowledged as inhabited by Catholics, it was not readily accepted as a Catholic area, since all Catholics were regarded as Irish Nationalists and therefore a threat to the status of Northern Ireland. Gerrymandering ensured that Unionist politicians controlled areas with a Catholic majority and no area could be regarded as beyond the actual, or symbolic, remit of the Orange state. Loyalist parades were allowed to pass through Catholic areas but attempts by Nationalists to parade or erect visual displays were often restricted or banned outright. Even the temporary erection of the Irish tricolour was seen as a challenge and an affront, and more permanent political displays or commemorations were almost unknown.

In the 1960s, these inequalities began to be challenged by the Northern Ireland Civil Rights Movement. The main thrust of the campaign focused on securing equal access to housing and employment, but a challenge was also mounted to the Orange hegemony of the streets. Demonstrators sought to carry their arguments into towns, which were regarded as the preserve of Protestants. They also began to challenge the 'traditional' rights of Protestants to parade wherever they wanted.

As ideological and political arguments turned into sectarian violence and outright warfare, Catholic areas in Derry and Belfast were enclosed behind barricades. As the forces of the state were excluded, people began to exert control over their own areas. A key element of this newly claimed control was to redefine the symbolic identity and status of the estates. The areas behind the barricades and away from interfaces became a form of sanctuary – places in which the Nationalist community, and to a lesser extent the Loyalist community, could begin to redefine itself on its own terms. These places served as sites of cultural and ideological resistance. Behind the barricades, the power of the state was restricted and the agents of the state were excluded, both physically and symbolically.

When the first barricades were erected in the Bogside in Derry in January 1969, the act of excluding the forces of the state was proclaimed by the slogan *You Are Now Entering Free Derry* painted on a gable wall in St Columb's Street. By the time the wall was repainted for the visit of the Home Secretary, James Callaghan, in August that year, it had become a key symbol of communal attitudes and collective resistance. In many ways, the appearance of the Free Derry mural marked the beginning of the contemporary Nationalist mural-painting tradition, although it was not until the 1981 Hunger strikes that such paintings began to appear widely and freely in Nationalist parts of Belfast and Derry.

The emergence of a sustained body of images from within the Republican community in the 1980s in turn stimulated other actors within the Unionist community to take up the brush, and, over the past two decades, the mural-painting tradition has been dramatically transformed. Initially, the walls were dominated by images of paramilitary figures and direct references to the conflict, but, slowly, the range of images has broadened, while the variety of styles has grown and the quality of the work improved. Murals are still used to mark out the territory of paramilitary groups in working-class areas, but they are also used to remember former colleagues, to honour political heroes and identify historical ancestors, to commemorate past events and mark allegiance with other national political struggles, to celebrate culture, language, sport and faith, to redefine and extend a sense of identity and nationality and to create a distinctive sense of place.

Mural painting has become a key element of popular culture and has been recognised and accepted as such. While many paintings are closely identified with the political conflict in some way, the brush and the spray can have increasingly been taken up by a range of other organisations: churches, youth groups, schools, community groups and individuals. These paintings often help to brighten up an area, but they also allow other voices and ideals to be represented, whether this is to reflect nostalgically on times past or provide a critical perspective on the present.

The Free Derry Corner mural has remained in place throughout the reconstruction of the Bogside, and although the wall is now isolated on a stretch of dual carriageway, it is far from a passive memorial. The mural is repainted regularly and Free Derry Corner has been established as the focal point for Nationalist and Republican commemorations within the city. In the past few years, several other large murals have been painted in the adjacent area by the Bogside Artists who have produced the major artworks from a sense of, and in collaboration with, the community. Some refer to the early events of the *Troubles,* such as the *Battle of the Bogside*: others address broader aspects of Nationalist political culture and commemoration, such as the Hunger Strikes or Bloody Sunday; still others are part of the opposition to Loyalist parades. Some have been in place for a number of years, others are painted on boards and attached to the back of the Free Derry wall for only a few days at a time. The area provides the most concentrated body of images in the city and some of the finest murals that have been painted in recent years. The Bogside Artists have made a marked contribution to this work, and their particularly strong images linger long in the memory.

The history of mural painting at Free Derry Corner has in many ways moved in parallel both with the revitalisation and redevelopment of the city itself and the resurgence of the Nationalist community in the area. Many of the paintings are memorials in some way or form and look back to the recent past of conflict and violence, death and disorder, but rather than indulging a morose nostalgia for the past, or a gloomy sense of circuitous entrapment, they rather seem to draw a line under such events: we will remember the past but we also need to move on. The murals thus act as a reminder of how things were and of where we have come from, but, rather than anchoring the present to a cycle of bitter recrimination, complaint and blame, they are part of a creative process which aims to situate the past within the present as something we must acknowledge and from which we can draw strength.

Mural painting emerged in the early years of the twentieth century as a means of marking territory, commemorating history, celebrating culture and defining identity. Nearly 100 years on, it remains one of the most dynamic forms of popular culture in the North of Ireland, but it is also still intrinsically linked to the social and political dynamics of the North. Most painting remains clearly identified with one community or the other: they are largely used to bolster one sense of identity over another and to help distinguish *us* from *them.* However, it also retains the potential to be taken up as part of a wider process that might serve as a medium for tracing common threads, shared ideas or alternative perspectives. Occasionally, paintings appear that illustrate new possibilities or that express critical or marginalised viewpoints and thus indicate that while the medium is now an established part of local culture, it still has a role as a means of representing our understanding of the past and our aspirations for the future.

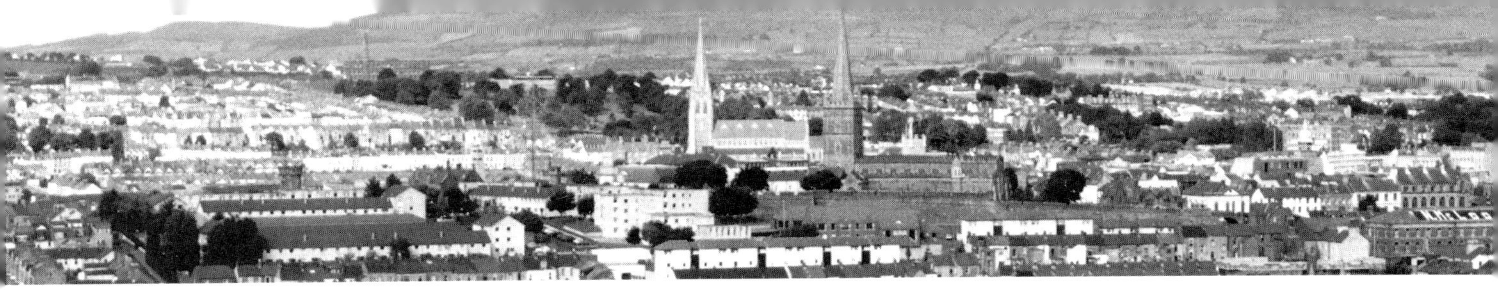

A BRIEF HISTORY OF DERRY

Derry derives its name from the old Irish word *Doire*, meaning an oak grove – particularly an oak grove on an island that is totally or partly surrounded by water or peat bog. Oak groves were sacred places for the Celtic peoples who once lived over most of Western Europe. Derry's original name is thought to be *Doire Calgach* (Oak Grove of *Calgach)*, a renowned pagan warrior of the period. Earliest historical references to Derry date to the sixth century AD when a monastery was founded there. The original oak grove, which gave its name to the city, was formerly an island in the River Foyle. The part of the river that ran past the island gradually dried out leaving a marshy area. In time, this area, for this reason, became known as the Bogside. Most of the civil conflicts that Derry has seen since 1969 have happened in or around the Bogside.

Oak trees occupied a numinous position in the Druid culture and in the ceremonies of the ancient Celts. Derry was almost certainly one of their ritual places. It was thanks to them that the Iron Age arrived in Ireland circa 500 BC, a full half-century after it had reached Europe. They were settled farmers, adept at metal work, storytelling and building stoned forts. They built thousands of circular forts in Ireland. Their culture was the foundation for the development of what we call Irish culture. The oak leaf has a special place, therefore, in the vast array of Irish symbols. To commemorate the fourteen people who were slain in the Bogside on 30 January 1972, the Bogside Artists painted a mural depicting all of the victims; fourteen oak leaves surround the central image.

Around AD 546, a Christian monastery was founded on the hill of Derry. According to legend, the Irish missionary, St Colmcille (AD 521–597), later known as Columba built the monastery of Derry. He founded many important monasteries in Ireland and Britain including Durrow, in the Irish midlands, and one on the island of Iona off the west coast of Scotland. Derry's monastery belonged to the group of churches that had Columba as their spiritual leader. It is believed that the first of them stood where the little St Augustine chapel of the Church of Ireland stands today. During the later middle ages, the old Derry monastery was taken over by the Augustinian order. The London colonists, who arrived to build the walled city of Londonderry in the early seventeenth century, used the monastery church as their first place of worship.

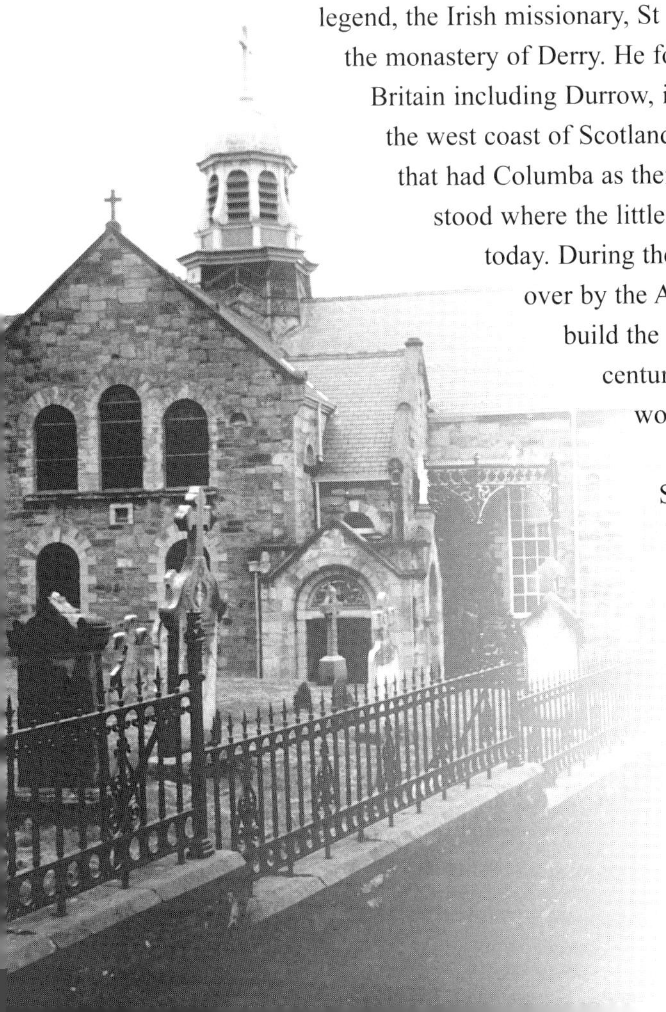

St Columba's 'Long Tower' was the first Catholic Church to appear in the city after the momentous events of the Reformation and Plantation. It is decorated in a grandiloquent post-Renaissance style. Originally built in 1784, the Long Tower occupies the precincts of another of Derry's famous medieval churches, the Teampall Mór, or Great Church. This was built in the 1160s, a time when a reasonably large settlement had grown up around the ancient monastery. The Teampall Mór served as the cathedral of the diocese of Derry throughout the middle ages. Like the distinctively Irish round tower of the same period (hence Long Tower) that stood nearby, all traces of the Teampall Mór disappeared in the seventeenth century.

Although the Vikings certainly sailed up the loughs and rivers of this area, the monastery in Derry escaped the worst effects of their raids, unlike many monasteries in the South, such as Clonmacnoise, which was looted ten times, or Kildare, sixteen times, during the ninth and tenth centuries. Derry's medieval resurgence began in the twelfth and thirteenth centuries when the local MacLochlainn dynasty moved into the settlement. Under their patronage, Derry prospered, the population grew; the monastery and its school thrived and prestigious buildings were erected. With the decline of the MacLochlainns, some of whom claimed to be kings of all Ireland, Derry's fortunes likewise diminished.

The famous skeleton depicted on the city's coat of arms tells of Derry's association with another aristocratic family, the Norman de Burgos, who built their great fortress at Greencastle at the entrance to Lough Foyle; they briefly owned part of Derry in the early fourteenth century. For all that, the settlement continued to decline. When the local O'Doherty family built a castle in Derry for their overlords, the O'Donnells, probably around 1500, it may well have been thought that a new era had dawned; but this wasn't to be. The recently built O'Doherty Tower facing the Guildhall is a modern attempt to commemorate that historic association.

Throughout the second half of the sixteenth century, English military leaders tried to conquer the province of Ulster, the only part of Ireland still outside their control. Around 1600, Sir Henry Docwra was despatched by Queen Elizabeth I (1533–1603) to occupy the town and use it as a base from which to launch military strikes against the native Irish opponents to her colonisation policy. This was during what became known as the Nine Years War, fought chiefly against the Gaelic O'Neill and O'Donnell clans. In 1608, Derry was attacked by Sir Cahir O'Doherty (a previous supporter of the English in Ulster) and the settlement was virtually wiped out. The attack came about shortly after the so-called 'Flight of the Earls' when the O'Neill and O'Donnell chieftains, together with their supporters, fled to the continent, leaving Gaelic Ulster leaderless.

The new king in England, James II, continuing with Elizabeth's strategy, resolved to subordinate Ulster once and for all. He decided to colonise the province with loyal English and Scottish migrants who were to be predominantly Protestant in religion. One part of this colonisation was to be organised by the ancient and wealthy trades' guilds of London. Between 1613 and 1619, Derry's Walls were built under the supervision and financial investment of London's

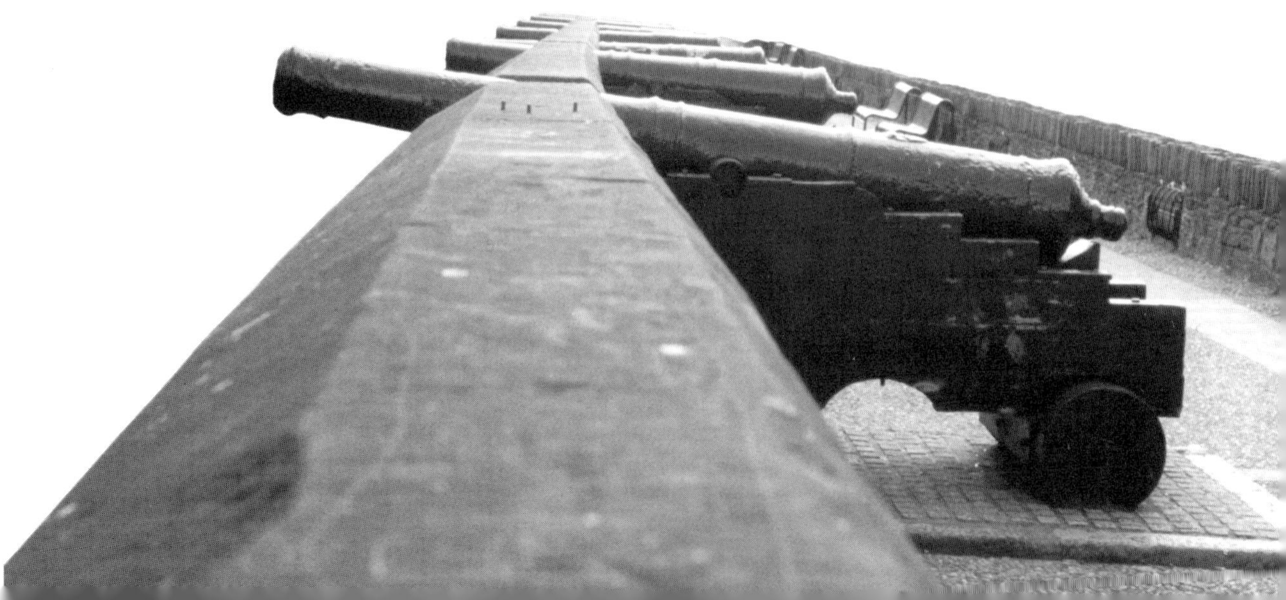

The Honourable The Irish Society and cost a whopping £10,000. They are considered to be the best-preserved medieval walls in Europe. The newly fortified city, and the county it was in, were renamed Londonderry in honour of this association. The city of Londonderry was the jewel in the crown of the Ulster plantations. It was the chief garrison of the North. By the 1680s, it still had only about 2,000 inhabitants, yet it was by far the largest settlement in Ulster. It was laid out according to the best contemporary principles of town planning imported from the continent. (The original street layout has survived to the present day, almost intact.) Derry was the last walled city built in Ireland. Among its new buildings was St Columb's Cathedral (1633), which was almost destroyed during the famous 105-day siege initiated by Catholic James II in 1689 in an inept attempt to wrest the crown of England back from William of Orange.

It was the thirteen Apprentice Boys who closed the Gates, and the city's Governor, Robert Lundy, who sneaked off with the help of Major Henry Baker and the Reverend George Walker, who would govern in his absence. They say Lundy was tried for treachery and banished from the city. His cowardice is remembered annually in a ritualistic burning of his effigy. More importantly, the narrative, as handed down from generation to generation, has been instrumental in elevating the notion of betrayal to an emotive level in Protestant consciousness. The siege, in which many thousands died of hunger, is of major significance in the Protestant epic. *No Surrender* also defines the spirit of the marching season when Ulster's Protestants celebrate the pivotal events of their history in some 3,000 parades – many of them confrontational from the Catholic viewpoint.

As a result of these events, two separate communities have existed side by side in the North of Ireland and in a state of economic co-dependency since the seventeenth century. In 1920, counties Cavan, Donegal and Monaghan were seceded from the ancient province of Ulster leaving a statelet of six counties – Northern Ireland – to be run by a 'Protestant parliament for a Protestant people'. For over fifty years, this regime was to be artificially maintained by gerrymandering, enforced emigration through unemployment and unfair allocation of housing, council elections based on property rather than population, segregated schooling, bigotry in the workplace, and a police force (Royal Ulster Constabulary) backed up by an auxiliary part-time cohort (B-Specials), both of which were 100 per cent Loyalist. The Protestants were then, as now, terrified of losing everything they had or were ever going to have, to an alien people apparently enslaved to an alien religion. This religious dimension helps explain both the passion and reverence many Protestants have for their history.

It was in this climate, and against all of these injustices, that the Civil Rights campaign began in 1968. It was inspired by Martin Luther King but very quickly reverted to the much older struggle of Republicanism against partition. Concessions were made but were all too late. Violent clashes, which began in October 1968, between police and protesters escalated to the point where, in March 1972, British Prime Minister Edward Heath disbanded the B-Specials and brought in direct rule from Westminster. This followed the pogrom of 30 January when the British Army gunned down fourteen innocent civilians during a Civil Rights march in Derry. The city, almost thirty years on, still awaits the results of an official ongoing inquiry into Bloody Sunday.

Derry at present has a population of some 120,000 people with slightly more females than males. It is a place where unemployment is still high. Over 70 per cent of the population is Catholic with the majority of the remainder either Presbyterian or Church of Ireland. The city deservedly enjoys a prolonged peace. During this period, it has initiated many new building projects and training programmes and works diligently through community-based initiatives towards a better future. A will to mutual tolerance and a respect for differences informs its spirit.

The Gasyard Wall Féile is rapidly becoming one of the most popular cultural festivals in Ireland and attracts thousands of visitors each year, much to the credit of its organisers, the Bogside and Brandywell Initiative, which is dedicated to the economic and social regeneration of the area.

The Bogside is by far the best-known section of the city. Its catchment area has a population of roughly 8,000. In some areas, the unemployment rate runs at 50 per cent on average – many of them long-term. Situated outside the Walls, it was originally a predominantly Protestant settlement. With the growth of commerce in the nineteenth century, resulting in the gradual influx of workers from the hinterlands, it became totally Catholic. It was a place of mainly small terraced houses, such as is typical of many working-class towns in the North of England. Today, it is in the process of extensive refurbishment.

With the establishment of the state of Northern Ireland, the Bogside was already a Catholic warren in the grip of severe unemployment, a situation that got even worse after the Second World War. There was severe rioting in the city from 1869 onwards while the population of the Bogside grew. Not a few of the additional population were people who had intended to emigrate but for one reason or other decided to stay. In 1919 serious trouble flared again. The months of April, May and June of 1920 saw forty people killed and many more wounded. From the 1920s onwards, the city was to experience continuous political conflict, kept largely at bay by the appeasement policies of the Nationalist Party. A general refurbishment of the Bogside began in 1963 and continued for a decade. The Rossville Flats, a centrepiece of the forthcoming *Troubles*, were completed in 1966. It seemed to many residents who were allocated these dwellings that their entire community life was being dismantled. The flats constituted one disaster among many. The RUC baton attack on protesters at Duke Street on 5 October 1968 is commonly held to be when the *Troubles* began. For most of the people living in the Bogside, it certainly was the last straw. One third of all civilian deaths in the city since then have taken place in the Bogside.

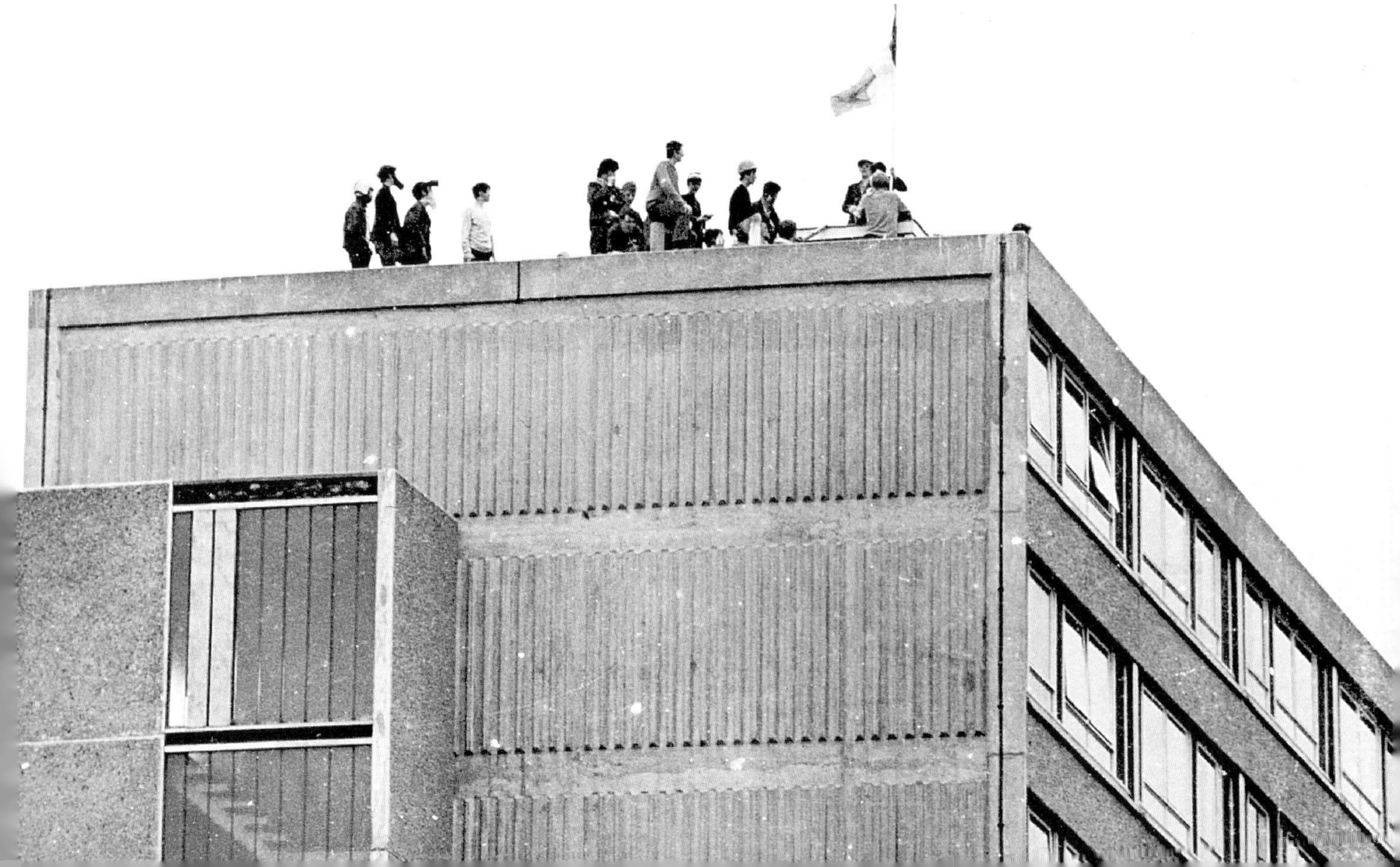

Despite its size and geographical position, Derry boasts quite a few famous people – not all of them politicians. Some of them are musicians and writers or affiliates of the theatre. Among its most famous citizens in the second half of the seventeenth century was George Farquhar, one of the restoration dramatists. Our reigning dramatist today is Brian Friel, a playwright of immense significance and international renown. We have two Nobel Laureates no less – John Hume and Seamus Heaney – both of whom attended St Columb's College. Éamon de Valera and Wolfe Tone were both incarcerated briefly in Derry's jail, of which only a single tower remains. Amelia Earhart, the first woman to fly the Atlantic, once landed at Derry. Her plane was lost over the Pacific in July 1937. Eleanor Marx, daughter of Karl, visited the city in 1891. Like her father, she took a keen interest in Irish affairs and wrote articles in the early 1880s about the treatment of Irish political prisoners in England, in particular Jeremiah O'Donovan Rossa. It was likely, in her capacity as worker for the Women's Trades' Union League – whose maxim was 'equal pay for equal work' – that she visited the city. She was Marx's youngest daughter and tragically committed suicide on 31 March 1898, aged just forty-two, two weeks after the anniversary of her father's death

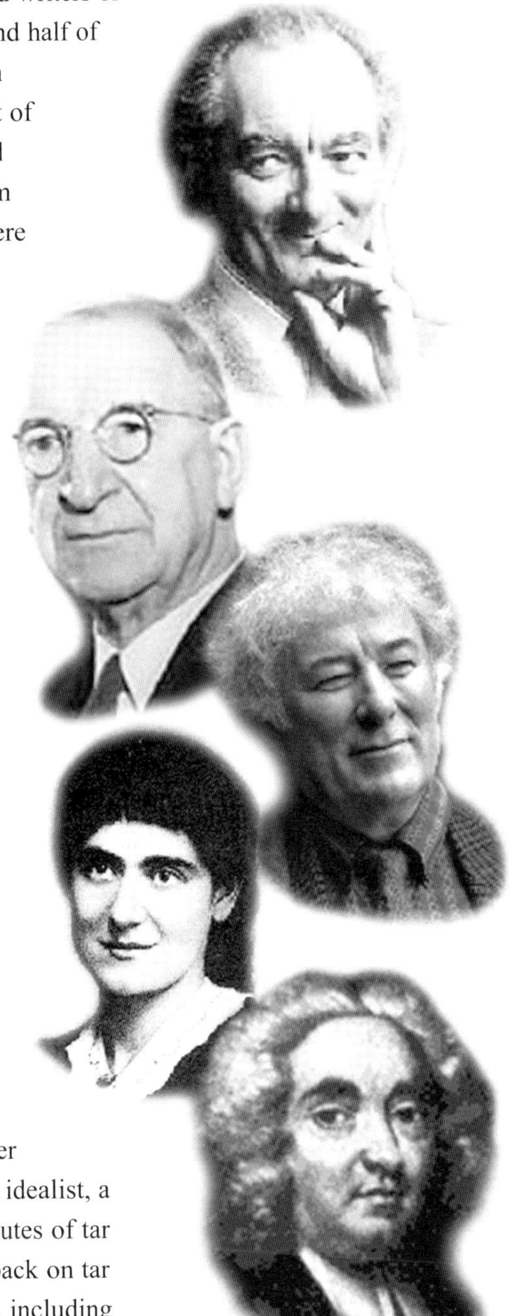

But of all the Maiden City's celebrated associates, perhaps the most colourful was Dr George Berkeley (1685–1753). He was an Anglican bishop and philosopher born at Kilkenny and taught at Trinity College, Dublin. He was also (1724–32) Anglican dean of Derry. At least he was appointed to the post until the then Lord Lieutenant, the Duke of Dorset, raised such an objection that Berkeley was instead made a bishop in 1733 and given the see of Cloyne to preside over. He died in London twenty years later, but not before he had established quite a reputation as a philosopher and fervent critic of Locke and [David] Hume. He is famous as an idealist, a devoted Platonist, and unashamed promoter of the medicinal attributes of tar water. It need hardly be said that modern medicine has turned its back on tar water. He believed that nothing exists outside the perceiving mind, including matter, an idea that has recently won converts in the UK with the creation of the National Lottery. British mathematician and philosopher Bertrand Russell (1872–1970) considered the bishop's proofs for the nonexistence of matter to have been 'quite ingenious'. Unfortunately, nobody takes 'Bertie' very seriously any more. Berkeley, on the other hand, is taken very seriously, with the resurgence of idealism among New Age thinkers and the increasing sophistication of pub quiz shows.

TESTIMONIALS

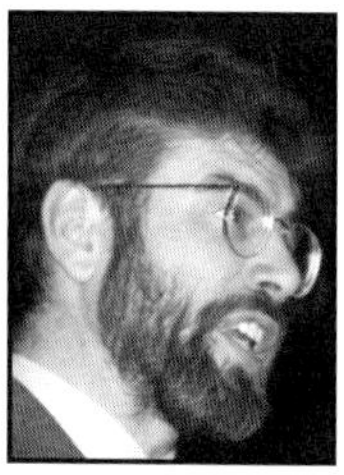

Gerry Adams, President of Sinn Féin; MLA, MP

Ba mhaith liom buíochas agus moladh a thabhairt di Ealaíontóirí Taobh an Bhogaigh as an tsaothar samhlaíochta seo atá déanta acu – na ceisteanna tabhachtacha seo a chur in airde, ceisteanna atá an – Tabhachtach don phobal in nDoire.

The contribution made by the Bogside Artists in recording the events of the last thirty years through their wall murals cannot be overstated. The artistic creativity and clarity of their message is to be commended.

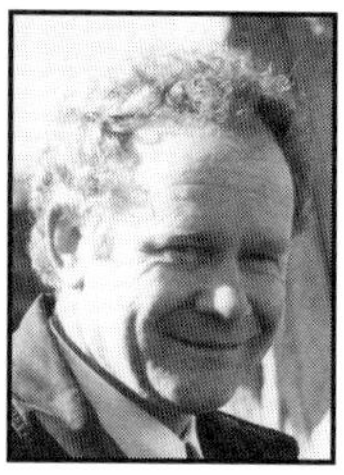

Martin McGuinness, MLA, MP, Minister for Education

The outstanding work of the Bogside Artists in recording events of significant importance in the recent history of our city has to be commended. The murals are recognised throughout the world and have become the biggest visitor attraction in Derry. I wish the Bogside Artists every success in the future.

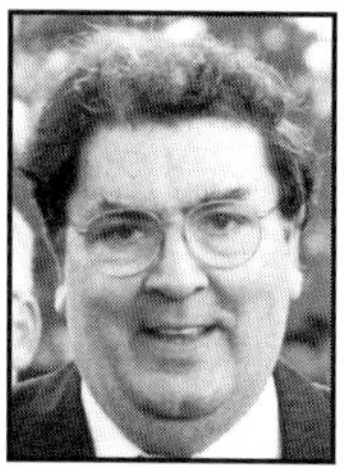

John Hume, Nobel Laureate, former leader of the SDLP; MLA, MP, Member of the European Parliament

I am amazed at the outstanding quality of this artwork.

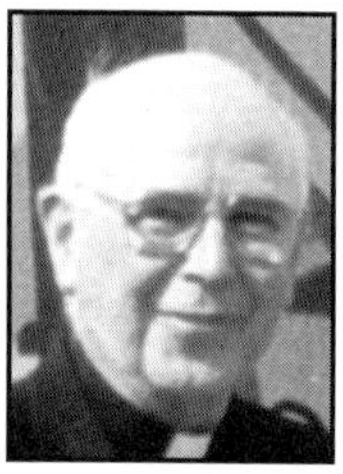

Most Rev Dr Edward Daly, retired Bishop of Derry

Outdoor political murals have been part of Northern Irish popular culture for many decades. Up until twenty-five years ago, this phenomenon was primarily an expression of Orange culture.

In the last two decades of the twentieth century, political murals have also become part of Nationalist/Republican culture, especially in some areas of Derry and Belfast. They have evolved from the rather crude graffiti of the late 1960s to the more professional, sharply focused and artistic depictions of the '70s, to the murals that have appeared in the Bogside and in West Belfast in the '80s and '90s.

These murals tell a story, make a political point or record events from recent local history. They are a powerful medium; they represent a genuine form of creative expression that has emerged from the community. The Bogside murals are splendid examples of original, popular and imaginative political art of the period and deservedly attract great interest from tourists and locals alike.

Nigel Rolfe – lecturer in sculpture and painting at the Royal College of Art, London

Bogside Artists: The Broken And The Fixed

Into the well of the earth, perhaps even the very well of despair, beneath the daunting Walls, under the thumb of political and cultural constructs of domination, outside and kept without, lies the Bogside.

It is unique; there is no place like it on earth, not only mapped out in terms of its geography of cultural boundaries, but as a living history of conflict and power. The *haves* and the *have nots*, inside and without, looking down and looking back, all the relationships are clearly exposed for all to see. To be there is to experience the planned architecture of repression, the town planning of oppression, dominated by those dark monstrous Walls, below something ancient and even medieval, beneath, disempowered and intentionally so. Under this overbearing dominance you would expect a spiritless community; but if anything, the effect has been completely opposite. Like a mythical spirit, even the name resonates, sets up hope and longing for the psychical hobgoblins of its own medieval antithesis. The spirit of this community is proud, defiant, beautiful, strong.

When you look at its rooftops from above, or pass through, you can sense it and nearly see it. These blue-grey roofs caught in the chimney smoke and mists of winter are unforgettable, a remarkable panorama. A very special place.

Artists paint pictures for many different reasons, to remark, highlight, bear witness, represent, clarify, expose, comment but above all to use an image-making process to dig below the surface of what is at first apparent with life itself. The move to make a painting is to remake the world. It is not the world itself, but from the world, secondary and plastic, and not concrete nor primary.

This is very driven work, by necessity, by anguish, by urban war that surrounds and qualifies all its citizens, by hope and by anxiety. Made in a place, from a place and made for it. Fed by dire events, awful histories, crimes of state, murder, mayhem, deep social unease. There is an urgency here, something direct and necessary. The chosen images are most usually re-presentations and reworkings of a photographic moment of profound local significance and symbolism. They are worked up, made large into and of the community that fostered their power and cherished their value, a community dispossessed of any normal routes of expression. These pictures are metaphors and signifiers of freedom and deliverance, deeply iconic, nearly religious, both in scale and subject, like mystery pageants of transformation. These are portraits, popular, realist manifestations, but on a huge scale whereby the community itself becomes a living museum to safeguard and preserve its own icons. They are important moments, held over and preserved but at the site itself, close by where the original event happened. They are monuments and shrines, reminders for those close and markers for everybody else. They hurt and they warn off. This is art of transformation, not only in scale and material but also in intellectual property. The subjects of these giant biopic portraits are somehow deified and qualified, a frozen moment of history becomes mythical. What are we looking at and what are they looking at? What time are we in and what time are they in? Are we looking back or are they looking on? Bystanders in some macabre and fantastic pageant

Scale has always been an issue of deification in portraiture, but there is a sense with these pictures that even though they are many times life-size, they are caught in a half-life. Washed out or broken open, terrifying and uneven, certainly not perfect or purely realist, but relying as they do on the style of pop-social realism, which, given the circumstance and background of their making, adds a destabilising strand, as they are not only celebrations, but are edgy and uncomfortable. They are difficult and not easy, haunted and, like their landscape, unforgettable.

Noel Sheridan, Provost of the National College of Art & Design, Dublin

A crucial question to ask of any art is, 'Who is it for?' This is not easily answered in the case of a great deal of twentieth-century modernism, but it seems clearer, at first glance, in the case of the murals in this exhibition. They are for the people behind and in front of them – but they may be viewed in different ways by both sides.

For those behind, the images can represent ideas of protection, strength and faith. For those opposite (or in opposition), the paintings may represent aggression, violence and fanaticism. And it is not just the abstractions of words that are transferable from one context to another; in many cases it could be the images themselves. Except perhaps when images of individuals are featured and then that iconography has particular and local relevance. Then again these images may provoke hate rather than respect. Whatever the intention, the reading is inevitably socially constructed.

Why, since I consider myself a Nationalist, am I so ambivalent? Why so 'on the one hand, but then on the other' about all of this? It may in part be due to the dubiety inherent in modernism (to which I also owe allegiance), but I think, too, that it arises from the learning curve we have all been on in the context of the peace talks. The depth of the complexity underlying the stark images has been surfaced and has become part of the frame of reference for both sides so that our reception of the images may alter.

They are wonderful visual achievements that only times of upheaval and revolution seem able to produce. But like David, Courbet, Manet, El Litizski and Malevitch, they are now for the museums and we can never recapture the fire of the time that forged these works. They are something else, but as long as they generate debate and thought, they continue to fulfil an important social role for art.

'Our fervent wish is that the peace process will give us time to put right what has been so drastically put wrong.' This is part of the statement by the Bogside Artists and their work has played an important part in that process. The murals we all await are the ones that will represent the new North. And if the artists in this exhibition are not part of the creation of that new imagery, then something has gone very wrong and William Kelly's argument against the contemporary self-reflexive *culture industry* will be fully justified.

Denise McCool – Co-ordinator, The Irish Immigration Center, Boston

The members of the Irish Immigration Center and the young people from South Boston were very impressed with the presentation. It afforded us a unique chance to learn first hand about the three artists and their community.

The Bogside Artists offered not only a concise historical perspective on Northern Ireland, but also addressed the current issues and hopes for the future of their work. At this important time in Northern Ireland's development, it is essential to promote many levels of discussion. The arts, in this respect, have often been underestimated as a tool for community development.

The Bogside Artists have shown, through this exhibition, that they have a role to play in striving towards peace and reconciliation in Northern Ireland. Long may they continue to document the life of their community.

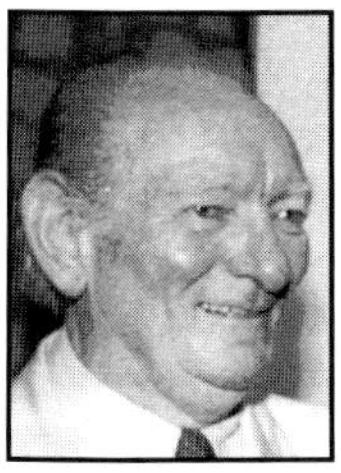

Brian Friel, internationally renowned playwright and author

The work of the Bogside Artists is celebrated locally and internationally, but it is their reputation that is important both to the artists and to their locality.

The work is remarkable in that it is simultaneously a vibrant response to events still vivid in the psyche of the community and, even as it testifies, it transcends those immediate passions and proposes an historian's distance and objectivity. The work says: You know the people in these pictures because they are your neighbours and your allies and you know what they endured; but have you thought about them in this way – as a people caught up in a chaos of tumultuous events and at the same time taking control of those events and shaping a new destiny? Because we, the Bogside Artists, believe that that is what has happened. That is what we are talking about.

This dual vision is made insistent by the theatricality of the events depicted, by the almost surrealism of the painting technique, by the political awareness that animates every event depicted, and, of course, by the very scale of the work and its dominant location in the centre of communities.

This is work of conscious ostentation, of deliberate defiance. It is work that Diego Rivera would have approved of. But it has delicacy too. Every mural explains – but it also embraces. Every mural instructs – but at the same time each has the intimacy and the consolations of a family photograph.

These murals tell the city about itself, what happened to it over the past seventy years and what futures may be available to it. I suspect the Bogside Artists have a lot of excitement squaring up each new virgin gable and a lot of fun endowing it with eloquence.

They are important people. I wish them well.

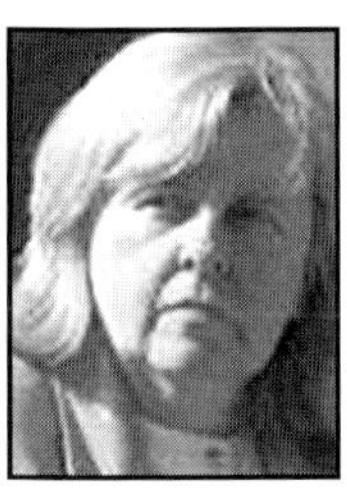

Bernadette McAliskey, Civil Rights activist

It is difficult to think of any social collective, ancient or modern, which has not expressed its history, beliefs and emotions through various forms of collective or public art.

With its first faltering steps and a crayon, or anything else that will make a mark, the human child is instinctively drawn to the best wall in the house. Somewhere, very deep in the human psyche, art is recognised as an integral part of human survival and progress.

Perhaps, this explains why *authority* considers any form of wall art not commissioned or sanctioned by itself to be a form of subversive activity.

Here, over many years, wall murals, graffiti, carefully crafted slogans and hastily daubed scrawls have documented our hopes, opinions, anger and grief, our determination to survive – our history.

As with all forms of art, some give greater testimony to the skill, craft and artistic genius of their creators than others: some give expression to that dark, razor humour that flourishes in the heart of the human hardship and others reflect the political sophistication of the message conveyed. All are valuable artefacts of our cultural, political and social present, documentation of our shared or contested past. We should treasure them.

Raymond G Helmick, SJ, Professor of Conflict Resolution, Boston College

The Bogside Artists give us the real People's Art of Northern Ireland's time of trouble. Their big murals in Derry raised the practice of mural painting to a level of sophistication, compassion and deep expression of their community's hurt that has not been attained elsewhere. The large paintings of this exhibit opened that whole treasury of the Derry people's experience to all of us who saw them at Boston College last year.

Ian Hunter, Director of Projects Environment –
a group devoted to the use of art in the pursuit of democratic rights

The Bogside Artists have pioneered a unique approach to art in the context of initiatives for community development and social change in Northern Ireland. Their murals and exhibitions' project are inextricably part of the history and culture of Derry, and, as such, are a worthy record of the people's struggle for social justice and civil rights. As artists, they have given generously and courageously to furthering the cause of community relations and education among younger artists and with young people in Derry. Now that they are gaining much deserved recognition as artists by the international community, I am convinced that their work in Derry will also come to be appreciated as an important social and cultural document in its own right.

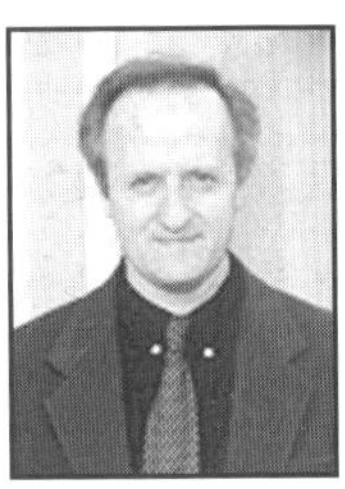

Dr Martin Melaugh, author of the CAIN website, Incore,
Magee College, Derry

As part of my work, I have, over a number of years, taken groups of academic visitors on a tour of the city of Derry. While it is often the case that the visitors know little or nothing of the history of the city, invariably they are well aware of, and are anxious to visit, the wall murals in the Bogside.

The large-scale murals painted by the Bogside Artists have become an important part of the physical, social, and political landscape of Derry. In contrast to other murals, which deal fleetingly with current political issues before being painted over in a few weeks or months, those of the Bogside Artists deal with major events and issues that will still resonate in another generation. The murals have taken on a permanent air that defied even the major renovation of the buildings on which they were painted.

When approached by the artists to produce a website, I readily agreed. At the CAIN website (http://cain.ulst.ac.uk), I was already aware of the widespread interest in the topic of political wall murals. CAIN had already included extracts from a number of books on the topic of murals, and these pages were proving to be of interest to a wide range of people. I was happy to include information supplied by the artists, as this provided a new perspective on the topic. The pages devoted to the Bogside Artists (http://cain.ulst.ac.uk/bogsideartists) give a flavour of their work on the wall murals, as well as other *street art* and exhibitions.

A SKETCH OF IRISH HISTORY

In a publication as brief as this, we can only touch on the key events. In being selective, some events will be left out and others that would require a whole book to themselves are only briefly mentioned. A history, even a brief one, is essential if the reader is to grasp the depth of feeling on both sides of the conflict in the North of Ireland. After all, Ireland has been locking horns with England for over 800 years. Christianity, incidentally, arrived in Ireland thanks to Pope Celestine's emissary, Palladius, some years before Patrick arrived to succeed him in AD 432. The fact that neither Henry VIII nor his daughter Elizabeth I succeeded in grafting the Reformation onto the country effectively set the 'religious' dimension to Irish politics that has survived to this day.

By 1601, Elizabeth had appropriated some 600,000 acres of the North for Protestant settlers, many from Scotland, leaving the remaining 50,000 for the dispossessed to live off. In 1609, James I reinforced this colony with his own stalwarts. By 1630, some 40,000 settlers, most of them poor Scots, had arrived in Ulster. Many of these were followers of Calvin and Knox. For almost a decade, wars between the Catholics and Protestants in Ireland grew until it appeared that the annexation would collapse. In 1641, Irish rebels thought to seize the opportunity afforded by the war between the royalists of Charles I and the Roundheads (Cromwell's parliamentarians).

Accordingly, in 1649, Oliver Cromwell was despatched with a large army to Ireland. He slaughtered the garrisons of Drogheda and Wexford, seized all the land he could for his financial backers and 3,000 of his troops, and drove Catholic landowners into Leinster, Munster and the West of Ireland. The slaughter at Drogheda took five days to complete and cost the lives of 3,500 men, women and children.

The confiscations of the 1650s set up a landlord class in Ireland whose source of wealth would be native tenants; it would form the backbone of the Irish ruling class. English landlords effectively supplanted both Gaelo-Norman lords and Gaelic chieftains entirely. Three million Irish were now governed by half-a-million foreign aristocrats. By 1700, 90 per cent of the land was owned by people of British origin, most of them non-Catholic. A system of 'shires' was introduced to form the thirty-two counties of Ireland.

Towards the beginning of the last decade of the century began the confrontation between Catholic James II and William of Orange that would have repercussions right up to our present day. In March 1689,

CHRONOLOGY OF IRISH HISTORY

circa 3000 BC
Megalithic tombs first constructed.

circa 700 BC
Celts arrive from parts of Gaul and Britain. Ireland divided into provinces. (This, according to a contributor, is reconstructed folk history and not based on archaeology.)

circa AD 350
Christianity reaches Ireland.

432
Traditional date for the arrival of St Patrick in Ireland.

700–800
Irish monasticism reaches its zenith.

795
Full-scale Viking invasion.

1014
Brian Boru defeats Vikings at Clontarf, but is murdered.

1169
Dermot MacMurrough, exiled king of Leinster, invites help from 'Strongbow'.

1172
Pope decrees that Henry II of England is feudal lord of Ireland.

1366
Statutes of Kilkenny belatedly forbid intermarriage of English and Irish. Gaelic culture unsuccessfully suppressed.

1534–40
Failed insurrection by Lord Offaly.

1541
Henry VIII proclaimed king (rather than feudal lord) of Ireland

1558–1603
Reign of Elizabeth I. Policy of Plantation begins. System of counties adopted.

1595–1603
Failed uprising of Hugh O'Neill.

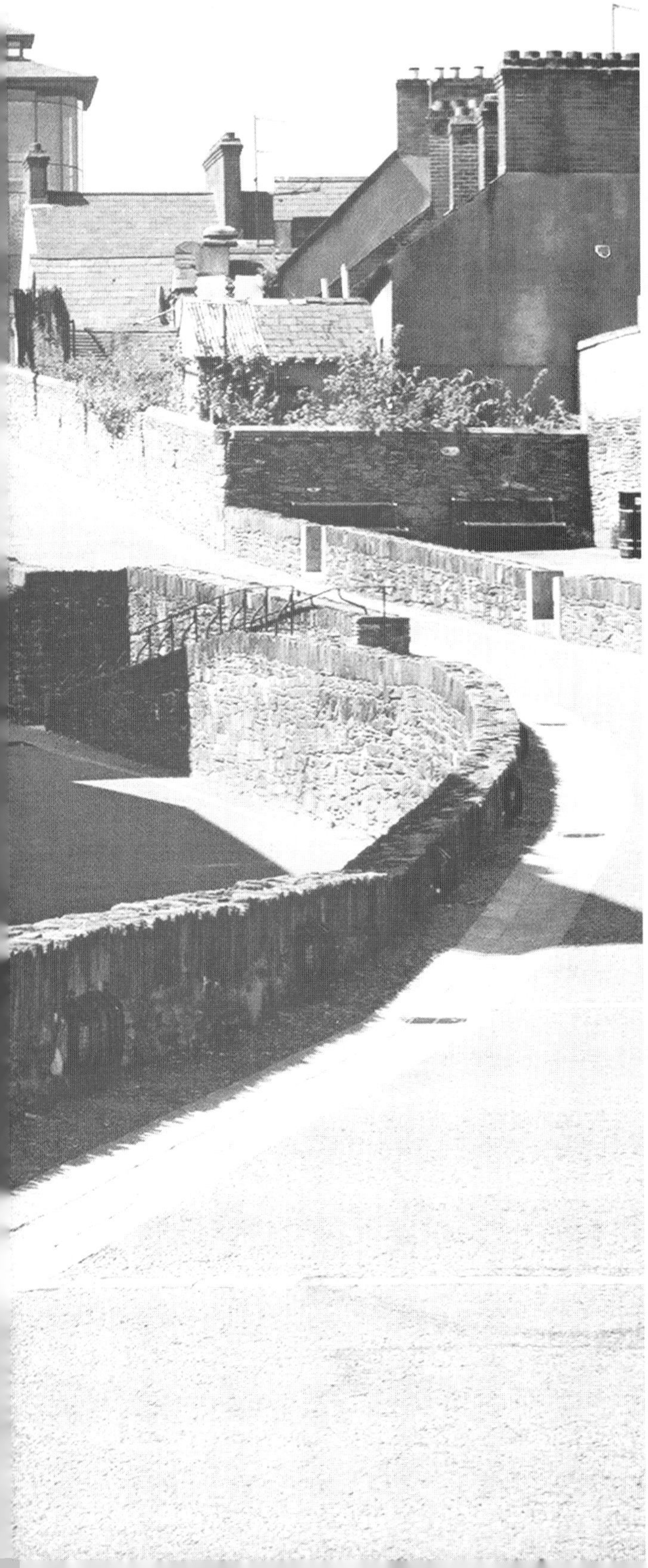

James laid siege to Derry, where 35,000 Protestants had gathered. The siege lasted fifteen weeks during which thousands died and the rest survived by eating whatever they could find. Dogs were allowed to feed off the dead only to be sold for meat themselves. Ten thousand took the offer of a general pardon from James to leave. On 28 July, British troops sailed up the Foyle to relieve the stricken town. James was later defeated at Aughrim and finally at the River Boyne – two significant dates that Ulster Protestants celebrate annually in over 2,000 marches. King Billy on his prancing white charger is a symbol of liberation for Protestants and perhaps their greatest and most revered icon.

Under the October 1691 Treaty of Limerick, Patrick Sarsfield, the leading Irish general, was allowed to leave for France with 12,000 of his soldiers. Such land that they had owned was taken by the Crown and the country was left without leadership. Almost immediately after James' defeat, the Protestant parliament in Dublin set about instituting severe laws against Catholics. These were known as the Penal Laws. They were punitive measures that were, initially at any rate, rigorously imposed. Basically, a Catholic had to swear an oath of allegiance to the English king and Protestantism if he was to be granted the right to work, teach or hold office. Bishops were banished: any attempt to convert a Protestant to Catholicism was an act of high treason; and Catholics were severely restricted with regards to what they could own and who would be entitled to inherit it. After the 1730s, the laws were less rigorously enforced. By 1793, Catholics could both own land and practise their religion with impunity. By then, over half the landed Catholics had become Protestants. Only 5 per cent of land belonged to Catholics.

Large numbers of indigenous Irish were now cottiers or labourers on land once owned by their families. So began the reign of the absentee landlord. The large majority of these were not so much 'absentee'; rather they lived in big country houses in Dublin and other main cities or on their vast estates. It should be noted that many Protestants, especially Presbyterians, suffered too from anti-Catholic legislation. In 1791, Wolfe Tone, himself a Protestant, founded the Society of United Irishmen. This was the time of the rise of the bourgeoisie throughout Europe. Still smarting over the loss of her colonies in America in 1783, England saw fit to appease the native Irish Catholics and granted those with sufficient property the right to vote.

The year1793 saw the beginning of a twenty-year struggle between England and France for dominion over Western Europe. The Protestants in the North reacted by founding the Orange Order in 1795. They were as obsessed by the thought of the mass executions of France's Reign of Terror as Tone was by his dream of independence. Inevitably, Tone solicited the help of the French for the uprising. The forty-three ships full of troops failed to land at Bantry Bay. The rebellion met with utter defeat at Vinegar Hill in June 1798, a significant event for Nationalists. In September, he tried again to land French troops in Ireland; this time via Donegal. His ships were intercepted and he was arrested. He slit his throat before he could be tried. It is interesting to note that Tone spent a short spell after his arrest in Derry's now demolished prison. His successor Robert Emmet's attempted coup of 1803 in Dublin fared no better. He was hanged.

Tone was an idealist, by all accounts, who was inspired by the noble vision of the French Revolution. He had never imagined total independence for Ireland, but, in the spirit of the times, sought the right for it to govern its own affairs without religious or racist bigotry. Between 1796 and 1798, it is estimated over 30,000 people were killed in Ireland. Thenceforth, to be 'Irish' now meant for Catholics to be Nationalist; for Protestants, Unionist meant British. Although Presbyterians had supported the cause of the United Irishmen, thanks to the persuasions of Orangeism, they now saw the struggle for independence as essentially Catholic and therefore antithetical to their interests. Irish Protestants would never again protest their Britishness.

According to Karl Marx, bourgeois England had a will to turn Ireland into its very own farmyard called 'West England'. They lost no time in bribing the Irish Parliament to pass the Act of Union. In those days, bribery was commonplace in political circles. It is likely that the 1798 rebellion was engineered by British agents whose job it was to provoke a rebellion that was guaranteed to be crushed. Passing the Act of Union would then be a formality that would meet with no resistance. Over one third of the leadership of the United Irishmen in Dublin had been infiltrated by British spies for this purpose. Religious antagonisms had also been fomented. Ireland had prospered during the long peace between 1691 and 1797 so that Dublin became the second largest city in the Empire and the fifth largest in Europe.

The 'brains' behind The Union may well have been William Pitt, who at the time was embroiled in the war with France. In parliament, he expressed his fears that Irish political autonomy would work against English interests, particularly at a time when a French invasion of

CHRONOLOGY OF IRISH HISTORY

1607
Flight of the Earls; leading Ulster families go into exile.

1641
Charles I's policies cause insurrection in Ulster and civil war in England.

1649
Cromwell invades Ireland.

1653
Under the Act of Settlement, Cromwell's opponents stripped of land.

1689–90
Deposed James II flees to Ireland; defeated at the Battle of the Boyne.

1704
Penal Code enacted; Catholics barred from voting, education and the military.

1775
American War of Independence inspires Irish unrest.

1782
Grattan's Parliament persuades British to declare Irish independence, but in name only.

1795
Foundation of the Orange Order.

1798
Wolfe Tone's uprising crushed.

1801
Ireland becomes part of Britain under the Act of Union.

1829
Catholic Emancipation Act passed after Daniel O'Connell elected MP.

1845–50
The Great Famine.

1879–82
The Land War; Parnell encourages boycott of repressive landlords.

1914
Implementation of Home Rule postponed because of outbreak of World War I.

Ireland was evidently a real threat. The Union wiped away any concessions Irish Catholics had hitherto gained. Both the abolition of the Irish Parliament and the lifting of protective tariffs put paid to Ireland's budding industries and curtailed its economic expansion.

Once again, the Irish had been left to the land. During the eighteenth century, demand had already increased rents six fold. 'The people had now before them,' Marx wrote, 'the choice between land *at any price* or starvation.' Surplus product was appropriated in lieu of rent plunging the whole country into the feudalism it thought to have escaped. Land, already exhausted from overuse, was given over to the cultivation of grain crops for export. Henceforth, the Irish question would become the *land question.*

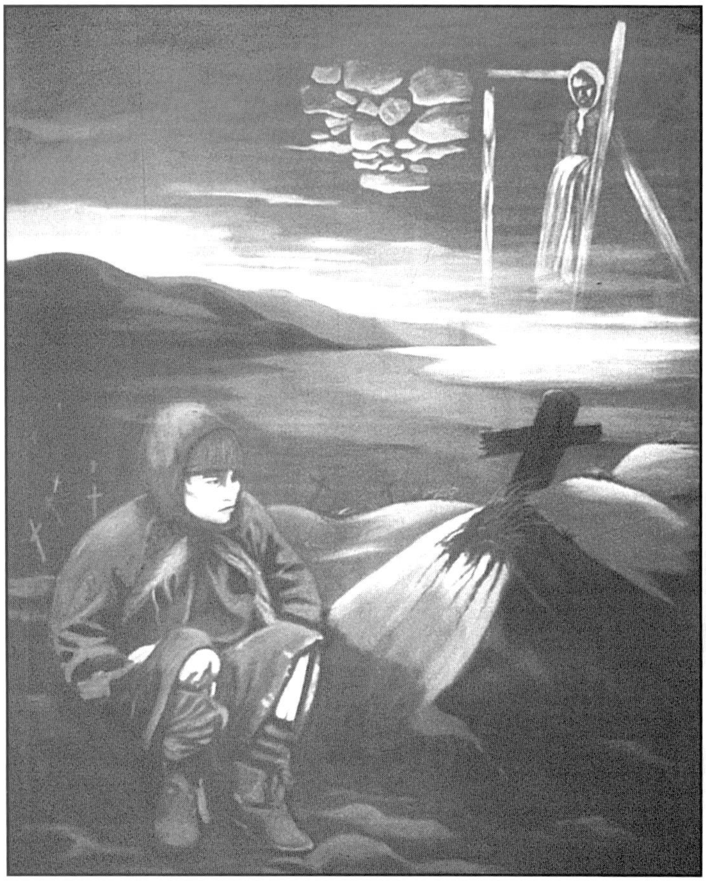

The Famine, acrylic on canvas. Protest to Peace exhibit, USA, 7ft x 6ft

In 1801, a new flag, the Union Jack, could be seen flying over public buildings throughout Britain and Ireland. The Act of Union would achieve its purpose of halting Ireland's industrial development and economic rivalry, turning the country into an assured supply of cheap food, raw recruits for the forces and easily exploited labour.

In 1823, the Catholic Association, founded by young lawyers and professional men, sought Catholic emancipation and a repeal of the Penal Laws. With self-seeking Daniel O'Connell at their head, they achieved this in 1829. Their next target was repeal of the Act of Union. This struggle for Home Rule polarised Irish society along the old lines. Throughout the 1820s, Orange Lodges proliferated all over the North. In accordance with the principle of 'divide-and-rule', England did much to encourage the divisions. Religious entrenchments would ensure a split within the lower classes in perpetuity, making 'the Orange card' the one to play in the endless pursuit of 'a majority in the House' no matter who was in office.

Between 1800 and 1841, the population of Ireland roughly doubled from four million to over eight million. What made this possible was the national diet, the potato; Sir Walter Raleigh had introduced it in the last decade of the sixteenth century. Its appeal was its nutritional value and its high yield. An area of two acres could support an entire family for a year. For this reason, plots became more and more subdivided for distribution among family members. So, by 1841, 300,000 families lived on holdings of less than five acres. Landless labourers leased land of an acre or less from other tenants and worked their farms to pay the rent. They lived off the potato yield from their own tiny patch. Over 130,000 families lived like this before the Great Famine, many of them to the west of the Shannon. By then, economic stagnation had already gripped the country. Agricultural prices had fallen while the demand for linen, of which Ulster had a virtual monopoly, had given way to that for cheaper cotton imported from America. The salted beef trade had also suffered for the same reason. While Ireland had been transformed into a farmyard, England had enjoyed great economic expansion and industrialisation. Irish landlords regarded industrial development as a risky venture because of the lack of iron and coal. Lack of an efficient banking system also deterred investors.

Ulster, however, had managed to circumvent these problems and a linen industry flourished for a while along the Lagan Valley. By 1780, this too had gone into decline – aided by Edmund Cartwright's power loom that made possible the mass production of cheap cotton cloth in England. All over the North of England, hundreds of mills sprang up. Robert Joy brought the new technology to Ulster and the Lagan Valley was transformed. By 1811, 30,000 people were employed in Ulster's cotton industry. This prosperity lasted only until 1825 when England saw fit to remove the protective tariffs that had made it possible. Fortunately, a new technology emerged that made large-scale linen production viable once more and the old markets were recovered and new ones created. Thomas Mulholland set up the first flax mill in Belfast in 1828. By 1850, dozens were operating in the Valley. Subsidiaries too, such as the makers of dyes and buttons, came into being to supply the industry, and towns like Bangor and Portadown blossomed. Local farmers who produced the flax likewise prospered. Thus, Ulster was providentially protected from the worst ravages of the forthcoming potato blight.

Nothing has had quite the impact of the Famine of 1845–50 on Ireland. One million of her population died and a further million and a half emigrated. Phytophera Infestans, closely related to bread-mould, and for which there was no known cure, everywhere attacked the potato crop. During that period, enough grain to feed the entire population was being exported to England for rent purposes. These exports continued while peasants were left to fend for themselves,

CHRONOLOGY OF IRISH HISTORY

1916
Easter Rising. After the leaders are executed, public opinion backs independence.

1920–21
War between Britain and Ireland; Irish Free State and Northern Ireland created.

1922
Civil war breaks out.

1932
De Valera elected.

1969
Rioting between Catholics and Protestants. British troops called in.

1971
Provisional IRA begins campaign to oust British troops from Ireland.

1972
UK and Republic of Ireland join European Community. Bloody Sunday in Derry.

1985
Anglo-Irish Agreement signed.

1994
Peace Declaration and IRA cease-fire.

1995
Seamus Heaney wins Nobel Prize for Literature.

1996
February, cease-fire broken by bombing of Docklands, London. British Prime Minister John Major demands decommissioning of IRA arms.

1997
IRA cease-fire resumes. All-party talks begin. The government of the South is included.

1998
Good Friday Agreement signed. Omagh car bomb kills twenty-nine; hundreds injured.

2001
IRA begins arms decommissioning.

trying hopelessly to coax rotting potatoes from wasted soil. Fintan Lalor, leader of the Young Irelanders, naively, perhaps, declared: 'Had the people of Ireland been the landlords of Ireland, not a single human creature would have perished.' Nothing, at any rate, has had more effect than the Famine on the Irish character. It deepened and softened the perception Irish people abroad had of their homeland and instituted a tradition of involvement in humanitarian causes all over the world.

The tragedy, however, was seen by many landlords as a blessing in disguise. Now, they could get on with the business of clearing the crofters from their land to make way for cattle and sheep. Well into the 1860s, evictions took place on a massive scale. Karl Marx, who lived through these years, took a serious interest in the Irish question. Parts of *Das Kapital*, particularly those dealing with capital accumulation, are evidently the result of his analyses of the Irish economy. He wrote: 'In 1855–66, 1,032,694 Irishmen were displaced by 996,877 head of cattle.' However much we may dispute the exactitude of the figures, the point is clear enough. What angered Marx was that in other colonised lands, ' . . . people were at least replaced by people.' The potato failure, as far as he was concerned, was the direct result of the exhaustion of the soil by capitalist rule and exploitation. Ireland was never again to return to its pre-1846 population level. Engels, who was married to Irishwoman Mary Burns (and later her sister Lizzie), and who had visited Ireland three times and even learned the language, said simply of Irish landlords, 'Those fellows should be shot.'

It is no surprise that after the Famine Ireland experienced a gradual resurgence of the old struggle for independence. This time, the Catholic Church took on the role of spokesman for the Nationalist movement. It denounced the ill-fated Young Ireland movement that collapsed in late 1848. Pope Pius IX had warned against it. The pulpit spoke out vehemently against all forms of socialism, communism, insurrections and trade unions. It would later speak out against the lockout strike in Dublin of 1913, causing it to fail. Leader and socialist James Larkin was so discouraged that he went off to America. In 1893, Douglas Hyde and Eoin MacNeill set up the Gaelic League to protect and promote Irish culture. In 1905, Arthur Griffith founded Sinn Féin, which grew rapidly throughout the early years of the 1900s, resulting in a revival of the Irish Republican Brotherhood that had been formed in 1858. Leader of the IRB, which would later become the IRA, was Pádraig Pearse.

The Home Rule Bill was left stranded by the commencement of World War I. It had already been defeated twice: first in 1886 and then in 1892. Resistance to it, especially from the House of Lords, was formidable. It proposed self-management for Ireland while leaving her international affairs to Westminster.

Catholic Church involvement in the cause had alienated Protestants, particularly those in the North where resistance was strongest. Edward Carson, who led the 100,000 Ulster Volunteers, vehemently opposed the bill and urged his men to join in the British war effort. In the South, John Redmond, constitutional Nationalist and chairman of the Home Rule Party, urged his followers to do likewise. His belief was that England, out of gratitude, would proffer independence. The result was that 200,000 men served with the British forces during the war. A large percentage of these ended up in the front lines; of these, 61,329 were killed.

At home, the struggle continued until 1916 when 1800 rebels set forth to confront 20,000 British troops in a very badly organised uprising. When the smoke cleared, 64 rebels, 216 civilians and 130 British troops lay dead; a further 357 were wounded. The army went ahead and executed fifteen rebels, including all seven members of the Military Council. Overnight, England lost all support among the ordinary people.

In 1918, seventy-three Sinn Féiners won 80 per cent of the vote for election to Westminster. They refused immediately to take their seats and instead set up their own government, Dáil Éireann. Their de-facto president, Éamon de Valera, was jailed; as a co-conspirator, he had been lucky to escape the firing squad, largely on account of the fact that he had been born in New York of Spanish and Irish parents.

In 1920, Britain proposed the Government of Ireland Act, which effectively split the country in two, leaving the Protestants to six counties in the North. The following year, Sinn Féin and British officials signed the agreement. The IRA, the successor to the IRB, resumed the struggle for full independence. Michael Collins was their leader, and the ensuing civil war between the Republicans and Free Staters raged on between 1922 and 1924. De Valera, meanwhile, had escaped from prison in England, and, after a brief spell in America to raise funds for the cause, he returned to Ireland and his presidency. In 1926, he founded the Fianna Fáil (warriors of destiny) party. De Valera was very opposed to the Union and has been associated with the death of his good friend Collins, who was gunned down between Bandon and Macroom, but there is scant evidence for this despite exhaustive fieldwork. Collins was well aware that in signing the treaty of 1921 he had signed his own death warrant.

Within a decade, the IRA had been outlawed. That did not prevent it continuing with its objective throughout the '40s and '50s. Finally, the Ireland Act of 1949 severed all constitutional links with Britain and established the Republic of Ireland in the South. Ulster Unionists in the North were granted their own parliament. It was to be a 'Protestant parliament for a Protestant people' and they did what they felt was necessary in order to maintain it. In October 1968, inspired by events in America, the Catholics of the North took to the streets in their demand for democratic rights.

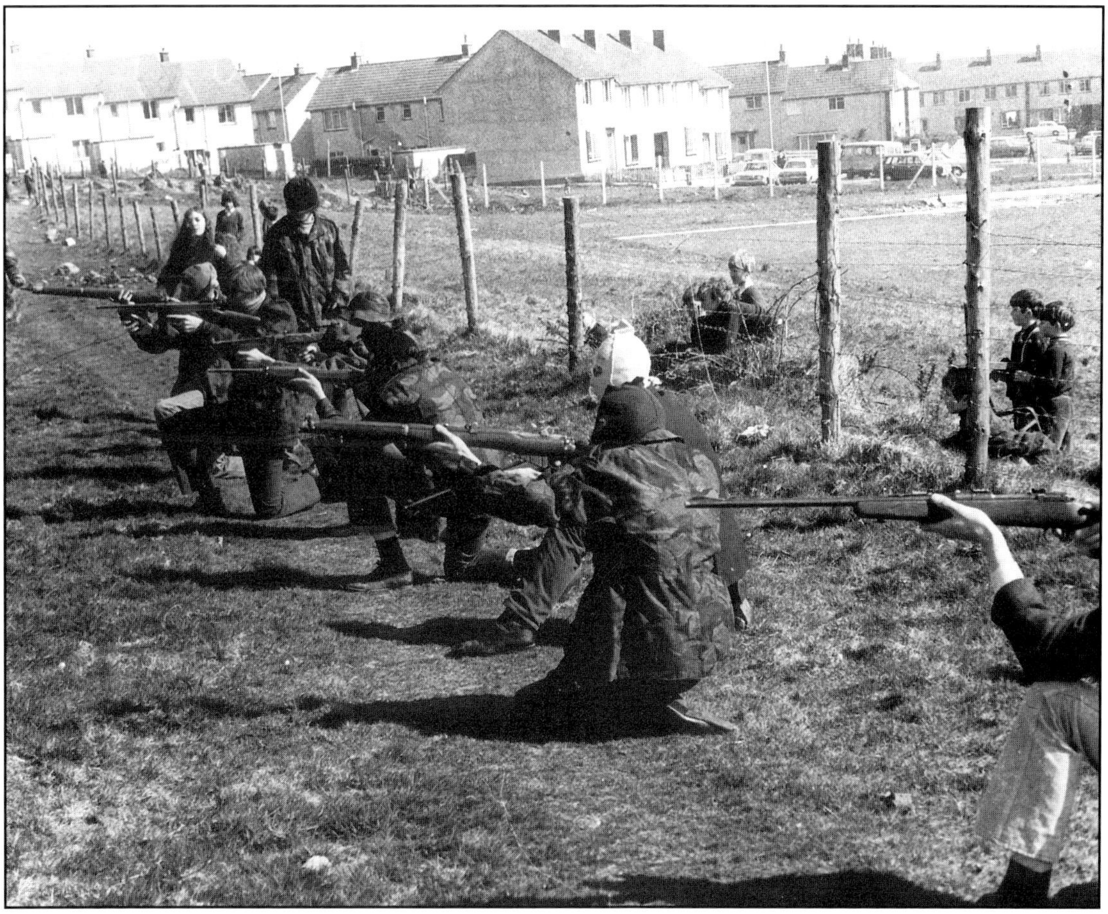

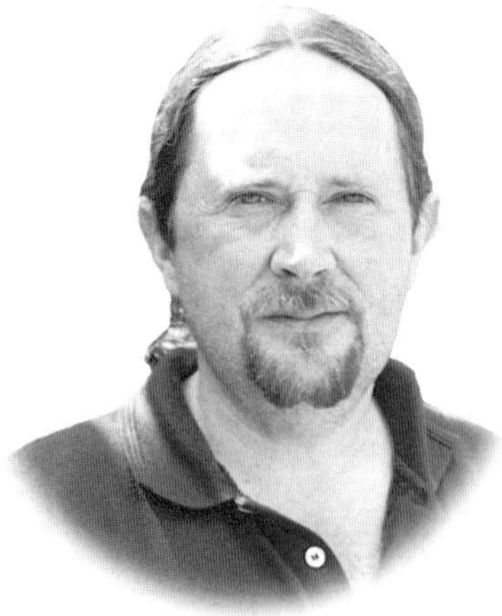

Tom Kelly

Apart from several intermittently brief stays in England in search of work, Tom has stayed most of his life in the Bogside. Outside of his role as a muralist, he also manages a small non-denominational Christian community in the heart of the Bogside called Wellspring; it places heavy emphasis on the Celtic arts.

'It's about getting back to what it was all really about in the beginning,' he will tell you. Part of Wellspring's agenda is to explore all aspects of Irish culture, particularly where it addresses the pure Christian message. Dance, music and art, especially in their Celtic aspects, are vibrant elements in Wellspring's ethos.

Prior to joining forces with his brother William and his lifelong friend Kevin Hasson, Tom worked for ten years in cross-community art projects in the city as a means of getting the two communities to understand one another.

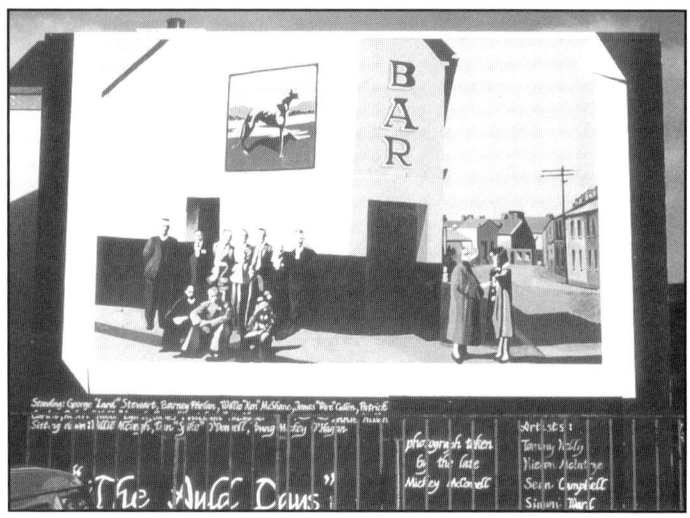

The Auld Days, Bogside 1994 – a heritage mural.

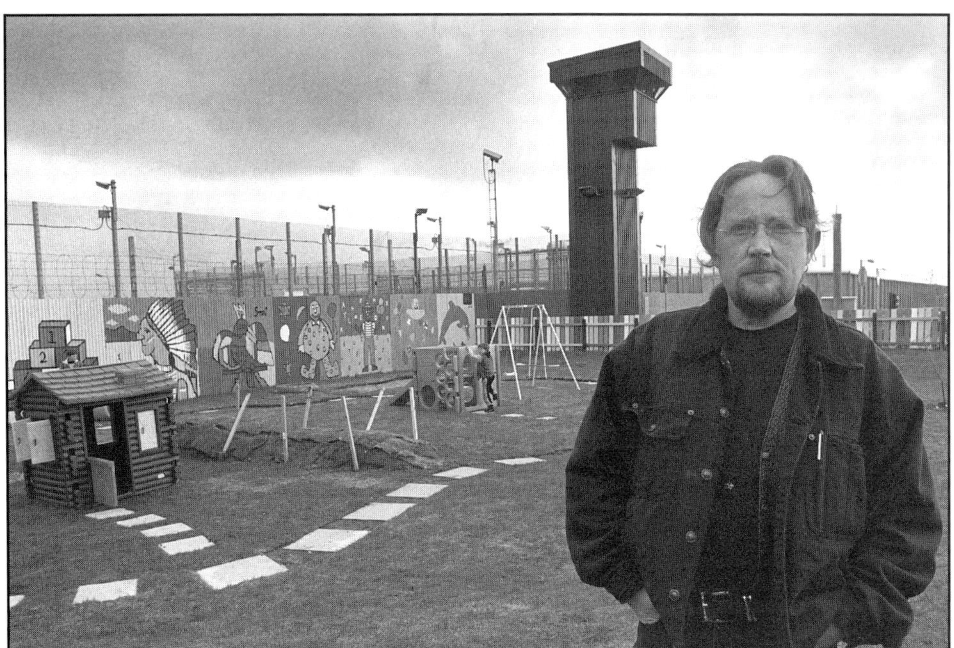

Children's play area, Magilligan Prison.

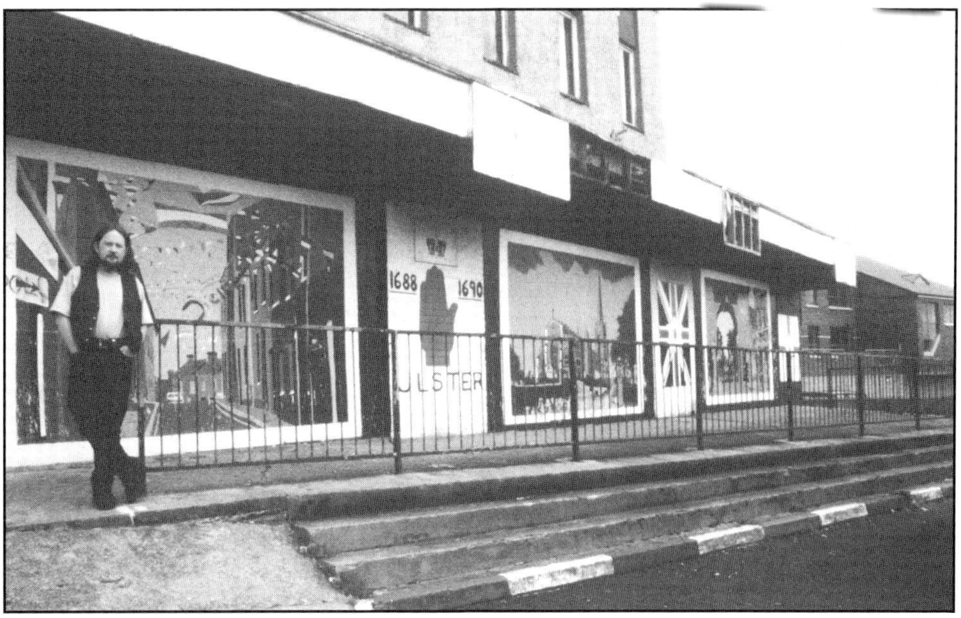

Past–Present–Future, a heritage mural in the Fountain Estate.

'I believed then, as I do now, that only in a real working environment, where people can be their true selves, can healing take place. Our society has done incalculable harm to our natural pride and sense of self-worth. Christianity addresses this.'

Tom supervised and completed many murals in the city that depicted life as it existed a long time ago. He called these 'heritage murals'. As a result of the refurbishment of the Bogside, none of them remains, except those that were completed in the interiors of schools, hospitals and community centres.

It was in this capacity as 'heritage-mural painter' that he was invited into the Fountain estate, a Protestant enclave close to the city Walls, to work with the young people of the youth club there. The Fountain is a conspicuously working-class estate that has seen its fair share of the *Troubles*. Paramilitary graffiti were painted out to enable Tom and his crew to do three murals there. So impressed were the residents with Tom's efforts, that, together with the young of the community, the residents organised a series of events to fund him on an expedition to Romania to help the starving orphans there.

The plight of the orphans in Romania had shocked the world, when, after a successful coup and the execution of tyrant Nicolae Ceausescu, the doors of the country's orphanages and hospitals were flung open. Half of Romania's 23 million population were without work. Those that had work earned barely enough to feed themselves. Parents too poor to feed themselves dumped their children on the state. The result was that over 150,000 orphans were being maltreated by a defunct and useless welfare system. Around 2,300 of them at that time were known to have AIDS, either contracted at birth or as a result of infected blood supplies. The brutal attitude of the new government towards these doomed children prompted a humanitarian response from the West. That was how and why the ordinary people of the Fountain clubbed together to send Tom to Romania. For Tom, it was a profoundly disturbing encounter.

'The colossal extent of the neglect and downright indifference to these abandoned children on the part of the government I found hard to take. People here do not understand how well off they are in comparison.'

Tom stayed and worked on and off with the young people of the Fountain for almost a year and got to know them very well. He is grateful to Jeanette Warke for giving him the opportunity. As one of the artists, Tom's Christian beliefs are very much in evidence in all of the murals so far painted.

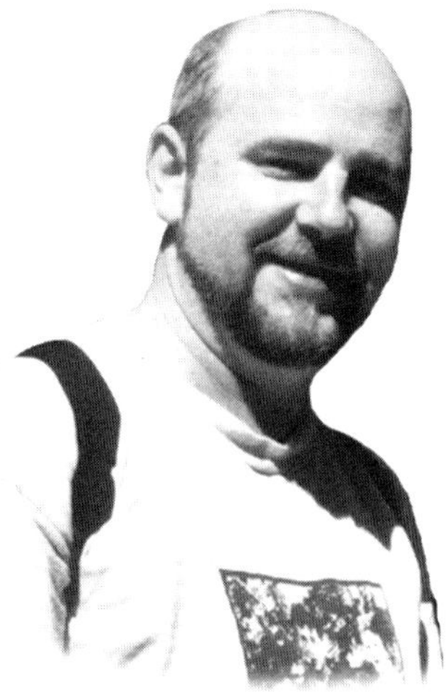

Kevin Hasson

Kevin's formal education began with the Christian Brothers' School in the Brandywell area of the city. It later moved to the Creggan and was renamed St Peter's. That was in the early 1970s.

'Art, even then, was the thing I was most interested in', he says. 'My father was the principle motivator in that regard. He was a very talented man who, in times of poverty, used his skills and imagination to entertain us. Creativity, therefore, constituted the environment I grew up in. My four other brothers are all talented either in painting, crafts or music, or in all three. In retrospect, I would say, without my dad we would have had some very bleak Christmases. He made our toys for us.'

For his first ever trip out of Ireland, Kevin, thanks to the persuasions of his girlfriend, found himself on a relief mission to the starving of Calcutta. Nothing could have prepared him for the culture shock. It was an experience that transformed him. On returning home again to the political maelstrom of Derry, he decided to make his way to Israel. 'By the time I reached Frankfurt, Germany, I was skint and decided to stay there. During my twelve years stay, I got to know a lot of people including German artists, painted a few murals and saw quite a bit of Europe.' There too, Kevin met his American wife to be. Once married, he settled down in America. Two sets of twins followed in quick succession, and, finally, he returned home with his family. He wasn't home a fortnight when he linked up once more with Tom, whom he had first met at St Peter's. Tom and Kevin had worked for a while in Doherty's Butchers before Kevin set sail for Europe. Art was the thing they had most in common.

The events of Bloody Sunday had a big impact on Kevin.

'Living in the Creggan, I was used to the sounds of gunfire. Usually it would last a few minutes and then stop. During the march on Bloody Sunday, shooting erupted around the Rossville flats. *It didn't stop.* All my instincts told me, 'This is different', and I ran all the way home and only when I reached the house did I feel safe. I was eleven years old at the time. But I will never forget that, nor the horror I felt too, when next day I learned the truth. As far as I am concerned, what took place on Bloody Sunday shaped the politics of the North.' In those days Kevin spent his spare time drawing what gradually became very familiar scenes in Derry. Three of these childhood sketches are reproduced opposite.

Kevin has high hopes for the major project the artists began in 1994 and which they call *The Bogside Modern,* viz a series of large murals stretching all along Rossville Street that will tell the history of the struggle through the key events.

'Ours is a commemorative art,' he stresses. 'We seek to give honour to the ordinary people who paid the price for whatever progress has been made.'

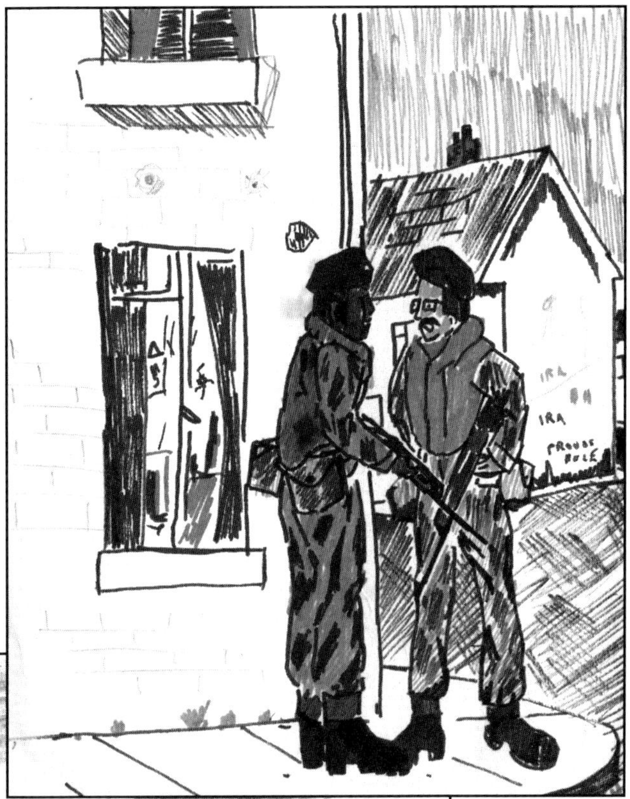

Of the murals so far painted, *Bloody Sunday,* depicting the death of Jackie Duddy, is special to Kevin. At the same time, he would not consider one mural as more important than the next.

'They are all equally well thought out and equally well painted.' For Kevin, who knows his history, the clear narrative of the murals that will comprise *The Bogside Modern* is what is vitally important.

'We get a lot of visitors coming to Derry from all over the world. Many of them come to the Bogside. Once they get there, they see our story, painted by ourselves. This will benefit all the people of Derry, at every level. It makes me proud to reflect that there has been a general increase in creative expression among the young of the city because of our work.'

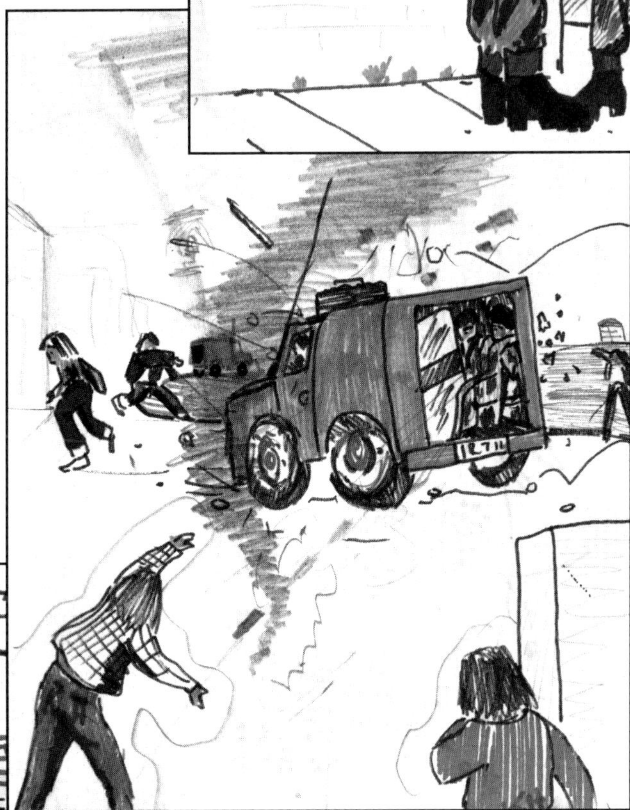

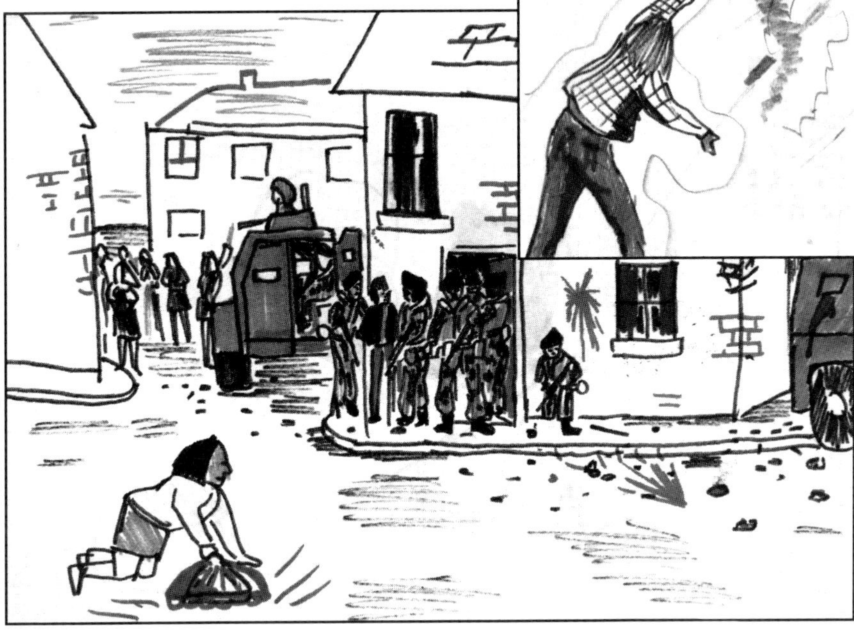

Kevin's childhood drawings of everyday life in the Creggan Estate, Derry, 1972.

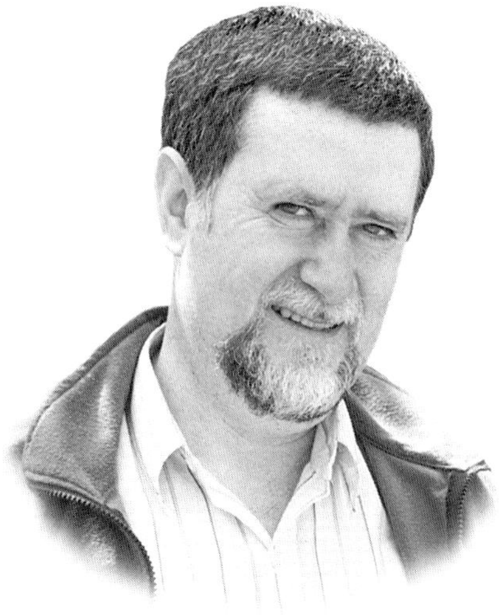

WILLIAM KELLY

Tom's older brother William likewise worked in England. First he went to Queen's University, Belfast, after a formal education at St Columb's College.

'I ended up studying French, because I liked the language, and Philosophy, because the world made no sense to me whatsoever.' William decided to leave after the first Christmas break. He went to Carlisle in England to work as a Post Office counter clerk, which lasted a year. He returned to study art at the Belfast Art College and later to take up a job back in Derry as an assistant librarian.

'That lasted a year too. It was the most agreeable job I had ever had. Around that time I met my future wife and moved to Dublin to resume my modest ambition to make my bread as an artist.' Three years later, he had his degree and a place in the dole queue.

'I had tried to get on the teacher-training course, but the interviewers, a man and a woman, knew well enough that I was both a socialist and able to think for myself, and so the drawbridge was quickly hoisted in the manner of a nun winding up the window of her car as a grinning drunk approaches. I was to have a similar experience when I applied to Cork, except the lady there, a redhead whose name escapes me, was even more freaked-out at the prospect of me at large on the premises misleading the church-going youth of Ireland.'

He moved to Wicklow with his wife and daughter and took a job at a sawmill.

'Working conditions were reminiscent of Solzhenitsyn's account of *One Day in the Life of Ivan Denisovich*.' A year later, he was back in Derry where he taught art part time at the local tech. That ended when he announced one morning to his students that anybody not interested in the subject of art should feel free to leave. 'They left,' he remembers ruefully. 'And I left later . . . about five minutes later.'

That's when William decided to resume his own work and try to make a living as a painter.

'After 14 one-man shows all over Ireland, I finally realised that class delusions and bigotry were as rife in the art world – more so, in fact – than anywhere else. Not even critics could be trusted to give an unbiased assessment of your work once they learned you were from the Catholic working class of the Bogside. It was a depressing fact, but one that I had discovered long before in the South with its pietistic hypocrisies and general antipathy towards the North. Although I had often met with the same response in England, I found 'my own', as they say, to be a whole lot worse.

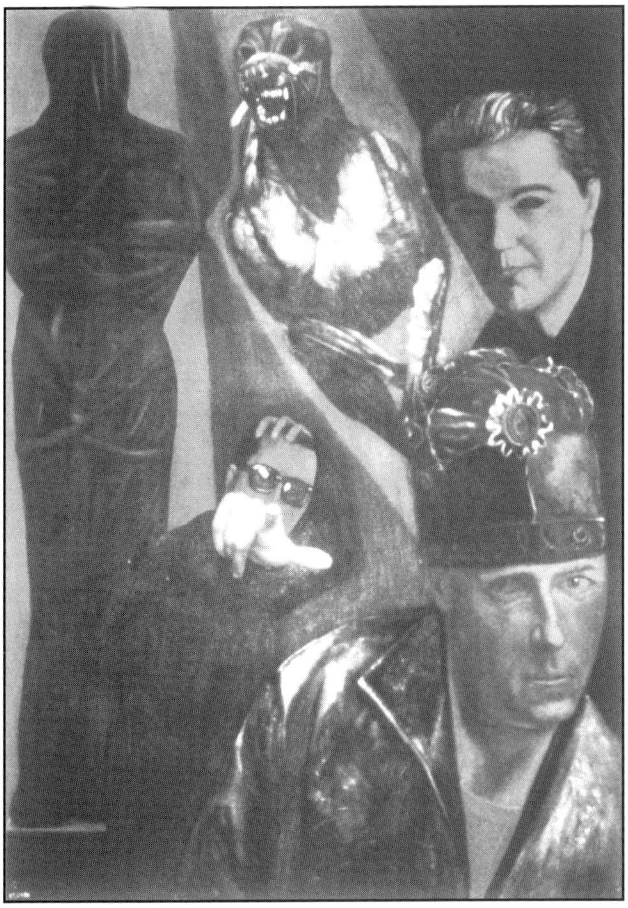

Paranoid? Limerick exhibition, oil on canvas.

The Irish really are irrevocably convinced that nothing good can come out of Ireland. If it is foreign, it has an edge from the start. Whatever it is the Irish are looking for, whether it be an interior decorator or a professor, they will instinctively seek elsewhere. It is particularly true of the arts; and it is as true of Dublin, Limerick and Cork as it is of Belfast and Derry. Incidentally, in all those years of work I never received a single penny from either arts council.' These were lessons that had a profound impact on his understanding of art and what it might be for.

'The year 1993 arrived and I was ready for change, because no change, not even jail, could have made my situation any worse. Being an artist had cost me dear, including my marriage. Up until then, and for a long time after, I was practising my craft in a one-bedroom flat on the fringes of the Bogside, in fact not a hundred yards from Bishop's Gate where James II himself had called on the city's citizens to surrender way back in 1688. The flat was as close to Dickensian squalor as you could get. Hitler had been invading Poland when the furniture was tacked together. Still, I refused to do any other work than what I had chosen to do. Given my critical outlook and my resultant penury, it was a natural progression for me to leave my romantic fantasies and join with Tom and Kevin to do some real art for a change. It is a decision I have never regretted. The *Troubles* of course, were raging all around. Photos of the stuff I did then, I can hardly bring myself to look at. Still, for me, it is as it always has been: it is the work alone that finally matters. *Meaning,* in a word: good artists find it and share it; bad artists visit hell on themselves and, by proxy, on everybody else. You will know them by their misery. As the world is evidently more desperately in need of meaningless bad news than meaningful good, they are generally well paid. We three are a happy bunch in the main.

The following was written a long time ago. We include it here because it not only describes our thinking then, but it has proved to be oddly prophetic. In fact, the whole drive towards novelty and self-aggrandisement in artistic form has accelerated. Now artists, who wish to make a name for themselves (and the market is so constructed that many are driven to do so), think in terms of the *grand gesture* or even the *grandest gesture*. If you can persuade an airport to divert its planes for your camera, or get thousands of people to strip naked and lay on the ground for a photo, or, in general, play God with people's time and lives, then you get to wear the mantle of *contemporary*. It's what's expected. It's *fashionable*. It's *way to go*. You are in or you are out. There is nothing essentially *contemporary* about any of it of course, at least not in the way that word expects itself to be understood. And taken to its logical conclusion, the vogue must finally demand, if it be honest with itself, that Cecil Blount de Mille be proclaimed the greatest artist of all time, because nobody with the possible exception of Adolf, got more people to line up for his flicks than did Cecil – not to mention the gigantic props pioneered by both. The vogue is an *ism* waiting for an ambitious critic to baptise it. Our viewpoint, then and now, has remained unaltered. We include this article here, because it helped gel our ideas into what we daringly call our 'manifesto'.

ARTICLE PUBLISHED IN *THE IRISH TIMES* ON 7 AUGUST 1993

After my last exhibition in Ireland at Limerick City's Gallery, opened by Michael Higgins, TD, and attended by future Taoiseach John Bruton, I wrote the following article for *The Irish Times*. Not only does it show my way of thinking at the time, but has proved surprisingly accurate and prophetic in its prognosis of the state of the art world. Soon afterwards, the Bogside Artists came into being.
William Kelly, September 2001.

Art today has become a service, a 'spiritual' service. The artist works within the milieu of pre-existing standards and expectations. He is the shaman of the age, standing shoulders with psychiatrists, advertising executives and media pundits. His wares, for the most part, are as spurious as any witchdoctor's powders and potions. This need not deter, for it is only those with *faith* who can be healed. Market credibility gifts the placebo with curative properties as well as exchange value.

As with any service, he or she who renders it is more important than the service itself. To have your hair done by Vidal Sassoon in your Armani jacket is altogether different from a visit to your local barber as you wear your Burton jacket bought in the January sales. Who we think we are determines whom we go to see and how much we are prepared to pay for the privilege. In the crumbling hotel called 'civilisation', the cultural suite is occupied by intellectuals (or at least men who think they know a thing or two about the business of art and are prepared to back their judgement). It is they who draw up the parameters, award the Oscars, distribute the prizes and blow the bugle of their latest 'discovery'. The rest is down to marketing.

What rules here is 'high profile'. The higher up the *ladder* the greener grows the grass. Neither 'high profile' nor prestige, of course, has any relationship to the product. What they have to do with is how people 'perceive' the product. Ergo, what they depend on is a niche in the public consciousness, or what the advertising gurus call a 'position'. Picasso does not revolve in the same orbit as Hockney. They are as different as Guinness and Coca Cola, which, incidentally, does not deter Hockney from cadging whatever ideas he can off Picasso.

Artists aflame with ambition, angle for 'position' by pitching at the best galleries; a single print hung in the Tate being hugely more preferable to a solo exhibition of large-scale oils in Hull. Media hype makes the running. And, as art has become a service, the hype must centre on the artist himself. Dali, for one, knew this well enough and his lesser cousins have not missed the message.

The trick of mesmerizing the public is to subdue its resistance and the method is . . . repetition. Repeat the assertion long enough and the public will buy it. Repetition is the modus operandi of every ad you see on TV: patterns, in other words, the stuff of which slot machines are made. Brand X really is the best, don't you know. Therefore, Picasso is the best, or Hockney, or Andre, or whoever. Other luminaries are ever in demand. And these market leaders set the parameters for the rest. It's not so much that the artist must compete with these, although many foolishly do, but, like satellites around the sun, they must find their own position. The credibility of the product is dependent exclusively on this consensual, uncritical acceptance. A 'bandwagon' in art is merely a niche that has already been established. If it survives, it is called a 'genre'.

And what are the standards? That is the question. The fact is that there aren't any. This means that the success or failure of the shaman is determined entirely by how much media hype he can win for himself. Warhol, an old advertising workhorse, was well briefed, so to speak, in the procedure. By aligning himself with Campbell's soup, which already occupied a high position in the collective psyche, he had successfully tacked his flag to his own ego. It was a merger. Repetition, the heartbeat of the advertising industry, is the method of his work. By sanctifying advertising ideology, he sanctified himself. Art and business, in other words, are identical. After soup it was Marilyn Monroe and then Mao, and so on. Andy never looked back. It was a marriage made in heaven – the poet threw in the towel and married the accountant, and they lived happily ever after, both blissfully unaware of the two little teeth marks on their necks.

Art and money is one and the same thing. There's an American chap called Boggs trying to enlighten us on this point by drawing and selling his own dollar bills – to the great merriment of his bank manager. The efficacy of the product, its value in moral or cultural terms, is merely irrelevant. Thus, the path to eminence for the aspiring 'artist' is as clear-cut as Tyrone crystal. Here it is:

1. Shock the audience if possible. (Kitsch still hurts a little. Porn not as much as it used to. 'Madonna' has already sanctified it. Think bricks or car tyres. The blank canvas has been done. Super-realism is only hypocrisy. Gigantism? Way to go. Well . . . when somebody outdoes Christo by tying a ribbon around the moon, there'll be nowhere else to go.)

2. Repeat your assertion. (Remember Andy's soup cans and silk-screens.)

3. Get the big galleries interested. (Don't worry about the 'work'.)

4. Get copies distributed of your 'pieces'. (Make friends with the media. Insult them. They forgive all in the cause of copy.)

5. Avoid all questions about the meaning of your 'work'.

There you have it. This is the royal road to success in the visual arts. The artist of integrity, if such still exists, is still dependent on all or some of the above for his success. The more he believes in himself, the more likely he is to find others more versed in the ways of the world to believe in him. It is a moral dilemma that has induced more than a few to bin their brushes. If Ireland has produced so few 'great artists', herein lies the reason. We still refuse to see ourselves as commodities in a free-floating market.

It is the *profile* of the shaman – his 'position', not the shaman himself – that gives potency to his wares. A drawing, after all, is *only* a drawing, until somebody tells you it's a *Modigliani.* The artist is the producer, the source, the factory, and even if the product is as efficacious or culturally important as a string of pearls – or a pile of bricks for that matter – it scarcely matters, for should he attain the position occupied by either in the collective consciousness, he will be a rich and successful man. This is why it is not talent that is funded by the government arts agencies, but *ambition*: not the exceptional, but the ordinary; not the honest, but the cunning; not the relevant, but the irrelevant; not the new, but the novel; and never the true, but the false.

Manifesto

We believe it is the artist's role to keep alive those values which are basic and human, and to resist those forces which seek to undermine and compromise that integrity. Our work, as the Bogside Artists, is purposefully directed to changing and bettering our society's view of itself. The individual, in this role, acts as an educator first and foremost. In our case, that education means fixing the past so that the disasters it speaks of do not happen again. As Bishop Tutu pointed out, we can only treat wounds that are seen, and seen clearly. That doesn't mean it is the artist's job to make people better or more human. After all, how effective has art been in that regard? Caligula saw himself as a poet. Nero, we are told, sang his own songs while Rome burned. Hitler, Goebbels and Goering all saw themselves as refined and sophisticated gentlemen who harnessed the brains of equally refined and sophisticated gentlemen to plan genocide on behalf of what was essentially an idiot's fantasy – the Superman, with the music of Wagner in one hand and a cudgel in the other. People caught in crossfire, whether it be in Jerusalem or Belfast, do not reflect on the contents of the Louvre, unless it be to wonder what good is any of it when the bullets start flying.

If the creative spirit depends on a truthful state of mind, then only those with a conscience have the right to live there. And once situated there, they must also be aware that they are in the service of a moral, and therefore a social, imperative to express that truth fearlessly. And because this service is essentially social, the artist's work is political, whether he wishes it or not. What we mean by political are the actions by which men strive to govern their affairs and create their social being. Art, in its roles of witness, messenger, and counsellor, has always been to the forefront in this context. It was primarily for the people of conscience that the Gulag Archipelago was built. For art can be a power of its own in the right hands. If the pen is mightier than the sword, the paintbrush is oftentimes a lot mightier than either. When, in fact, we speak of art being transpersonal, we are speaking of its social character, for it is its social character that determines its ultimate efficacy.

The ship called Modern Art would appear to have lost her way. Not only are its maps no longer reliable, but its navigation equipment is knackered. In Ireland, consciously or otherwise, the ideology implanted by the old colonialism still holds sway. So much so, that you could be forgiven for thinking it is the Tourist Board that controls modern Irish culture. That which is truly contemporary in Irish art, or outside the established European traditions, is barely tolerated. It has always been like that. Middle-class values and their adherents decide what is art and what isn't. Inevitably, as with editors of newspapers and television programme controllers, they manoeuvre themselves into a position whereby they can promote these values. Their masters in business and conservative politics facilitate their rise to eminence. This is why there are no great paintings or sculptures from Ireland's Great Famine period of 1845–50 when a million people died and over two million were to emigrate over the following decade. Still less will you find a contemporary painting depicting the 1916 uprising.

Were it not for our writers, in fact, there would not have been any artistic commentary on those times at all. That this attitude should still prevail in the face of over thirty years of dire political conflict is nothing short of bewildering. In the corridors of these august institutions, conservative delusions rule. In vain do you argue with these people that what we refer to as 'great art', whether it be European or not, had its roots in social conflict, for social change appears to only come about by conflict. Only when we learn to make social change without crucifying each other will we be able to lay claim to being truly human.

Picasso, and before him Manet, had taken a swipe at the moral hypocrisies of their day; Manet's Olympia is the precursor of Les Demoiselles D'Avignon. Neither was acceptable in his own time. Marcel Duchamp's entire output follows from the same reaction to prevailing cultural values. Magritte's work speaks of man's social alienation. Honore Daumier and George Grosz, both powerfully influential artists, were social critics first and foremost. Käthe Kollwitz and Francisco Goya were brutally honest reporters on human social injustice. Whole movements, like Dadaism, Surrealism and German Expressionism, were essentially reactions against social, and therefore political, restraints. Let us not forget that Picasso himself was a lifelong card-carrying member of the Communist party. On his studio door he had once written in bold letters, 'Je ne suis pas un gentilhomme!' Whatever else you might think of that, he at least made his position perfectly clear. And let us not forget the era of the witch-hunts, conducted by the Un-American Activities committees, when artists again were singled out as the chief enemies of the state. Prominent in the game was Richard Nixon, incidentally. Criminals, even petty ones, do not like witnesses. Messengers can only present the message. The counsellor is more likely to lose his head in the dungeons than get an invitation to the wingding at the palace.

The Bogside Artists are seen as political activists stumbling from overt conflict to a diffident handshake with democracy. That's whenever they are taken seriously, that is. Ironically, back home we are seen by some as non-reactionary artists who are, by that token, unrepresentative of their community. To ourselves, we are three men who are simply engaged in documenting our history in a way we think appropriate: nothing more, nothing less; what you see is most definitely what you get.

The poet Seamus Heaney, objecting vehemently to having been included in a British anthology of poetry, explained himself thus:

'What is the source of our first suffering? It lies in the fact that we hesitated to speak... It was born in the moment when we accumulated silent things within us.'

Well, with due deference to the great poet, we have not hesitated to speak. We felt strongly that the daily media outpourings of tribal cant and unsubstantiated vilification concerning all those who stood up for civil rights since 1968 required a response that would endure long enough for the truth of our human dignity to prevail. We re-appropriated our own story.

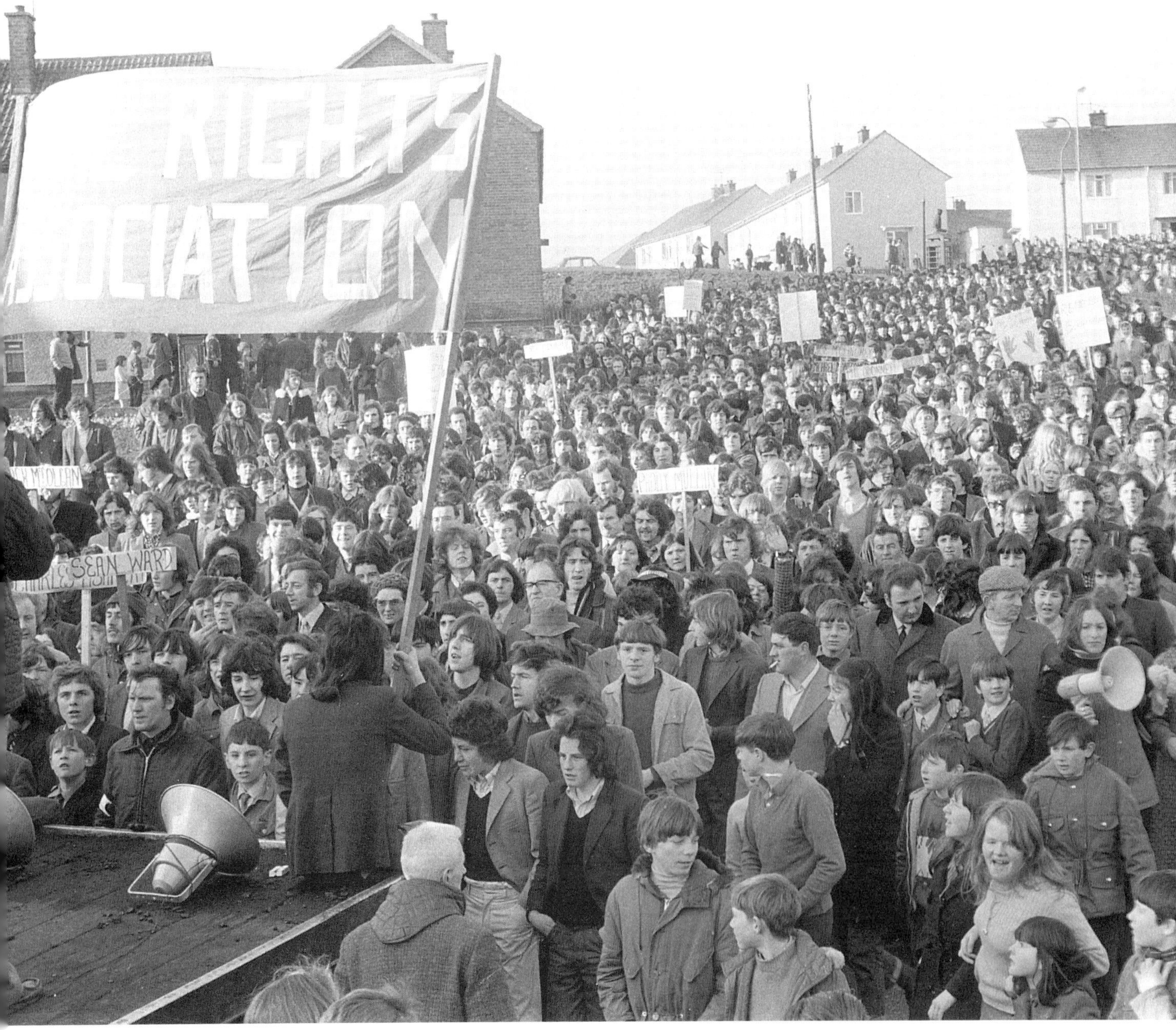

Wall Painting

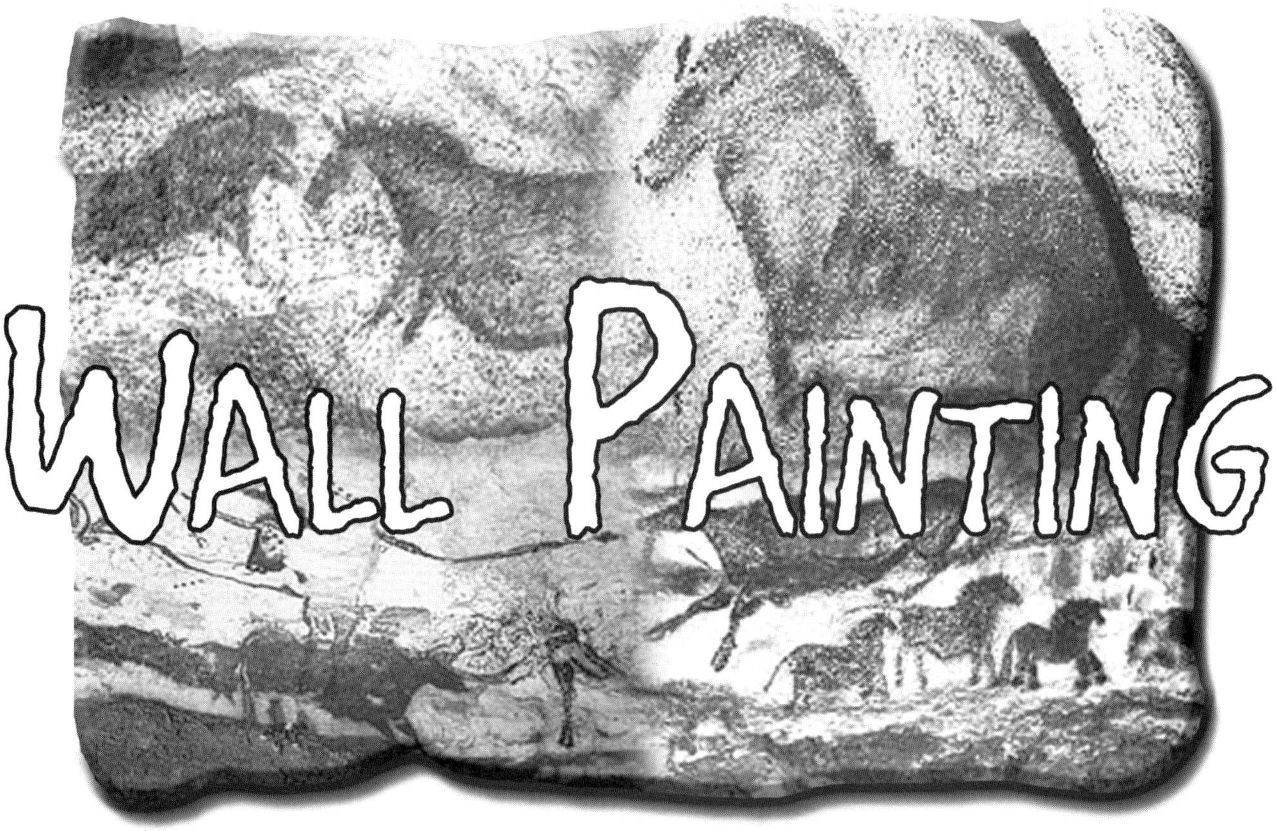

Apartheid was a politics of space more than anything . . . much of the Apartheid legislation was denying people the right to move. It's all about space, restricting space . . . Claiming art is also reclaiming space.

David Koloane, South African artist

Wall painting goes back to the caves of Australia's Northern Territory, of Lascaux and Altamira and beyond. The Egyptians were masters of wall painting as were the Buddhists of India, China, Japan and Tibet. The preparation of a wall using plaster gave rise to fresco painting, which itself goes back to Minoan and Greek times. From these derive the Graeco-Roman frescoes still superlatively alive in the remains of Pompeii. Giotto (1267–1337), recognised as one of the great initiators of the revival of classical art known as the Renaissance, was essentially a wall painter. Thenceforth, most of the great Italian masters from Masaccio (1401–28) onwards, produced works in the medium. Michelangelo's Sistine Chapel is, in fact, an enormous fresco.

Since their arrival on the scene in the 1920s and '30s, *Los Tres Grandes*, Diego Rivera, Jose Orozco and David Alfaro Siqueiros, have been seen as the prototypical political muralists. What is not so commonly appreciated is that they did their work *after* the revolution proper, at a time when several parties vied for Nationalist support. The years of armed revolution were between 1910 and 1920. Rivera (1886–1957) was travelling around Europe between 1907 and 1921. His first important commissions came from the Mexican government, which was anxious to promote Mexican cultural nationalism. The murals participated in supplying the stuff of vote-catching myths. Of the three, it was Orozco and his preoccupation with the human propensity for greed, deception and violence that had the biggest impact on Jackson Pollock who worked with him. Pollock always saw himself as a muralist on canvas. Rivera is still the most discussed of the

Mexican muralists, although critics find his didacticism offensive. He was a friend of Leon Trotsky who was assassinated in Mexico City by Ramon del Rio in 1940. These days, throughout America, wall painting is undergoing something of a revival. Its efficacy lies in the fact that it is a direct and powerful way to place an artistic statement in the public forum.

Cuban artists have either been exiled – or exiled themselves – to America and elsewhere. Artists like Carlos Alfonzo, Luis Marin and Daniel Serra-Badue are well respected. In South Africa, the work of Willie Bester, Manfred Zylla, Sue Williamson and Denise Penfold, to name but a few, has confronted social iniquity with honesty and vigour. Zylla is unique among them in seeing the need for community involvement in the making of public art statements wherein they can express their anger and frustration at the injustices they experience.

In Northern Ireland, mural painting was once regarded as a strictly Protestant preserve. Orange symbolism and mythic Williamite imagery were its substance. Since the beginning of the nineteenth century, and in line with the governmental policy of physical segregation, street bunting, flags, pavement decoration, floral displays, banners, as well as murals, have been the weft and weave of Protestant culture. It wasn't until 1969, and, specifically, with the mural in the Bogside called *Free Derry*, that Republican painters saw in murals a way to express their responses to political and social events. Free Derry Corner has become profoundly totemic in that sense. The Bogsiders were signalling not only a reclaiming of physical space and political space, but psychological space. They were claiming a right to choice.

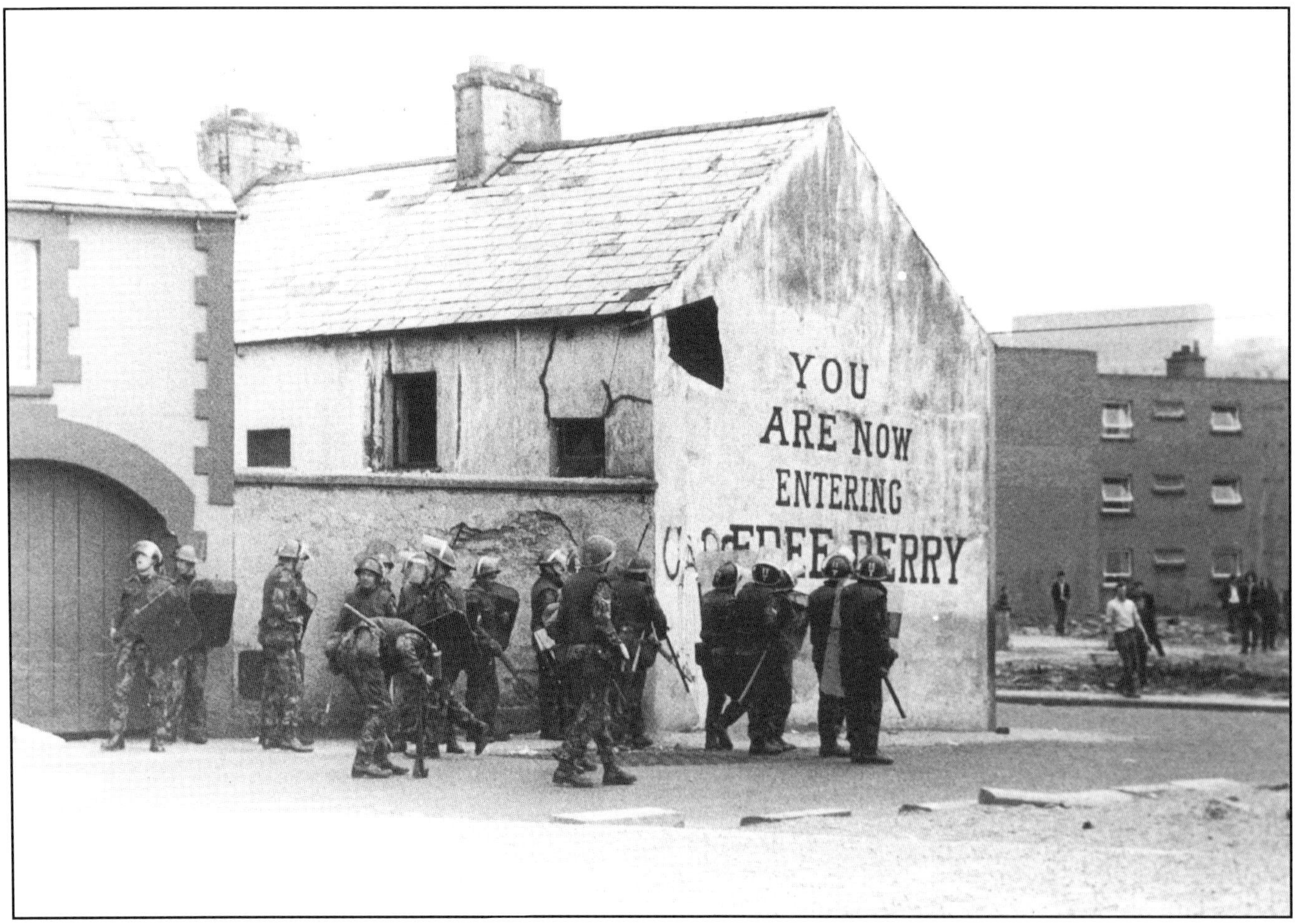

In the early 1980s, Republican murals proliferated throughout the North, as indeed they once proliferated in working-class Protestant precincts during the anti-Home Rule era. Nowadays, many of them seek to emphasise the Irishness of Nationalism. In this pursuit, artists call on ancient folklore and history, as often as not using interlaced borders and patterns that characterise Celtic art. Even so, many of these murals are associated with paramilitary groups rather than with Nationalists expressing merely a sense of identity. The same cannot be said of Loyalist murals, although of late, Loyalist painters appear to be taking an interest in their own history and traditions for their own sake in much the same way as Republicans. One hesitates to speak of culture in either regard as an existent fact, because it is clear to all of us that culture is more media influenced – and consequently of a sameness everywhere – than many of us would care to admit. It could also be argued that this embracing of indigenous culture, which is by no means peculiar to Northern Ireland, is a reaction to the relentless homogenisation that constitutes the global 'other culture' of the electronic age. Islamic fundamentalists fear this as much as anything else that characterises the threat posed by the West.

Not all artists either have the opportunity or the will to express such views on city Walls. However pretentious it may sound, we too work on canvas. Such work is currently on tour in America and Australia. *From Protest to Peace*, the name of both shows, describes the work well. Briefly, what are on view are the collective responses of three men born and raised in Derry. We feel that only by telling our story can some light be shed on the hidden and not so hidden political determinisms that have shaped our past and will continue to shape our future. Only by objectifying the past can we hope ever to exorcise its dominion over us. It is a necessary part of the healing process, as true for the individual psyche as for that of the collective – if indeed the two can ever be separated. And it is as true for Protestant people as it is for Catholic.

The work is what it is. We know full well that we are outside the mainstream of modern art, and purposely so, for we understood from the beginning that we had a story to tell rather than a career to promote. The *story* is what is important. We are not aspirants to the rogues' hall called the *Collectibles*: Bakelite phones and Victorian clocks are also collectible. HP sauce is famous and has been around longer than any of us – since 1899 in fact – and will probably still be around when all the celebrities we now applaud are gone and forgotten. Our work raises questions about art and artists in general that are best addressed in an educational context. That is why we show mostly in community art centres and universities. We welcome the opportunity to explain the simple fact that we do not march to the beat of any drum, unless it be that of human freedom.

As with any art, the work itself can evoke all sorts of responses. The child's unclouded view or the man-in-the-street's gut response often contains more wisdom and intelligence than the most pedantic conceptual edifice. What you bring to the work, as an honest observer, is just as important, if not more so, than what is gifted to you. We do not play down the contextual significance that lends itself to the work. Neither are we militant propagandists, tribal fantasists, or proponents of the *us*-versus-*them* delusion that is still causing such evils around the world. We are simply human beings, born in a certain époque and in a particular set of circumstances, who practise the art of painting and like to think, however naively, that we are free to do just that. That we have chosen to paint the world and society into which we were born should not be wondered at, any more than one should wonder why Goya created his Desastres de la Guerra etchings, Kollwitz her prints, Dylan his songs, or Solzhenitsyn his novels.

OUR CV

The artists are no great advocates of CVs, irrespective of the importance placed upon them by art schools and colleges. Alas, it is clear why these institutions are driven to do so: because the artist has it tough enough in other ways and needs anything that will help him move forward and, we hope, make a living. That said, it is a fact that in the art world it is an area in which deception is easy and prevalent. Just as a slide can give a completely false picture of an artefact in terms of colour, dimensions, texture and so on (almost always flattering), so too, and even more so, can a CV.

For instance, it is common practice for a painter to send a single drawing or print to be accepted by a foreign gallery where it will figure with hundreds of others in some annual event to do with mail art. In his CV, he will state: 'Exhibited at the Gallery of Modern Art, Tokyo.' The same applies to inclusions in magazines or newspapers. In many quarters, the artist's CV is more important than his/her work. The carefully polished CV becomes the pebble by which they hope to bring down the giant of anonymity and seize the crown referred to in the trade as 'established'. To the status quo, only the 'established' artist really matters. Many students are encouraged in this pursuit by tutors who themselves missed the crown by a mile and were placed in the stocks of art education for their failure. There are artists whose singular achievement has not been anything they produced at all . . . merely their CVs. That in itself should tell you something about the state of the art world.

What follows is as close as we can get to where we have been and the sort of attention we have received. It is provided for those refugees from televisual narcosis who may be still in possession of the faculty the Ancients once called 'curiosity'. To list magazines, books and newspapers where our work has figured would be impossible, as we are not aware of all of them and, even if we were, we see no point whatever in listing them; they are too numerous to mention. We mention only a few of those to which we have ourselves contributed, as such texts may be of interest to those willing to take the trouble to track them down.

Derry – The Calgach Centre (the artists' studio), Jan '98

Mildura, Australia – The Mildura Arts Centre, Victoria, Feb '98

Sydney, Australia – ACU (Australia Catholic University), St Mary's Campus, May '98

Sydney, Australia – The University Sydney, College of The Arts, May '98 (These two exhibitions, running concurrently, marked the first-ever collaboration on an art exhibition by these institutions.)

Boston, USA – Bapst Library, Boston College, July '98 (This show, hosted by Professors Raymond Helmick and John Michalcyzk, marked the first time ever the magnificent Bapst Library was given over to an art exhibition.)

Orange County, USA – Rocklands Community College, Sep '98

New York – The Irish Centre, Manhattan, Dec '98

Boston – The Boston State House, May '99 (The show here was extended from an initial week to over four.)

Boston – Boston College, The Rolesham Arts Centre, Oct '99

Philadelphia, USA – The John Moore College Gallery, Sep 2000

Philadelphia – Villanova University Gallery, Sep 2000 (The show heralded a unique collaboration between these colleges.)

Our touring show in the USA is already the most comprehensive explication in art form on the subject of the *Troubles* to have come out of Ireland. It comprises paintings, texts and photographs. A second exhibition also toured Australia. The following is a detailed itinerary:

Mildura – Mildura Arts Centre, Victoria, Jan 2000

Perth – The Perth International Fringe Festival, Feb 2000

This exhibition at the PICA gallery was put together by the artists especially for the festival; they used text, slides, film and cibachromes of work already on tour in Australia. They also painted, in public, a large-scale mural at the gallery during the show.

Adelaide – The Red House Community Gallery, March 2000

Port MacArthur – The Fountain Gallery, April 2000

Adelaide – The Onkaparinga Arts Centre, May/June 2000

Ballarat – ACU, July/Aug 2000

Melbourne – ACU, St Patrick's Campus, Sep/Oct 2000

Newcastle – Newcastle Regional University, Nov/Dec 2000

Sydney – ACU, St Mary's Campus, Dec/Jan 2000/01

Brisbane – ACU, McAuley Campus, Jan/Feb 2001

Brisbane – The Queensland Irish Association, Feb 2001

This tour is also continuing: from Limerick to Philadelphia and New York; to Sydney and Perth; the Bogside Artists have given numerous talks on their work. They have deliberately opened a wide-ranging debate on the role of the artist in society, focusing specifically on the meaning of politics vis-à-vis the dimension of cultural expression. Their work has appeared in numerous magazines, periodicals, newspapers and books. They have also written many articles for newspapers and magazines including *Hot Press*, *Fortnight*, *The Irish Times* and *Exhibita*. They have so far featured in seven documentaries: in particular, *What You See Is What You Get*, a BBC forty-five minute film devoted to the artists and their work, which was broadcast just a few weeks before the Good Friday agreement – the bedrock of the present peace process. In addition, the artists have given radio interviews on their work from Boston to Sydney. They recently featured in a documentary called *Walls For Change,* by Cindy Leaney, which was broadcast nationally in Canada and North America. The artists will continue with their tour of the USA and will be showing in new venues prior to a retrospective at Trenton Museum in the metropolitan district of New York in February 2004.

THE PETROL BOMBER

It was the era of flower power, Zen, dope, alternative lifestyles, dropping out and dropping in, and the High Priest of it all, Timothy Leary (recently dropped 'around'). Protest was the name of the game. Shocking the establishment was a fad. It was the era of *Easy Rider* and *Woodstock,* where half a million people spent four days in a swamp to hear an endless parade of spaced-out pop stars do their thing. WASP values were on the ropes. The war in Vietnam filled the papers daily. Jimi Hendrix and the Beatles were on the crest of a wave and our own Phil Coulter was to win the Eurovision Song Contest with *Puppet On a String*.

On 5 June 1968, Robert Kennedy was gunned down in Los Angeles while the world was still trying to get to grips with the assassination of Martin Luther King on 4 April as he spoke from the balcony of the Lorraine Motel in Memphis, Tennessee. Nixon had appropriated the Whitehouse on a 'peace with honour' ticket for withdrawal of troops from Vietnam. The first went there in March '65. Within a year, 385,000 bewildered Americans in uniform were walking through the paddy fields wondering what they were doing there. By the time Lyndon Johnson cried, 'Hold, enough!' to the barman and Nixon had seized the wheel, the war had cost 58,000 lives, too high a price even for America. But it made an awful lot of people rich, that being the name of the game.

On 20 July 1969, Armstrong and Aldrin set their all-American boots on the chaste surface of the moon, much to the delight of the then president, 'Tricky Dicky' Nixon. Despite his looks, and with all the charm of a poison apple, Richard Milhous Nixon had eventually managed to get himself elected as the thirty-seventh president of the USA. For this deranged soul, the world and all its problems had been created so that he could write his memoirs.

Shortly afterwards, on 9 August, another moon-man, Charles Manson led his devoted 'family' of worshipful devotees to a mansion in Bel Air to kill his 'arch-enemy', Sharon Tate (eight months pregnant at the time) and six of her friends. It was one horror story from many. The actress and wife of Roman Polanski had been stabbed sixteen times and her friend Rose LaBianca forty-eight times, a clear case of 'overkill', an epithet spawned in the hells of Vietnam and as shameless in its brutal absurdity as its contemporary derivative 'ethnic cleansing'. After the trial, people in the USA drove around with 'Free Charlie Manson' stickers on their cars. We were all appropriately shocked, and still are.

Spurred on by the patent lunacy of Vietnam, Afro-Americans saw fit to march for civil rights. From 1955 to his death, Dr Martin Luther King worked tirelessly to expose the inhuman heart of American politics. Influenced by Gandhi, he used the media, mass demonstrations, marches and sit-ins to effect reforms in education, housing and jobs. And in so doing, he set the style for civil-rights campaigners for evermore. On 28 August 1963, King had led a march of over a quarter of a million people to the Lincoln Memorial in Washington. There, he delivered his famous 'I have a dream . . . ' speech. It seemed to many that the dream was over when forty-three people were killed at Newark and 7,000 arrested during the summer riots of 1967. Detroit had a similar death toll with 388 families left homeless and the government lumbered with a bill for $500 million. Some 164 riots occurred right across the USA that year from New York to Los Angeles. It was all happening in 1967; that was the year the Northern Ireland Civil Rights Association was formed.

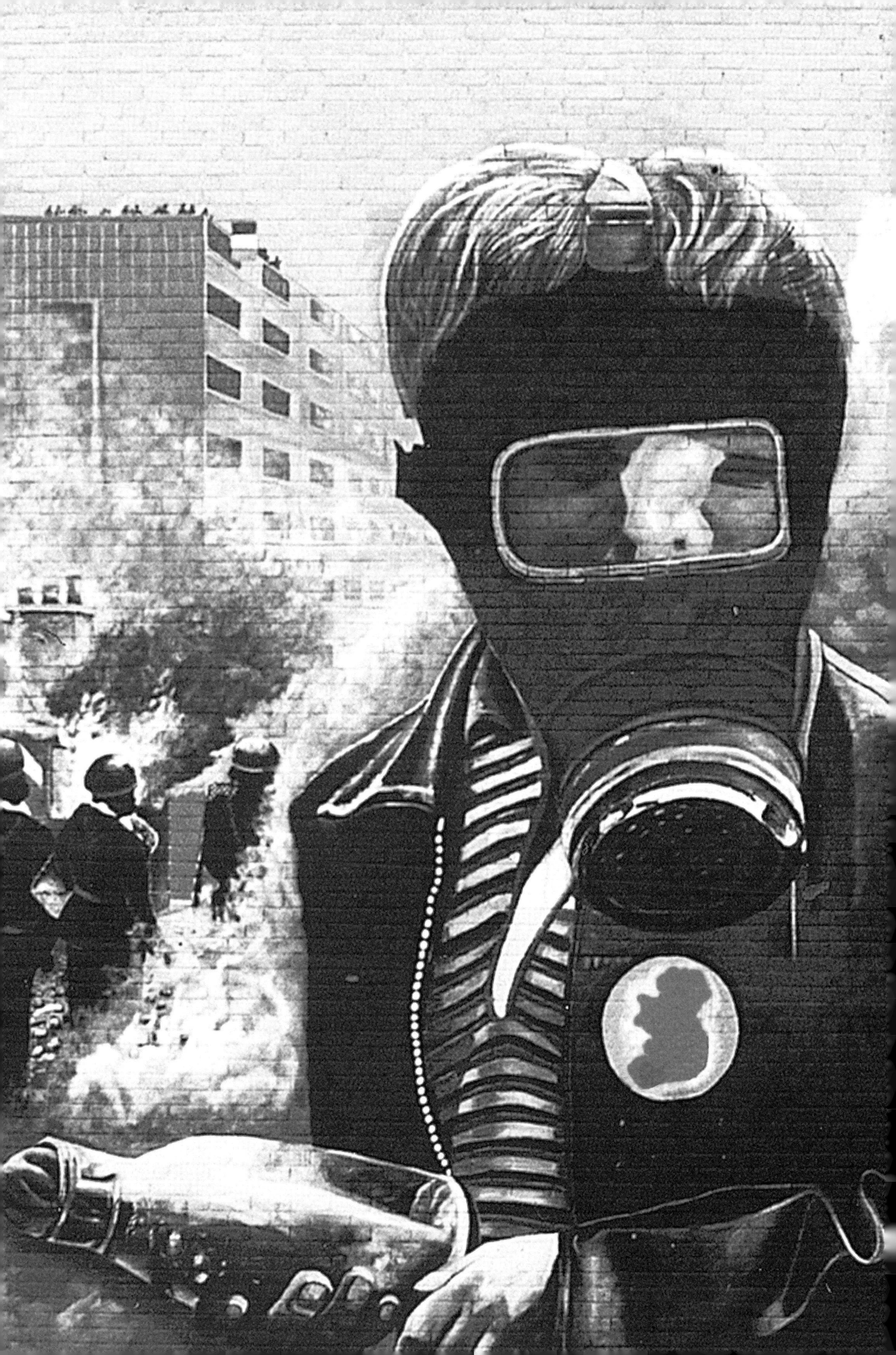

The May '68 riots in Paris did nothing to ease the general angst in the Bogside, or anywhere else for that matter. They began with students marching against the general quality of French life and their predestined stations in society. The barricade battles between the students and police inspired workers at Nantes, Renault, Lockeed and Unulec to down tools. Banks, insurance offices, hospitals and factories were taken over by their employees. The situation was finally brought under control by the trade unions and the Communist Party, but not before over 12 million people had gone on strike, sickened by years of Gaullist rule and oppression. The minds of fervent socialists everywhere grew heady at the possibilities. Paris, of course, was no stranger to either riots or street barricades. Between 1827 and 1849, the capital saw both no less than eight times. The last barricades had been erected almost a century previously, during the Paris Commune of 1871. Charles de Gaulle quit office in 1969 and died the following year, requesting that nobody from the government attend his funeral.

Bogsiders, like everyone else, watched the ubiquitous mayhem on television. What the events brought home to many was that *politics* lay at the core of all aspirations for justice and equality. Not to know at least the rudiments of socialist theory left you on the 'inside' looking out, when you should have been on the 'outside' looking in. Worse, you should have had the wit to know you were on the 'outside' to begin with. Only the 'outsider' was really hip with what was going on. As the years rolled by, leading outsiders of the époque gradually moved indoors to accept their knighthoods and Grammies, and even grow petulant at falling record sales. Revolution in song, film or book was then good business – and still is. Foxy guys, who went on to create absurdities like the Sex Pistols and the Punk phenomenon, knew well enough the marketing potential of youthful rebellion and how both could be used to remove the fantasising factory worker from her hard-earned pocket money.

The mid-1950s movies of James Dean were far from dead in the '60s. The 'misfit', the outsider second only to Hamlet, Jimmy Dean was the thinking man's Presley. He had become a cult figure, especially in France. His legacy lingered on in mythic form. You were for or against, in or out, hip or square, Mod or Rocker. To us in the Bogside, a chap on a scooter was still only a chap on a scooter – and probably Protestant – while in certain places like Brighton, England, the same was seen as a declaration of war on wheels and dealt with accordingly.

The year 1969 witnessed the smash hit film *2001, A Space Odyssey* and Elvis Presley's hit song, *Suspicious Minds*. We longed for the former and hummed the latter while wondering who was running the show, as lost to all intents and purposes as the Afro-American trudging through the jungles of Vietnam; the Northern Irish not only qualified as 'outsiders', they spoke for the entire colony.

Back in our boxes in the Bogside, we looked to *The Liver Birds* or *Dave Allen* to cheer us up. Yasser Arafat became president of the Palestine Liberation Organisation. He wore a cloth thing on his head and apparently shaved with rusty blades; that was all we knew – or wanted to know. Sammy Beckett got the Nobel Prize for Literature for deep-freezing the human race into a state of suicidal depression. Shakespeare was undergoing another revival on the box and Bob Dylan was gazing upon the chimes of freedom flashin' while humping his crucifix from one exotic bed to another. Mary Quant had been killing us all slowly by inches for almost two years, *give or take a few weeks*. Frank Sinatra was doing it *My Way* or no way. Tammy Wynette was on her third husband when she conceived *Stand By Your Man*. She was destined, two husbands later, to beget an even bigger smash with *D-I-V-O-R-C-E*. Women everywhere were beginning to think that a career, multiple lovers and holidays abroad were preferable to serfdom, an ape, and perpetual dosages of *Coronation Street.* The Rolling Stones, meanwhile, had succeeded in planting into the minds of the gullible the notion that they were the *real* Beatles, because they were more misbehaved, had long hair to prove it, smoked pot and even wore their own clothes too and everything!

Added to all this anarchy and confusion, Derry had other problems to deal with that were soon to leave the realm of mere student debate and emerge into the arena of brutal reality. NICRA had had little success taking its grievances to Stormont and Westminster. In mid-1968, they decided to organise street demonstrations to bring attention to eighteen months of fruitless campaigning. William Craig's hard-line intransigence was the major stumbling block. He would eventually be the one to let the genie out of the bottle.

Towards the end of the year, thousands of people were brought out onto the streets of Derry. Mass demonstrations, reminiscent of Dr King's and given widespread publicity by the media, began to bring pressure to bear on the Unionist Government at Stormont. Initial demonstrations were allowed to pass off peacefully. Unionists, however, were beginning to detect the spectre of Republicanism walking in the ranks of the righteous and felt their entire regime seriously threatened. The march, planned for 5 October 1968, and made up of every shade of revolutionary political opinion that existed, was perceived, even before it took place, as a dangerous act of insurgency.

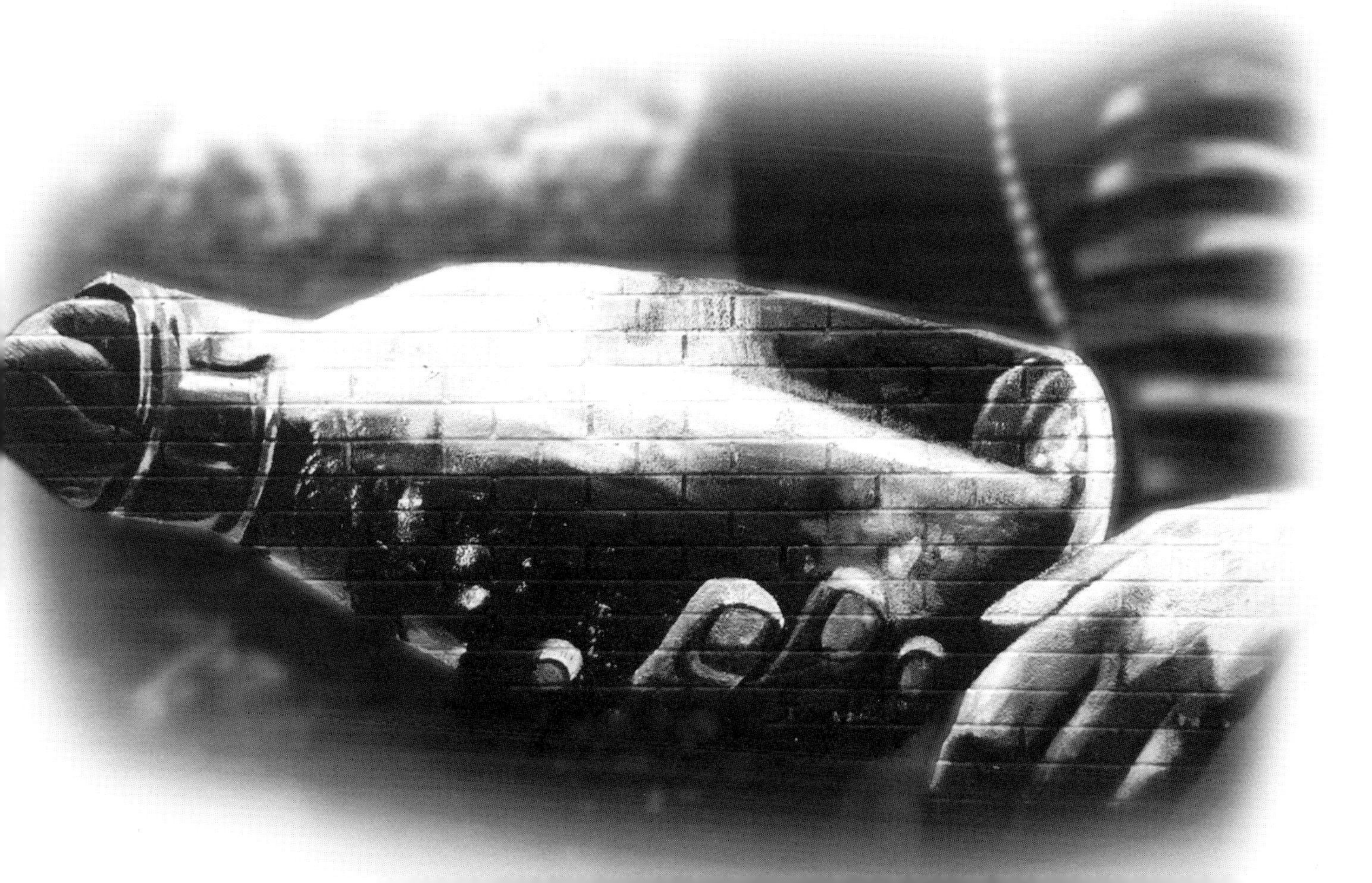

THE PETROL BOMBER MURAL

For a mural to be successful, it must take into consideration the restrictions of the materials it has to contend with. In this case, the gaps between the bricks and the texture of the wall itself proved formidable obstacles. The surrounding environment must also be taken into consideration. With this in mind, we decided that black and white would satisfy both the demands of the locale, the dramatic nature of the subject matter as well as the vitally important notion that history is the record of something that happened some time ago. We knew that large masses would not only be read better from a distance, but would also integrate cogently with the surrounding architectural space. Given the site of the mural, an illusory perspective, in general to be avoided in this type of mural, could be used to some effect. This device is seldom successful in a large-scale outdoor painting unless it be trompe d'oeil, which has no object but to titillate. In this instance, however, given the form and shape of the dominant figures and the fact that the perspective would in no way detract from its content, it was deemed appropriate. Thus, from the technical viewpoint, the success of the image, in terms of its form, was assured.

The original design was derived from a photograph taken by Clive Limpkin. This is not to be wondered at, as artists have used photographs since the days of Degas. In the service of historical accuracy, we must use photographs of the given period. Our inspiration in this case had another source: the chap behind the mask is a full cousin to Tom and William. This provided an added incentive for the artists. Several more images were collated from other sources and a sketch drawn up that expressed what the artists wished to express. We were present on the day of the battle and remembered it well.

The completed cartoon was then transferred to the wall, using the tried and tested method of squaring-up. The design itself is basically X-shaped. The artistic canon known as the 'golden mean' was used in conjunction with these diagonals to isolate and give significance to key elements in the picture, such as the badge on the child's jacket, the bottle he holds, and the small group on top of the Rossville Flats. All in all, it's as classical as it can get, in the strictest meaning of that word.

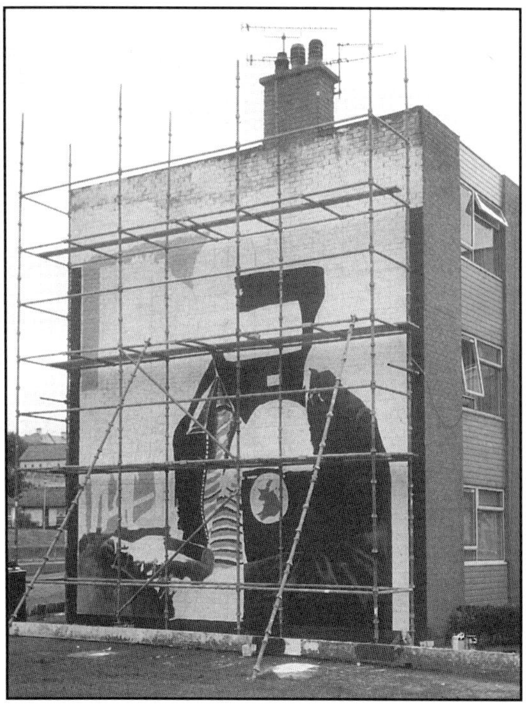

Of all our murals, it is the one that appears to have the most appeal. Just as Michelangelo's Statue of David ushered in the new Republic and

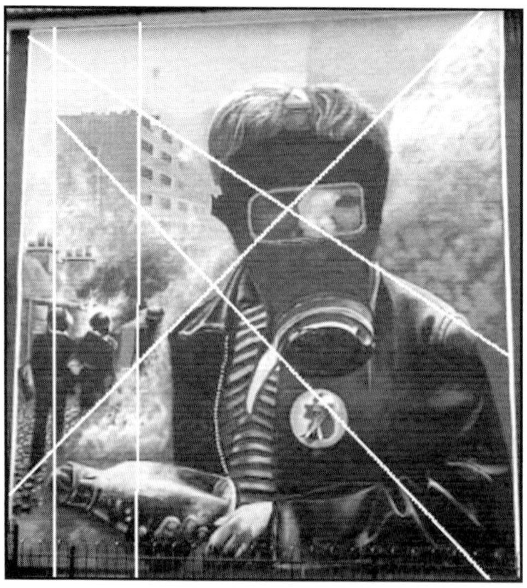

demonstrated Florentine virtues and self-reliance, so also does *The Petrol Bomber* mural put a face on the struggle for civil rights and gives voice to the resolve of oppressed peoples everywhere; it owes its popularity to that. A student in Peking – or an urchin in the streets of Sao Paulo – will relate to it without any difficulty. Just as the greatest truths seek their natural expression in simple parables, so too the most effective visual poetry is without props or frills. Mural artists in general, when faced with a large area, make the obvious mistake of packing it to the gills with imagery. If you expect your work to be read at a glance or from a distance, this is not the way to go.

The esteem in which our mural is held says a great deal. It says a great deal to art critics. And it says a lot too about our social values, which still nourish the delusion that a man with letters after his name alone deserves to be listened to, while an unlettered man need not be listened to at all. This is one of the middle-class delusions and perhaps the most pernicious that the wall painter has to contend with. Chaps who stroll the streets of London on their way to the Stock Exchange to spend the day hoovering their fellow man generally have degrees the length of their arm. Who needs them?

History will assuredly dub this 'the age of the pedagogue', an age when the beguiled and the gullible knelt before the televisual cult of the technocrat and the 'expert' and waited to be told how to live . . . in wraparound sound. Doctors in psychiatry, who are more screwed up than their patients, give endless advice on marriage and relationships. Doctors of medicine, who are known to be among the highest class of alcoholics in the country, give us advice on good health. And so it goes on. Kids who have no interest in specialising in anything are made to feel small and stupid because they do not have a degree. In Japan and elsewhere, academic failure leads to numerous suicides per year. The magic of art is that it can make nonsense of all that. The reward for us, the artists, is that *The Petrol Bomber* will go on saying it, even after the sun has set – and even after the heroic struggle of the people of the Bogside has become nothing more than a dusty chronicle for oddball academics to transform into lucrative lecture tours for the benefit of students, who figure it is better to have a degree than to be a decent human being. Many of them operate on the principle that their 'superior intellects' give them the right to do so.

PEACE

A new hope has been born
In this our troubled land.
A new dawn has broken;
Child, stretch forth thy hand.

Don't look back with your father's eyes
And see things long past.
Look to the new dawn, child of hope,
And peace, at long, long, last.

Patrick Coyle

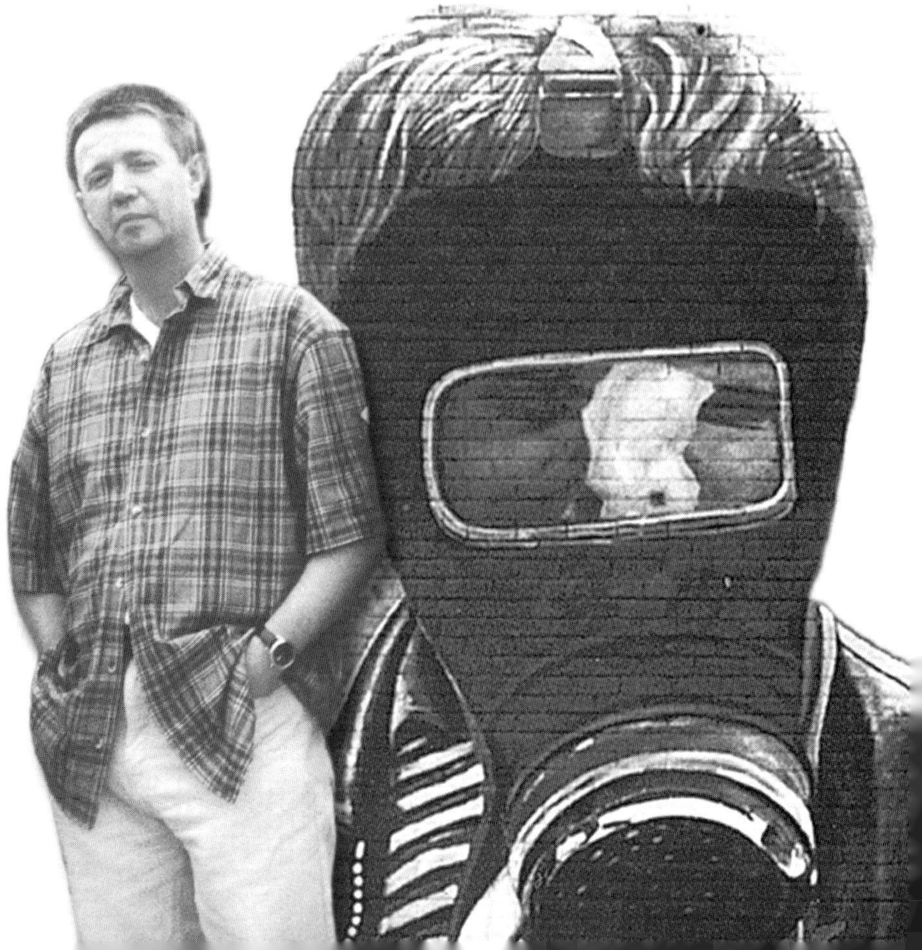

BERNADETTE

When Bernadette Devlin was elected to Westminster for Mid-Ulster in April 1969, she was only twenty-two years of age, the youngest woman ever to have taken a seat in the House of Commons. In 1968, she had been a psychology student at Queen's University, Belfast and a member of the People's Democracy movement. Later she would become, along with Eamonn McCann, one of the principal organisers of the 1 January 1969 protest that met its Waterloo at Burntollet Bridge outside Derry. On that fateful day, the RUC, in collusion with their B-Special civilian force, laid into marchers and inflicted serious injuries on many of them. Thousands gathered in the Guildhall Square to greet the bloodied survivors. Serious rioting flared up in the city, and, in the early hours of the morning, the RUC invaded the Bogside, beating up on anybody they came across and smashing windows as they went. On 19 April, a pitched battle took place with the police. Sammy Devenney was beaten up by them in his own home and died later from his injuries.

That same month, Bernadette was elected. Backslapping palms in the House of Commons were soon to turn to shaking fists when she took part in the *Battle of the Bogside* through 12–14 August of that bizarre year. That wasn't supposed to be in her script as a dignified Member of the House.

As with their counterparts in Paris, students in Northern Ireland, especially those at Queen's University, saw themselves as the intellectual phalanx of the working class. They were still sensitive enough to identify with Martin Luther King's crusade, still close enough to the real world to recognise its problems as their own, and still far enough removed from their allotted starting blocks in the rat race to be able to reflect intelligently on what could be done. Less than a week after the formation of the PD, the first Civil Rights march in Derry prepared to take place in Duke St, near the train station in the Waterside area of the city. It never got started.

The night before the march, NICRA wanted to call it off, because Home Affairs Minister William Craig had imposed a banning order and a confrontation looked to be inevitable. After much discussion, it was decided to proceed. The inevitable happened. RUC police, of whom there were 130 in position front and back of the crowd, without provocation, tore into those at the front of the march. One hundred, out of approximately 400 assembled, were taken to hospital; quite a few more received treatment elsewhere. Official figures put the casualty list as: four policemen and seventy-seven civilians injured. Still others were drenched by two water cannons as they tried to get across the bridge. This was the first time water cannon had been used in Derry. Riots soon developed as word reached the Bogside and the fighting lasted until the early hours of the next morning.

Press photos of the RUC in action were seen all around the world, leaving the British Government facing serious pressure to take a more active role in the governance of the Six Counties. The forthcoming *Battle of the Bogside* would provide the much-needed nudge in that direction and Bernadette Devlin would take a major role in this event – and in the events that followed.

Prior to the 12 August 1969 annual Apprentice Boys' march in Derry, moderates and Catholics had called for its ban. After the police brutality of Duke Street and Burntollet, it was clear to all that the parade was as provocative as it was ever likely to get. The night of 11 August saw barricades set up in the Bogside manned by the Republican and recently formed Citizens' Defence Association. The stage was set for the *Battle of the Bogside*.

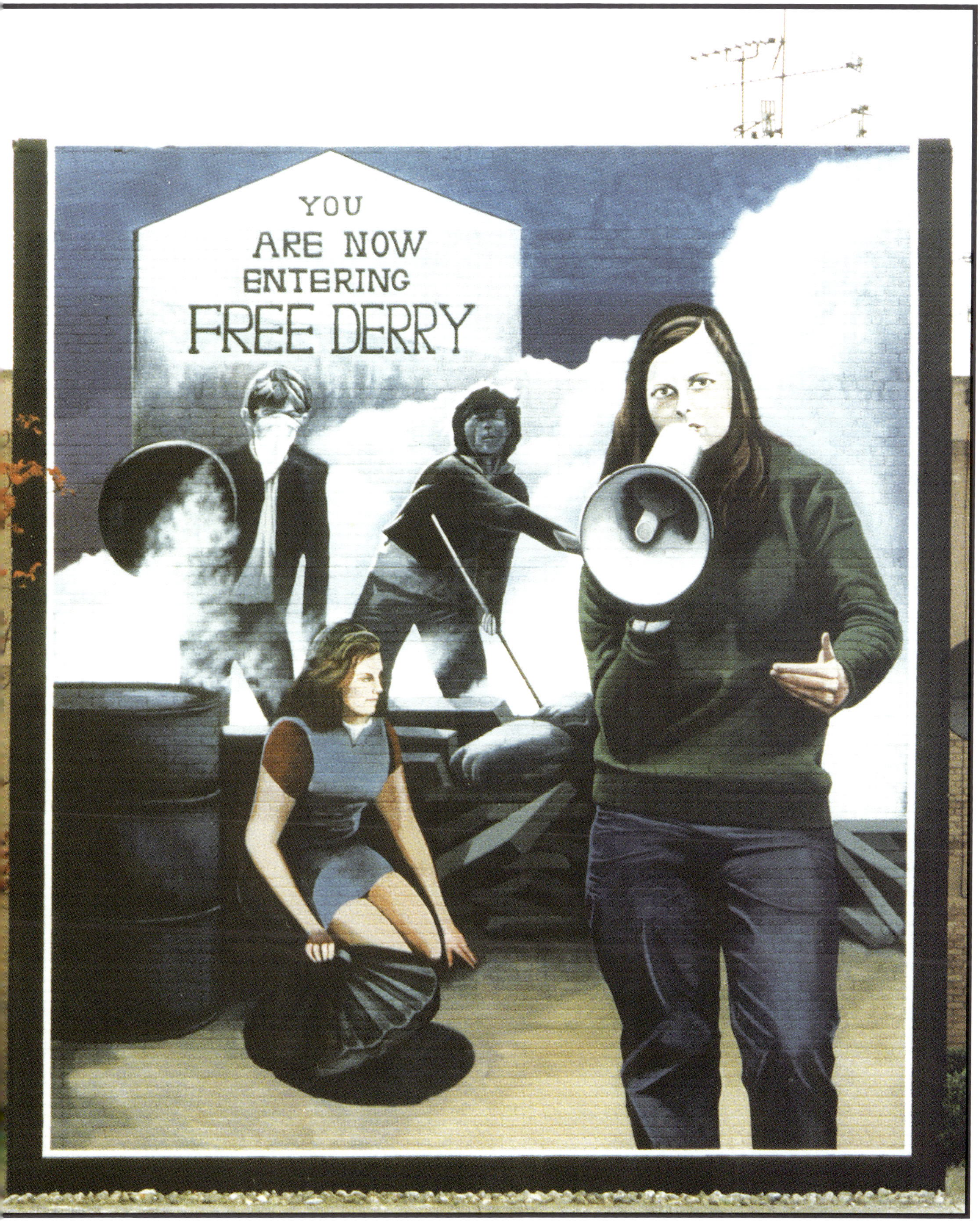
YOU
ARE NOW
ENTERING
FREE DERRY

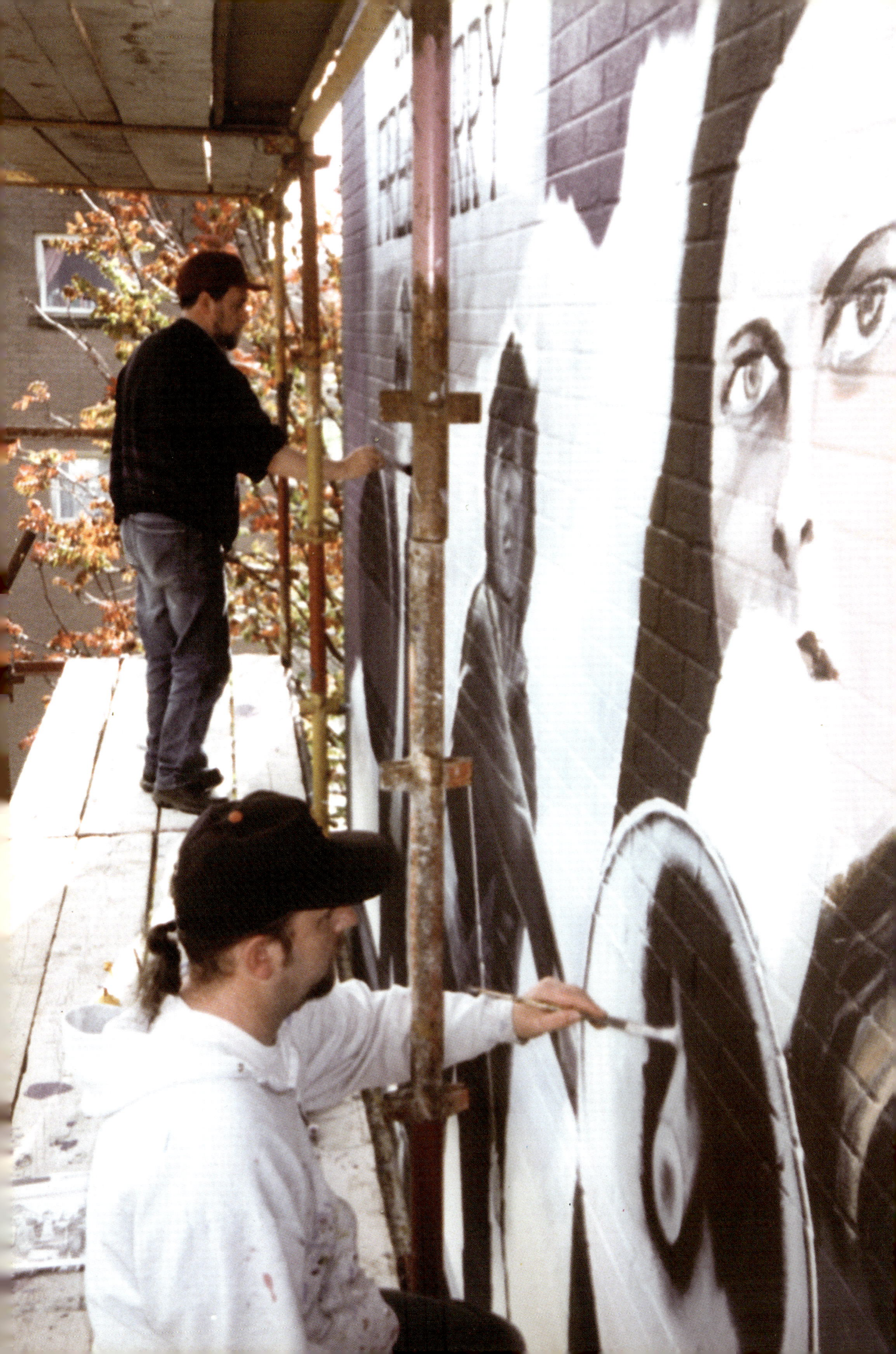

The ensuing battle lasted from 4.00pm, and, for a further two days, it was all tear gas, rock throwing, petrol bombs and barricades. Lorries were coming in with rocks; kids were running around with gasmasks and crates of bottles. The gas was everywhere. For years later, in fact to this day, people complain of its effects. They also say that all the birds left Derry on that day and stayed away for years. In the midst of it all was the MP for Mid-Ulster marshalling her 'troops' through a loudhailer. The famous picture of her breaking a paving stone was to circle the globe. 'Throw them hard and throw them straight!' she shouted. It worked too. The police retreated. Then the B-Specials turned up, armed to the teeth. The crowd sensed that this was the real thing and an unnerving quiet descended on the rioters. Next, it was learned that the British Army, in the manner of the cavalry coming to liberate the homesteaders from the marauding Apache was headed across the bridge. The 'Boggies' had won.

According to Bernadette, the army came in, not because NI Prime Minister Chichester-Clark had asked for them, but because the idea of a private army calling itself the B-Specials irked the sensitivities of British Prime Minister Harold Wilson. The Bogsiders, at any rate, were glad to see them that day, although the wisest among them, especially Bernadette, knew full well the honeymoon wouldn't last.

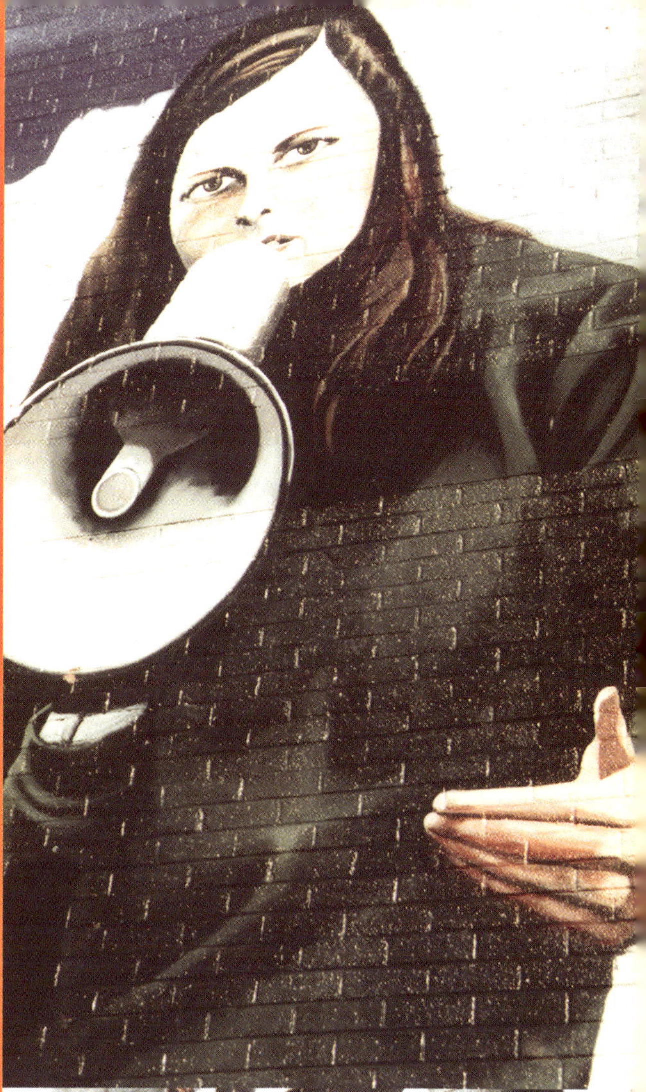

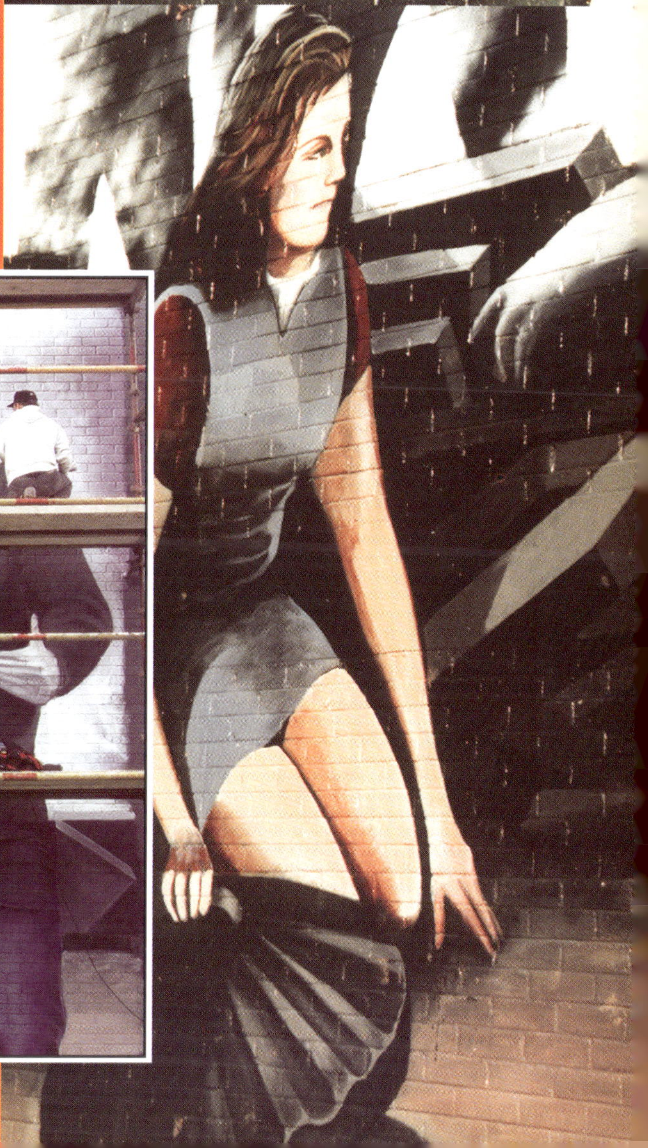

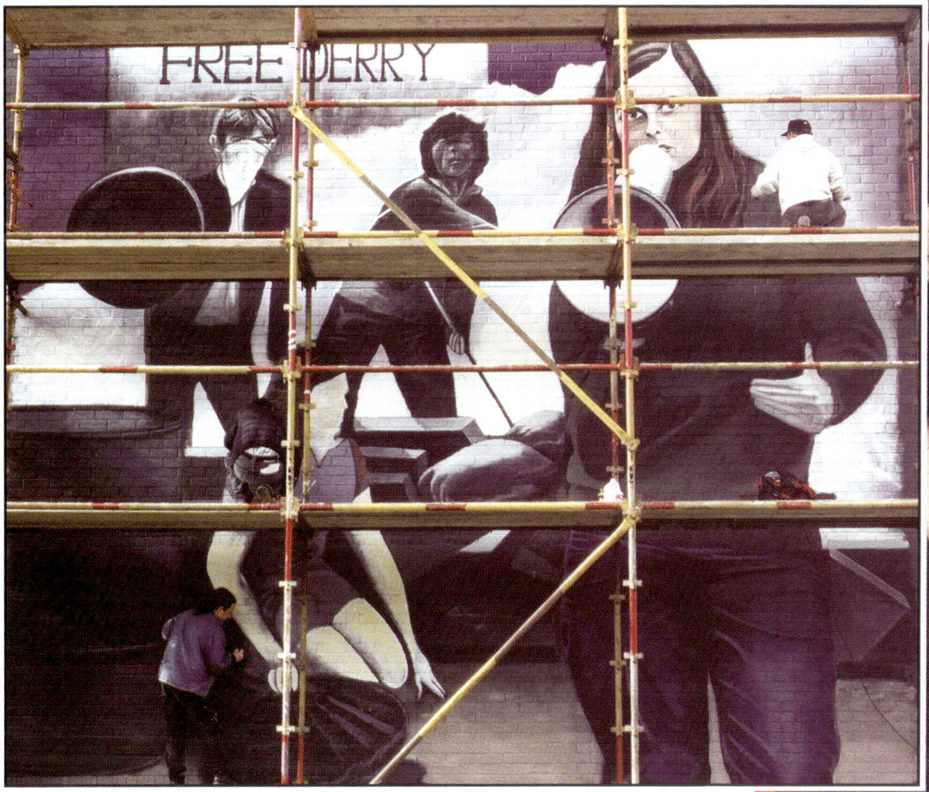

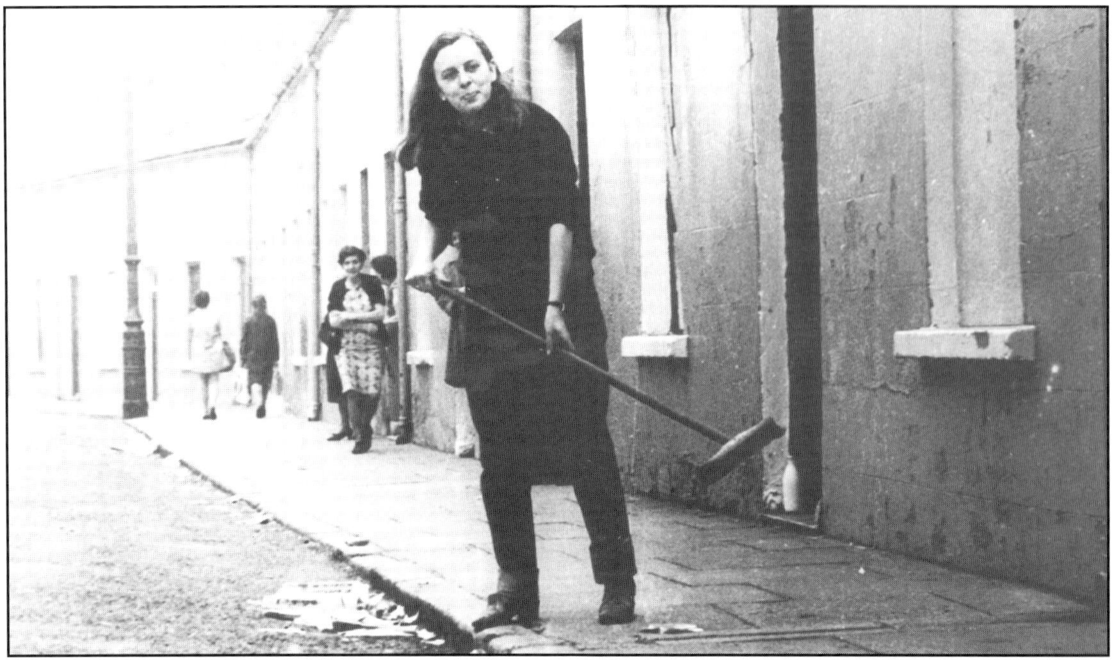

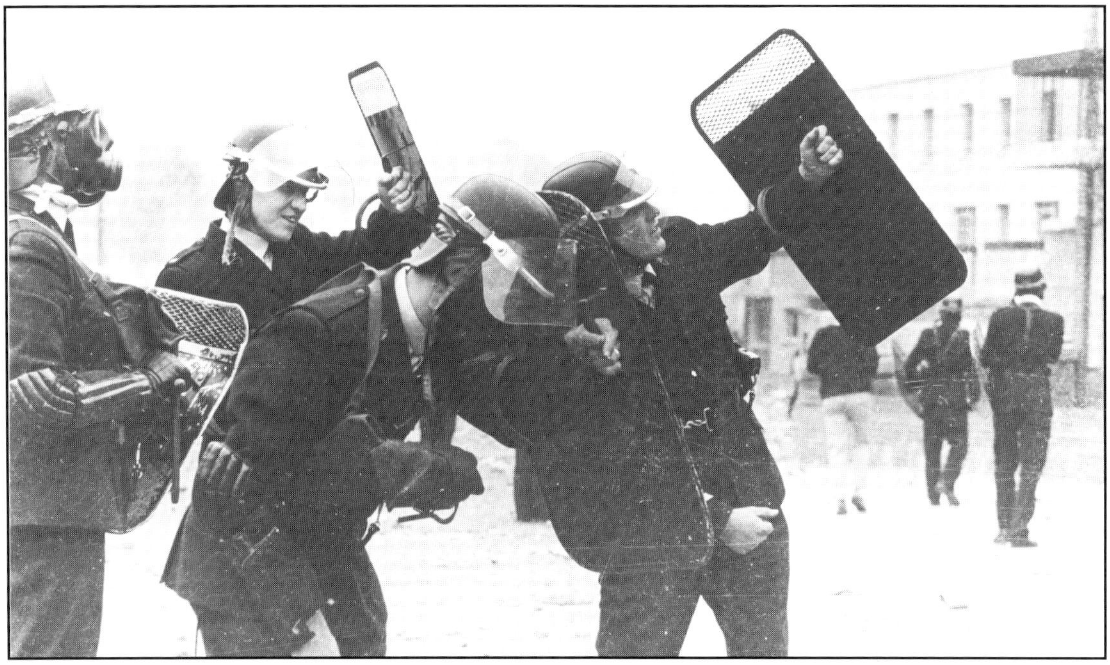

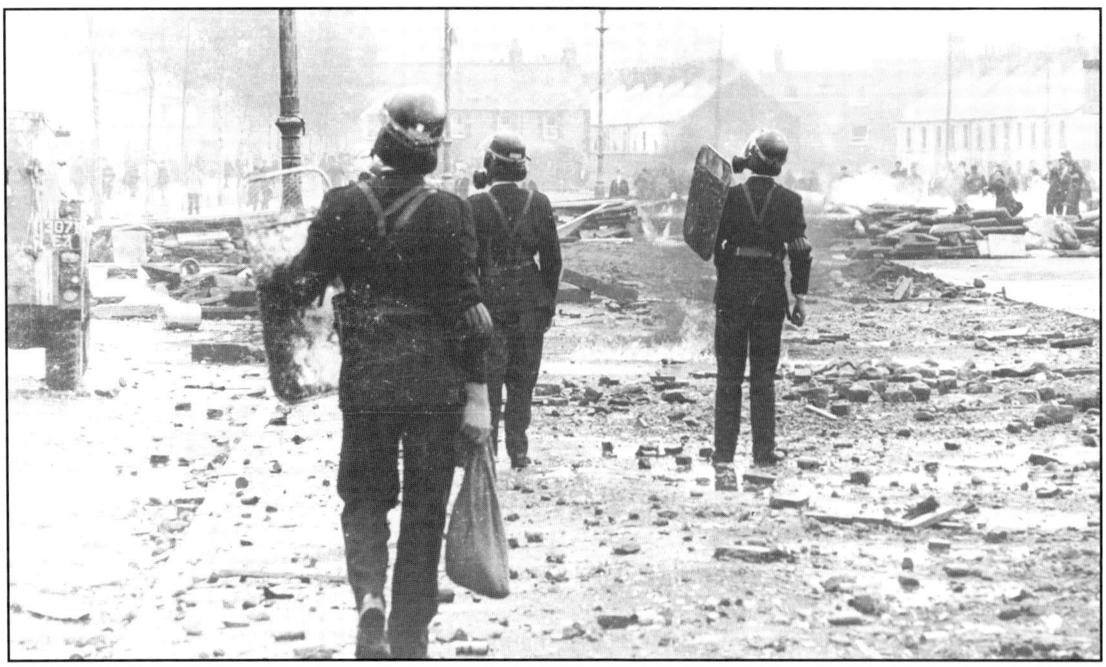

BERNADETTE MURAL

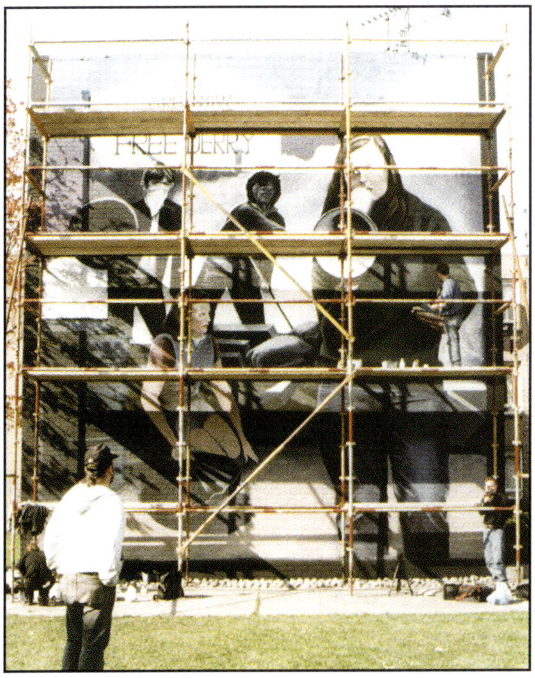

Although we made Bernadette clearly the main figure, the mural is also homage to the vital role played by women in the struggle for civil rights. The first idea that presented itself to us was, of course, the well-known photograph of Bernadette breaking the stone into throwable pieces. On reflection, we felt she was more than that, and that this act would not show her in her more important role as speaker for the people and fearless thinker, for both of which she will be always remembered. 'Bernadette at the loudhailer' was the image we all remembered from the time.

This was the first colour mural we tried, although it has to be said we had no colour photographs to work from, and the black-and-white photos we managed to get were not of the best quality.

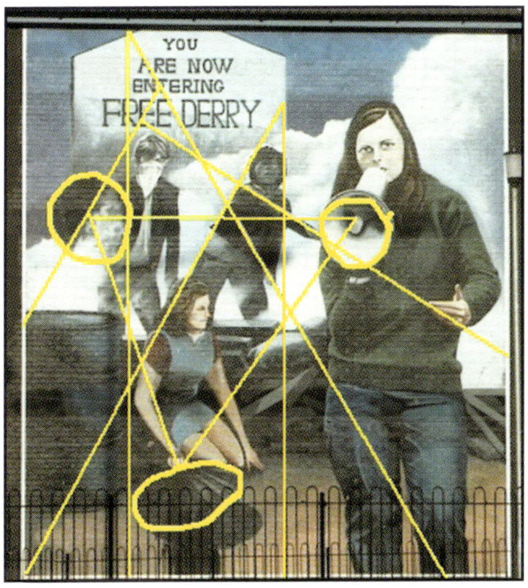

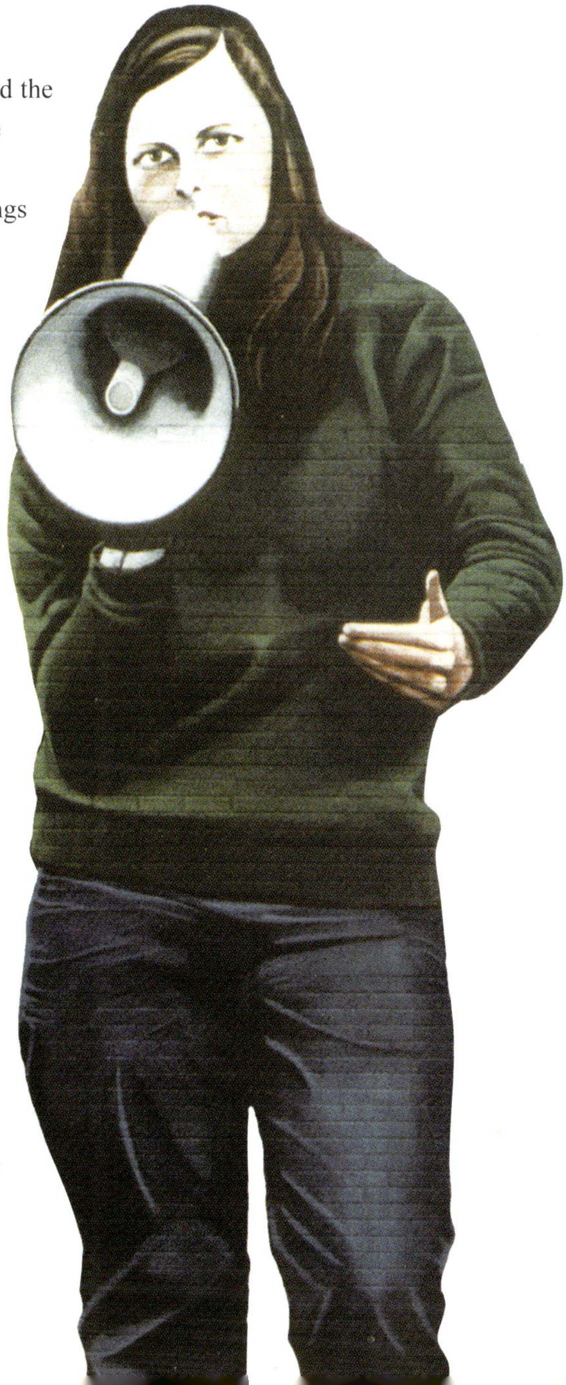

Both the colour harmonies and the design are kept very tight, the triangle motif being predominant throughout. In monumental paintings of this type, the triangle is almost inescapable as a design element. You will find we placed them judiciously all over the painting as a sort of thread tying the entire image together.

In terms of content, we were painting a mural especially for women. It is a tribute to them. It would accordingly have been unthinkable to paint it in black-and-white, especially as, in terms of equal rights, women everywhere still have a long way to go. We hoped that by painting it in colour, it would be that bit special. Of course, colour brings with it a different set of problems entirely.

While we were painting the figure of Bernadette, a woman approached to inform us that Bernadette's jumper on the occasion was mauve or purple, but definitely not green. We had to point out to her that our green was a symbolic colour and that purple would not have worked in any case. Her insistence on fact, as opposed to 'artistic licence', brought home to us how vitally important historical accuracy is to a lot of people. Lessons like that have to be considered very carefully.

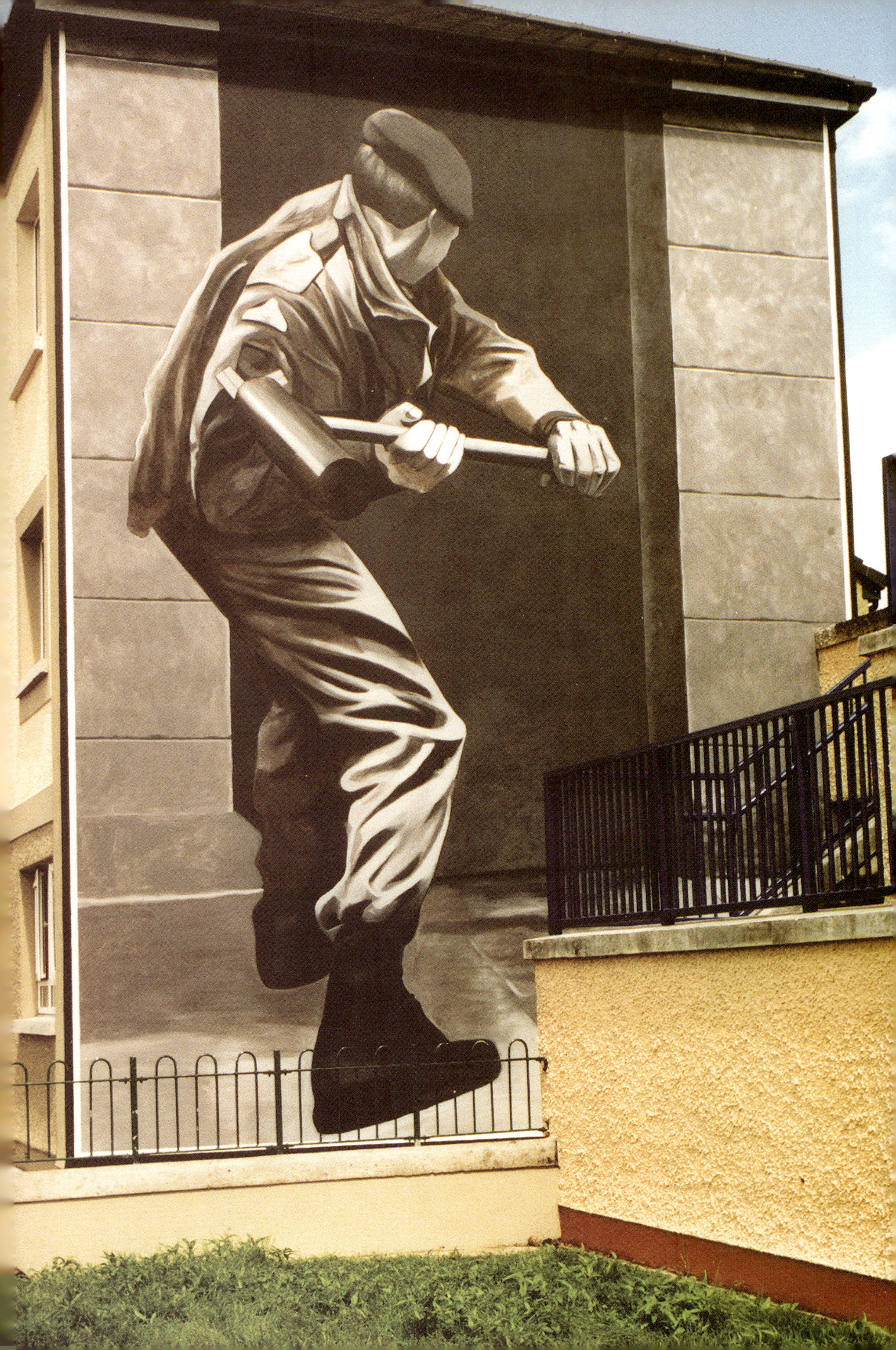

OPERATION MOTORMAN

Following the brutal murder of Ranger Best by the Official IRA, and the outcry that followed it, a cease-fire was announced on 29 May 1972. At 4.00am on 31 July, a massive contingent of British troops, supported by tanks and armoured cars, stormed over the barricades of the Bogside and into Creggan. 'Operation Motorman', as it was called, involved thousands of soldiers, armoured vehicles, Centurion tanks and bulldozers. Its purpose was to restore state control to the no-go areas of the Bogside and Creggan. It was the biggest mobilisation of troops seen in Ireland since World War II. The anticipated showdown with the IRA never materialised, as volunteers had already escaped over the border. Two people, 15-year-old Daniel Hegarty and IRA man Seamus Bradley were killed during the operation.

A few minutes before the invasion, the sirens had sounded throughout Free Derry to alert the citizens. Daniel Hegarty, eager to see the spectacle as any kid would, and in particular the big tanks, left his home at 22 Swilly Gardens in Creggan never to return. He was shot dead at a range of less than eight feet; the British Army has consistently claimed he was a terrorist. Similar discrepancies in submitted evidence surround the shooting of Seamus Bradley, who was almost certainly unarmed at the time of his killing.

Daniel's father, Alec, has recently launched a campaign to clear his son's name. Statements made subsequently by soldiers identified only as 'A' and 'B' are profoundly contradictory. No investigation was carried out by the RUC at the time. Mr. Hegarty has called on British MP Andrew Hunter to name his son's killers and has strenuously denied that his son was linked to any paramilitary grouping. The campaign continues.

In his memoirs, the then British Prime Minister, Edward Heath, now in his mid-eighties, revealed that he had ordered naval ships on standby at the mouth of the Foyle to bombard Derry should the troops meet with any resistance. He also had RAF planes on standby. He was fully prepared to use them too, irrespective of the inevitably huge number of casualties that would have resulted. Lunacy of this magnitude is beyond comprehension. It raises the question of what kind of thinking must have preceded the debacle of Bloody Sunday if measures as psychotic as these were being considered so soon afterwards. Of course, if tests for sanity were mandatory for all candidates to high office, the world would grind to a halt overnight and Hollywood would have to fold up its tents and go home.

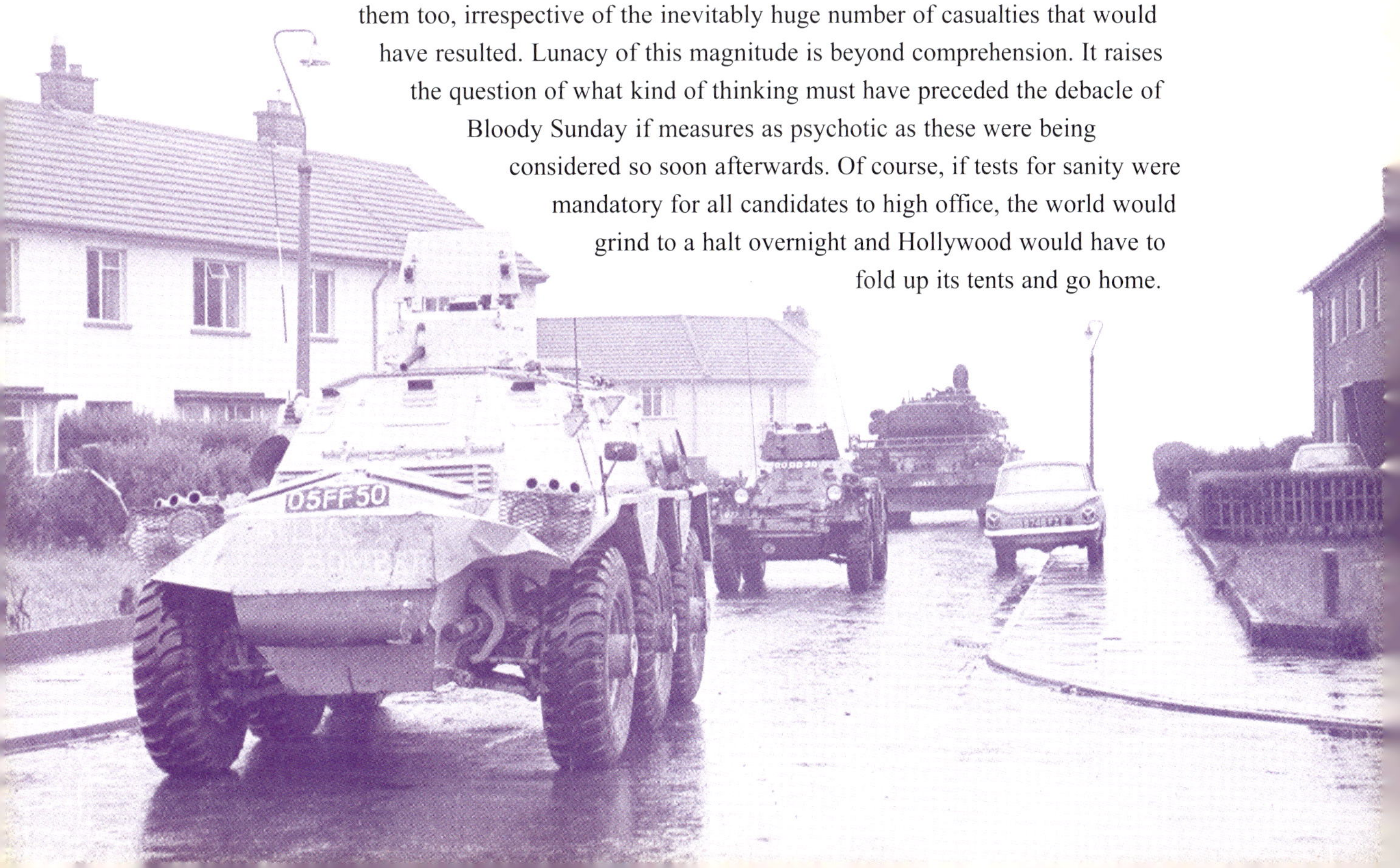

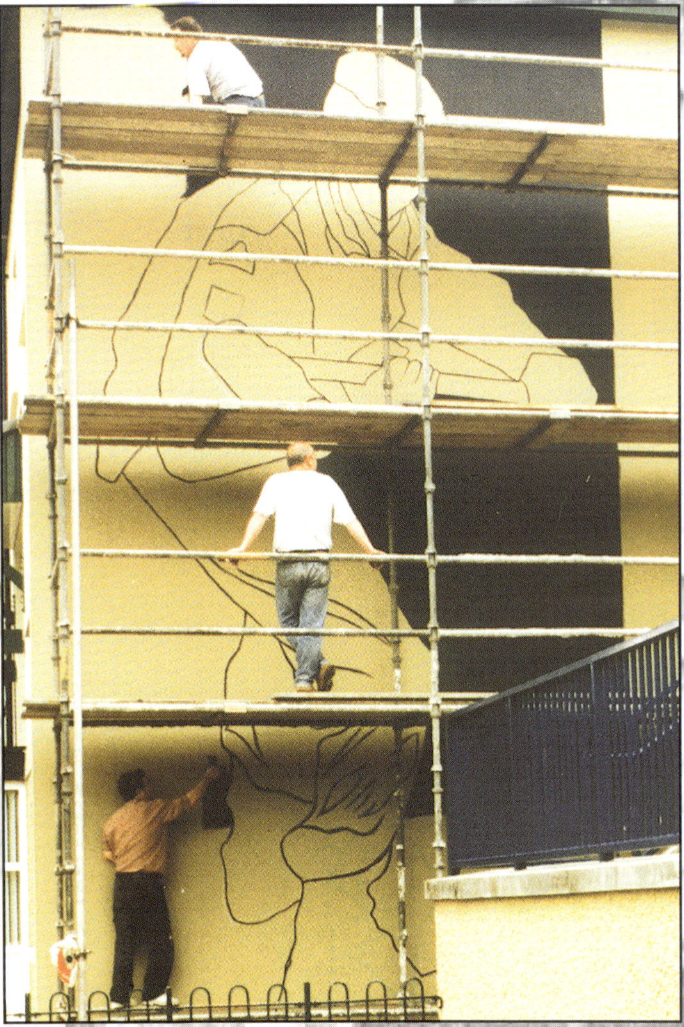

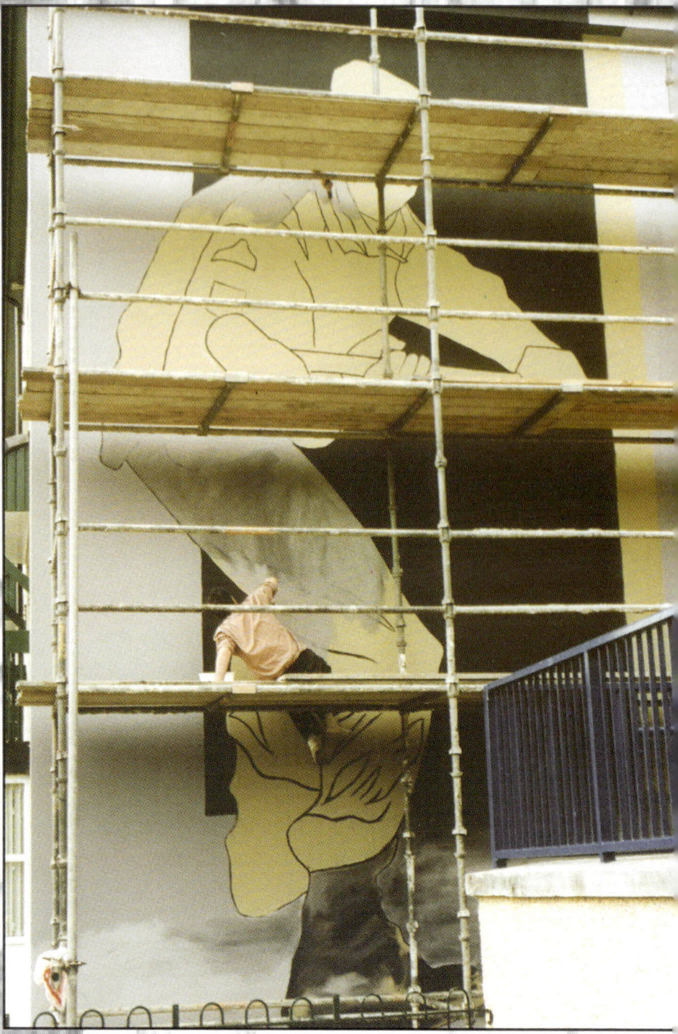

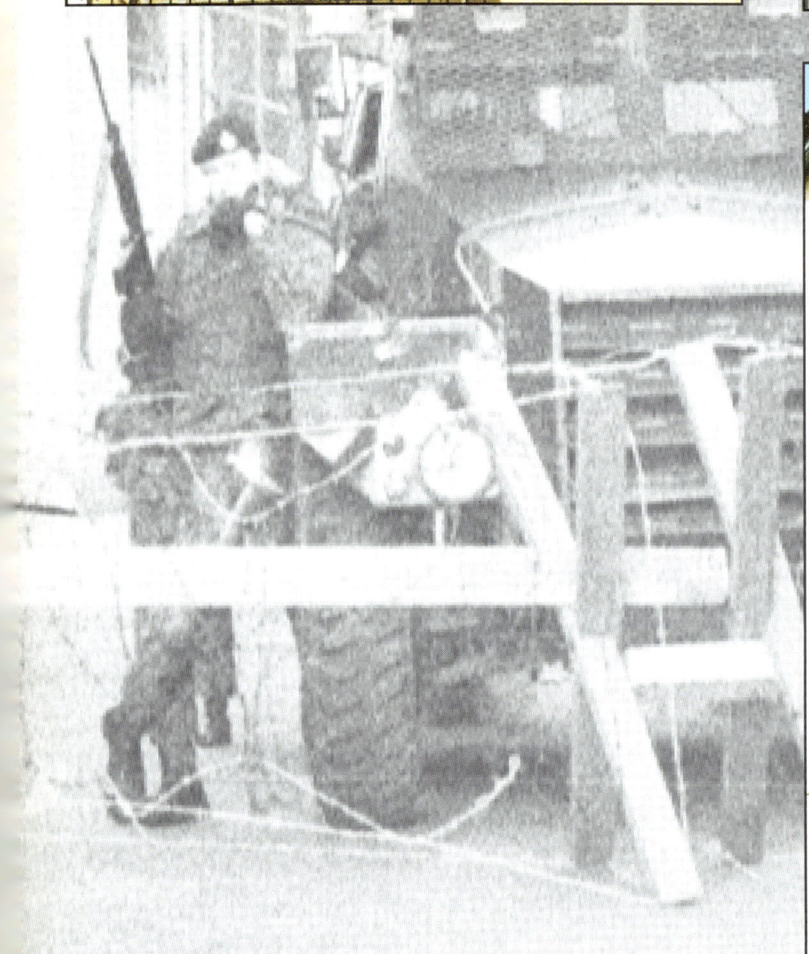

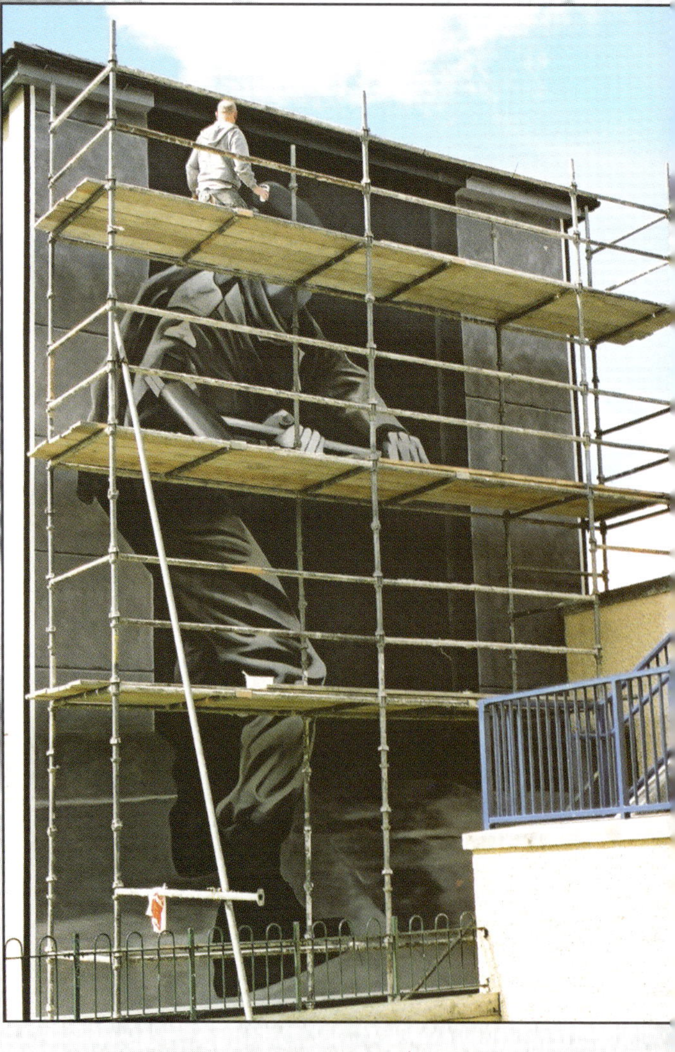

Onwards and upwards – the artists at work on the Bogside Gallery, 2001.

OPERATION MOTORMAN MURAL

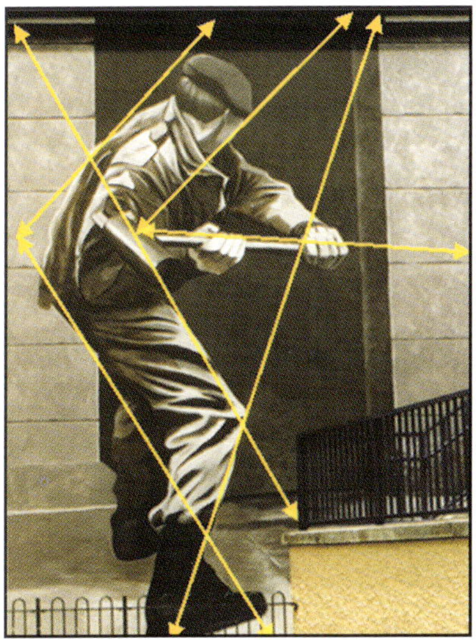

Our intention with this mural was not so much to convey the enormity of the event itself, which of course would require a cast of thousands and more walls than we could get, but to communicate something of the ferocity of the onslaught.

It seemed to us that the photo of a soldier pounding in a door sufficiently satisfied our requirements. Very little had to be done except change various elements of contrast to make the thing as dramatic as possible. Highlights are exaggerated for this purpose and the hands were enlarged. We darkened the door to provide additional contrast and to make the object look solid. We tried three different shades of dark grey before we got it right. We toned down the walls so that the soldier would be more visible against them and accented the lines between the bricks. We also omitted the highlights from the upper part of the wall for the same reason. The diagonals of the paving stones we left until last. Most importantly, we darkened the shadows on the figure so that the highlights, by contrast, would dramatise the soldier and give the spectator a clear view of the violence depicted.

Black-and-white painting doesn't lend itself to much leeway by way of 'special effects'. Too far towards white, and the highlights take on a chalky and artificial aspect. Too far towards black, and the shadows become too graphic and banal. Finding the mean, so that the shadows are not too black and the highlights not too white, is the key to the problem. Then, it's a question of what type of black to use as your base, as there are twelve different possibilities. In this case, we decided on two ranges of tones: a cold range for the walls of the house and a warm range for the soldier's uniform. This worked to bring the soldier out of the background without having to rely on tonal contrast alone to effect the magic.

More to the point, the image also satisfies our subtext, which we keep in mind when designing all our murals. If the image can go beyond the merely parochial then it will gain in meaning; this image does that. It becomes an anti-war painting as much as an historical recording. Its ultimate effectiveness is due largely to the size and positioning of the figure. On the wall adjacent, we will be adding more elements in the saga of 'Motorman'. Edward Heath's mental capacity is, however, well beyond our frail powers of depiction. We await the return of Walt Disney to do it justice.

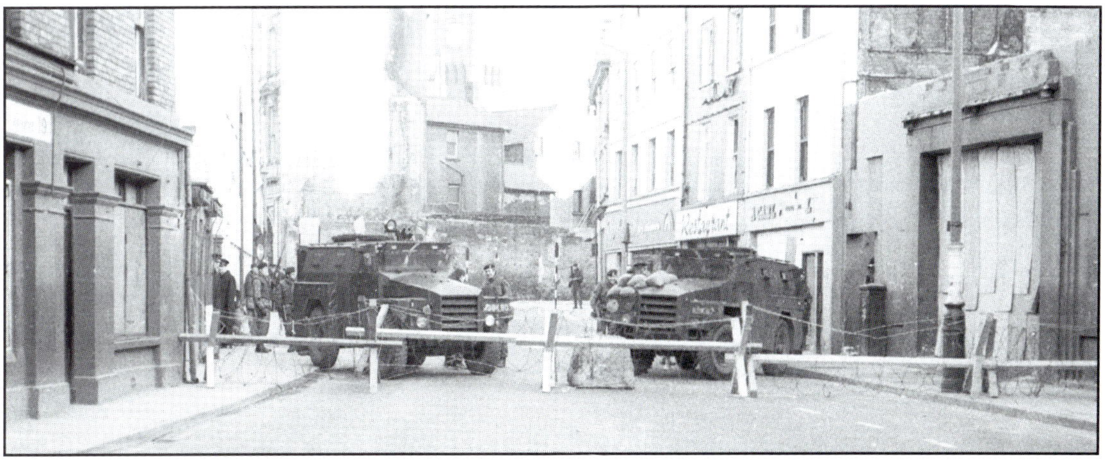

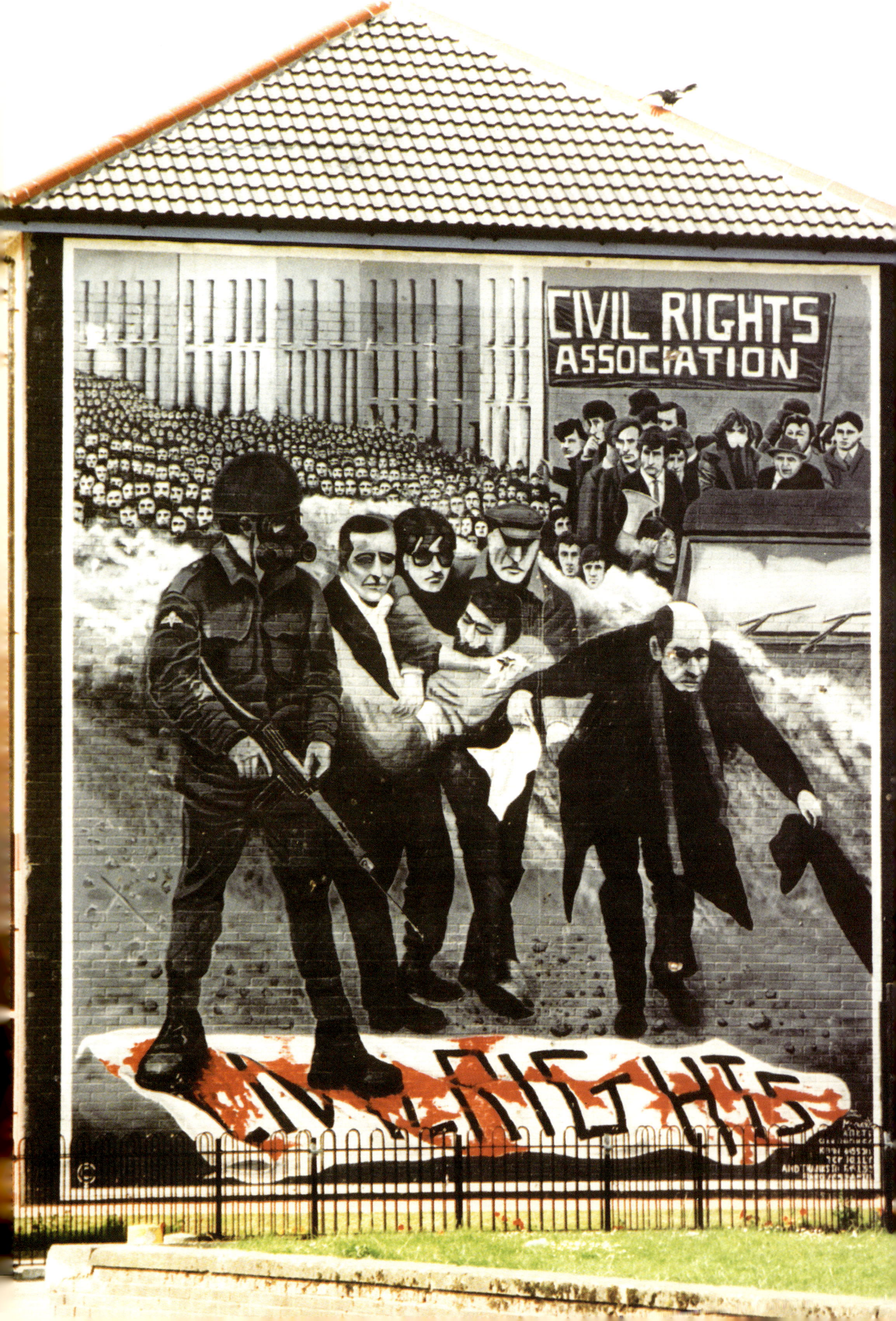
CIVIL RIGHTS
ASSOCIATION
RIGHTS

BLOODY SUNDAY

NICRA had planned a march for Sunday 30 January 1972 to protest against the imprisonment of over 900 people, most of them Catholic, during the previous year as a result of the introduction of internment without trial by the Unionist government. Derry, in those days, had a population of 55,000, the vast majority of them Catholics. The Bogside and beyond was a no-go area, policed effectively by the IRA, but considered a lawless warren by both Commander Ford, chief of the Land Forces in Northern Ireland, and Edward Heath, the British Prime Minister. Both were under pressure from Unionist MPs to rectify the situation. Decisions that would prove catastrophic were taken well in advance of the date of the proposed march. On 26 October 1971, Ford ordered Brigadier McClellan, who was in charge of the troops in Derry, to ' . . . recreate the state of law in the Creggan and Bogside as and when he could.' Lt Col Derek Wilford, Commander of 1 Para, a buffoon of a man by any standards, was ordered to prepare his troops for the march. Nobody paid much attention to RUC Chief Superintendent Frank Lagan in Derry, who had cautioned McClellan about the use of military force during the demonstration. Heath, for his part, was well aware of the plan at least five days previously.

Some 20,000 marchers, young and old, started from Creggan at 3.00pm en route to the Guildhall Square. They were unaware that 320 of Wilford's Paras, out of a total of 1800 troops stationed in Derry that day, were waiting to divert the march to the Bogside. A small group of youths broke loose as the demonstrators headed for Free Derry Corner and low level rioting flared up. The army responded with CS gas, rubber bullets and water cannon. At 3.45pm, two live rounds were fired by the army, injuring two civilians. One of them, John Johnson, died a few months later from his injuries. At 4.07pm, the Paras, at their own request, were permitted to invade the Bogside. Twenty-seven minutes later, thirteen people, most of them young, lay dead; a further fourteen were seriously wounded.

Details, facts, articles, films and books that would be written about this pogrom could fill a small library. Next day, the House of Commons was in pandemonium. Reverberations spread around the world. In the Six Counties, young Republicans became embittered and many joined the IRA, a consequence foretold to the House by Bernadette Devlin, whose account of the incident was repeatedly interrupted by the Speaker.

Later, Home Secretary Reginald Maudling announced that ' . . . the government has decided that it is right to set up an independent inquiry . . . ' What followed, were it not a matter of such profound seriousness, would have merited the pantomimic skills of Gilbert and Sullivan.

Lord Widgery, despite his military background in the British Army, was appointed sole and 'impartial' arbiter of the Tribunal of Inquiry, although the Tribunals of Inquiry Act of 1921 allowed for a panel of three. Together with Lord Chancellor Hailsham, he had attended a meeting on 31 January at 10 Downing Street. There, he was advised by Prime Minister Heath that the subject of the inquiry was not the sort that 'those who designed the 1921 Act originally had in mind.' Nor should the recommendations made by Lord Salmon as to procedure be necessarily considered 'relevant in this case'. Heath also advised Widgery that ' . . . it has to be remembered that we are in Northern Ireland fighting not only a military war but a propaganda war.' Basically, Widgery was instructed to make sure that the army came out smelling of roses. And Widgery, with his 'lean and hungry look', knew too well what was required of him and how to deliver it.

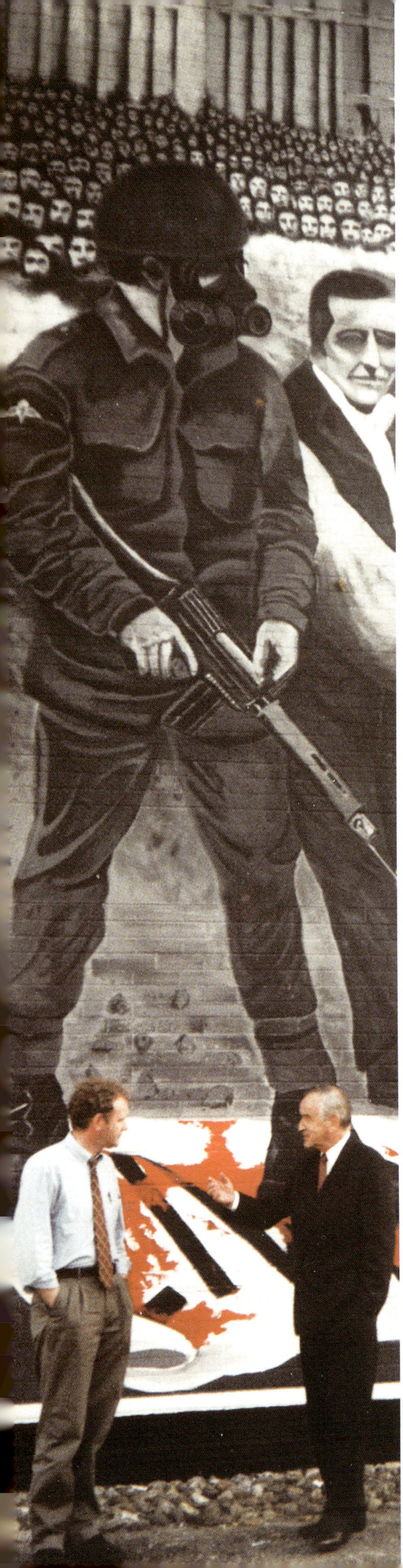

Not surprisingly, protests concerning the proposed structure, notably from MPs Fitt and Hume, were ignored by the government. An embargo of twenty-five years minimum was placed on information gathered by the inquiry. Right of appeal was denied. The Catholic bishop of Derry, Dr Edward Daly, who had ministered to the dead and dying on that day, summed up Widgery's conclusions succinctly when he stated: 'Widgery found the guilty innocent and the innocent guilty.'

Unsurprisingly, the army was exonerated. Later, 1 Para was to be commended for its 'heroic' actions by the Queen, a gesture later exposed for all its hypocrisy by those soldiers themselves who had the courage to state the truth of what really had happened. It was a whitewash to end all whitewashes and a bitter insult to the families and relatives of the deceased. Later, it would be discovered that vast quantities of evidence, including 500 independent eyewitness accounts, as well as taped conversations between the army and the RUC made by radio buff James Porter, had been labelled inadmissible evidence by Widgery. Much of this evidence would have proven that snipers had fired into the crowd from the city Walls, killing John Young, William Nash and Michael McDaid.

Earlier statements submitted by soldiers were not made available to the counsel for the next of kin, thus effectively extinguishing the process of cross-examination, which would certainly have exposed an orchestrated strategy of deception. It would have revealed the appalling fact that these same soldiers were reciting from a prepared script. Widgery waxed lyrical: he was impressed, he wrote, by the demeanour of the soldiers. They gave their evidence ' . . . with confidence and without hesitation or prevarication and withstood a rigorous cross-examination without contradicting themselves or each other.' Truly, Franklin Roosevelt was thinking praise, not chicanery, when he said: 'Old soldiers never die, they just fade, fade, fade away.' But chicanery is what was most certainly dished out to the world's press by the tribunal's 'findings'. The Widgery Report was to remain the official British record of events for almost twenty-five years. During that time, new evidence unearthed by men such as Professor Dermot Walsh of the Law Department at the University of Limerick, and the persistent demand for justice by relatives of the deceased, made a new inquiry imperative.

On 29 January 1998, in response to the tireless efforts of the members of the Bloody Sunday Justice Campaign that had been formally established in 1992, Prime Minister Tony Blair announced a new Tribunal of Inquiry into Bloody Sunday. It is made up of three senior judges from England, Canada and Australia.

BLOODY SUNDAY MURAL

Bloody Sunday depicts the fate of the campaign for civil rights. It shows the death of Jackie Duddy. Also prominent in the picture is Bishop Daly, who was a key figure on that fateful day when fourteen individuals lost their lives.

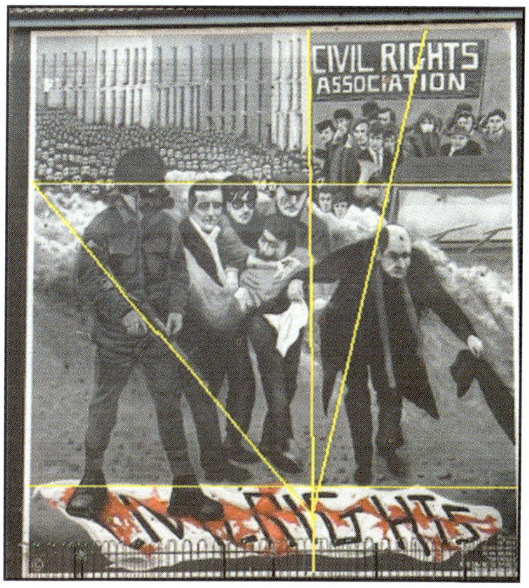

Again it is painted in black-and-white and is the result of a photomontage compiled from film footage. The bloodstained banner upon which the soldier is standing speaks a great deal for the price people pay everywhere for democratic freedom. In terms of media coverage, it is second only to *The Petrol Bomber* as a chronicle of a specific event that had dire repercussions both in the North of Ireland and beyond. More young men joined the IRA after Bloody Sunday than at any other time afterwards.

The design in this case was very simple. We had to convey a feeling of tragedy and to make it clear that what compounded the tragedy was the nature of the march itself. We included the crowd and the background to the march. The soldier points with his rifle to the blood-spattered banner and looms large as an oppressive presence. Nothing more needed to be done but to depict the event with as much historical accuracy as possible.

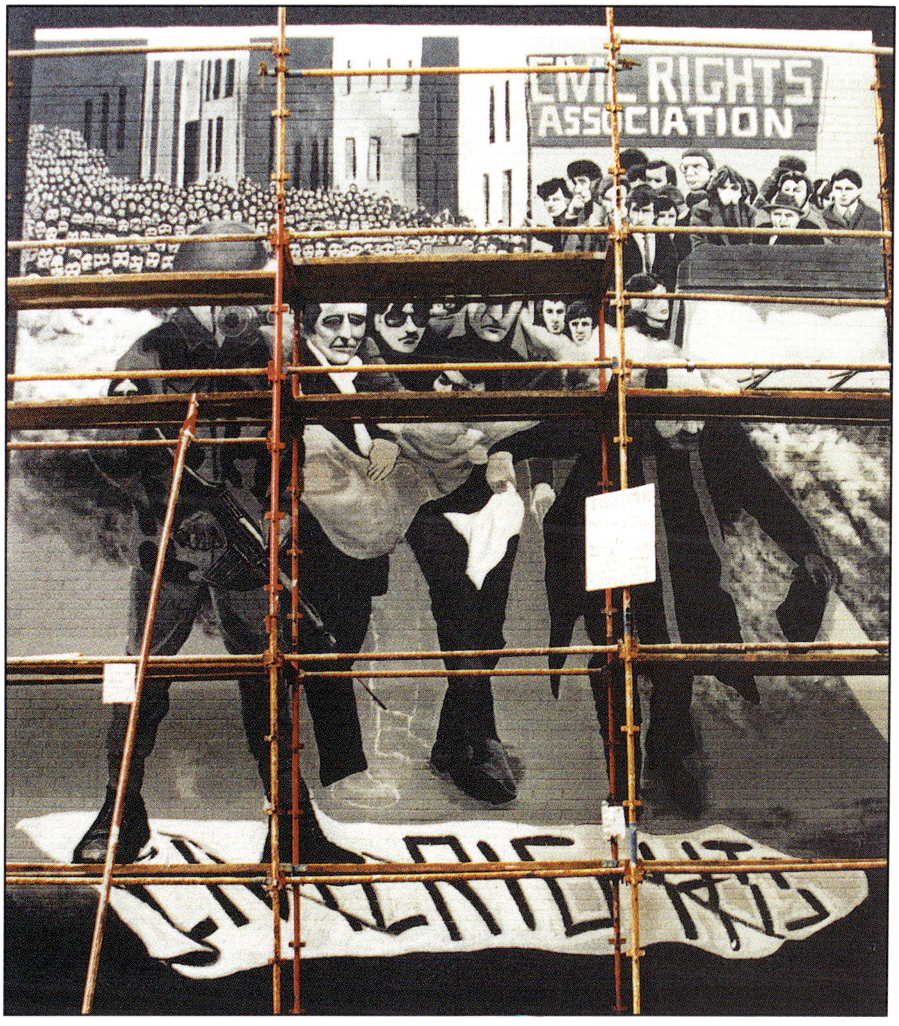

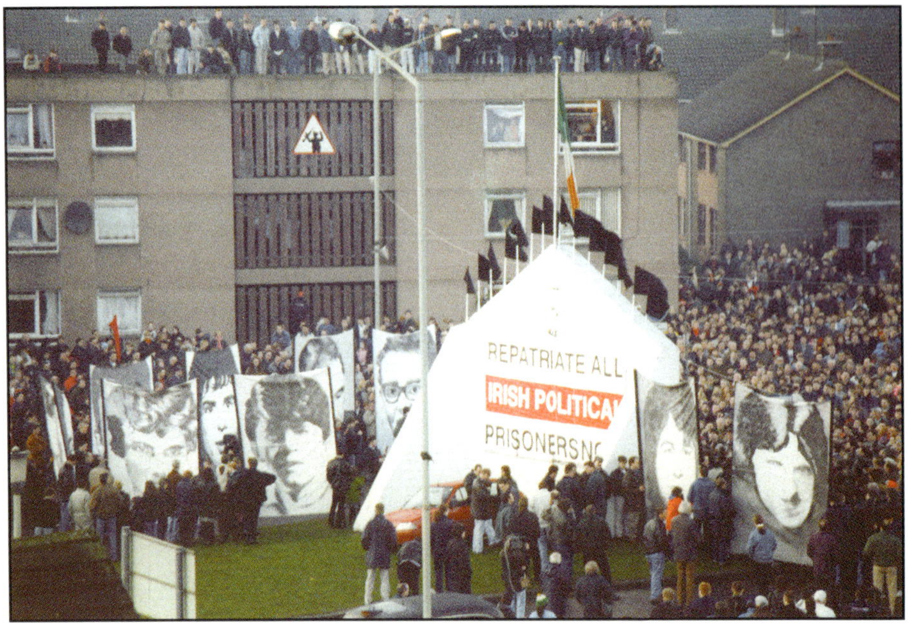

Bloody Sunday march with banners, Free Derry Corner, 1998.

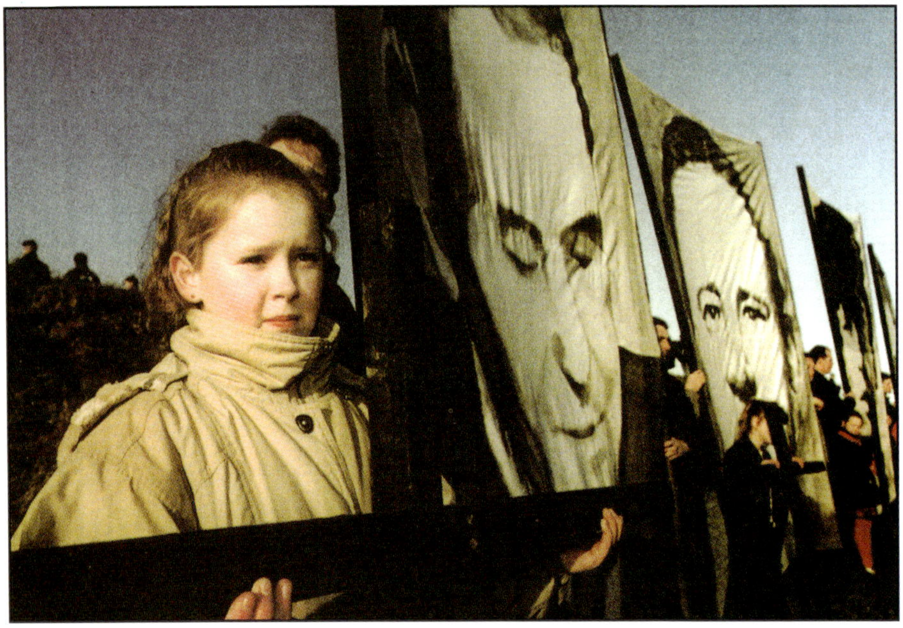

Child with cross and banners, 1998.

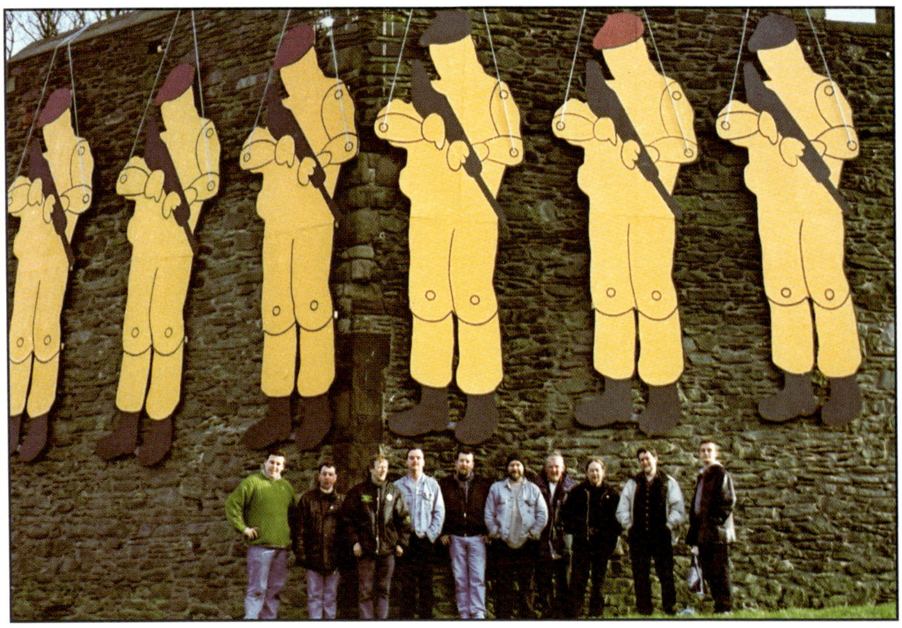

Puppet soldiers on the city Walls – the Bogside Artists and helpers.

PUPPETS AND BANNERS

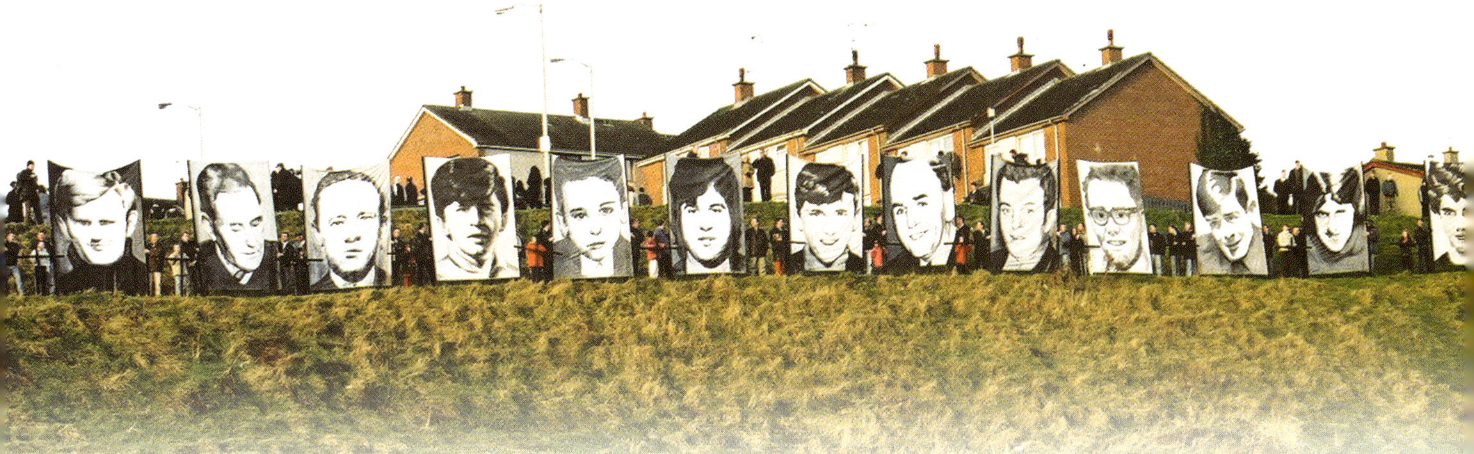

We felt we had to quantify and articulate the collective feeling of the people of the Bogside with regard to the Bloody Sunday tragedy. It is, for the people of the Bogside, *the* pivotal event in their history. By painting large portrait-banners of all fourteen victims, we were able to raise the narrative of the massacre out of the inanity of mere historical fact and into the dimension of human feeling. The following year, we constructed and painted six large puppets depicting the soldiers of the Parachute and Anglian Regiments who had been responsible for the debacle. The puppets, painted in lurid yellow to highlight the cowardice of the act they represent, were suspended from the Derry Walls overlooking the scene of the massacre; the banners were held aloft on the apartment block opposite Free Derry Corner. These banners have been almost a standard feature of the Bloody Sunday commemorations.

Both these projects formed the basis of a forty-minute documentary made about us by the BBC. Broadcast on 1 April 1998, it received the second highest viewing figures of the night. From the reviews, it was clear to us that the film had gone a long way to de-demonising both ourselves and the people of the Bogside. As that was our avowed intention from the beginning, full credit must go to producer and director Seán Maguire, who made a film that touched people everywhere at a time when it mattered most. Not for nothing did we title it *What You See Is What You Get*, for the damage that has been done by misperceiving what actually exists by both sides cannot be overestimated. The documentary was broadcast a couple of weeks before the Good Friday Agreement was signed.

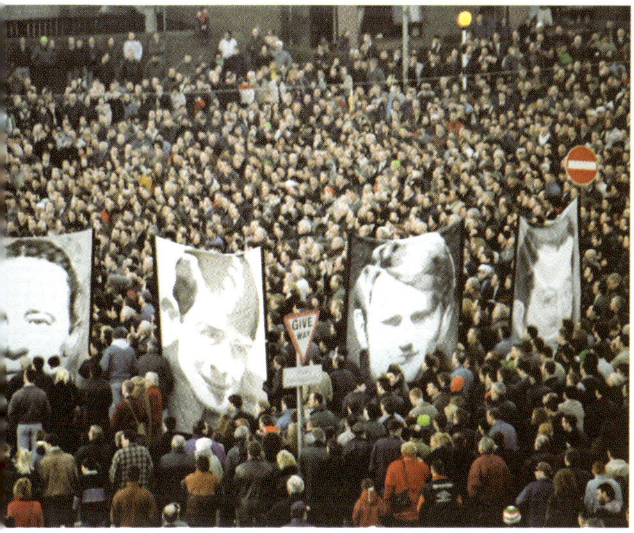

The dead of Bloody Sunday among their own.

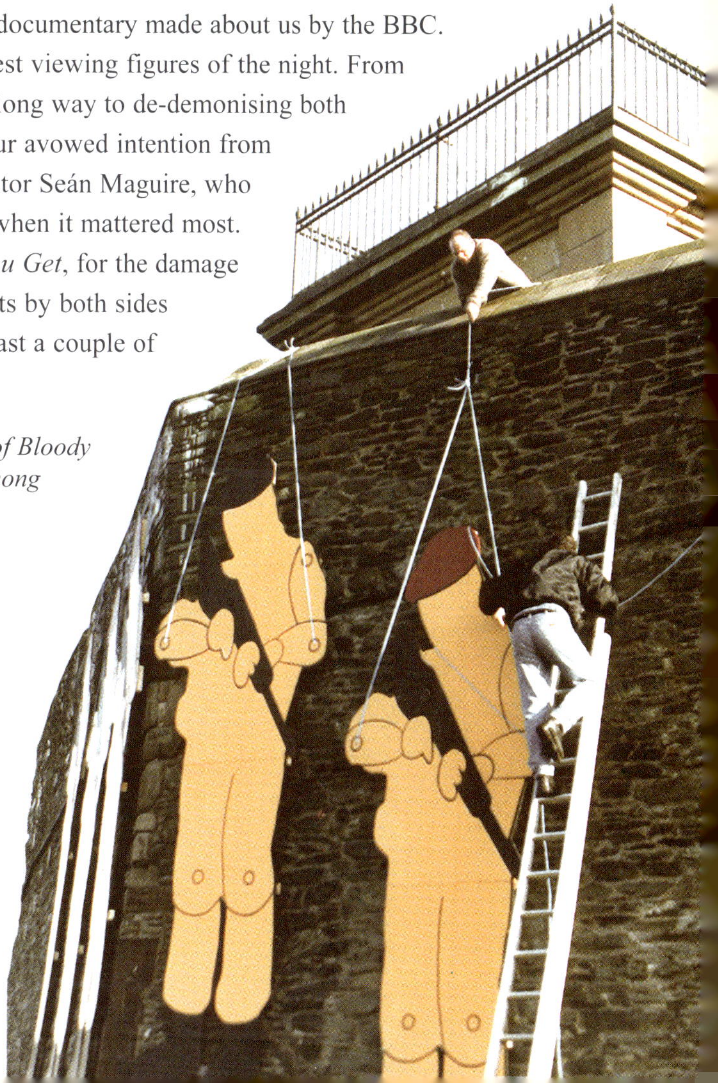

HUNGER STRIKE

As a tactic, the hunger strike had a long history in Ireland. It was a way of shaming your enemy, a way of achieving justice and had been used in many other countries, such as India and South Africa. St Patrick is reputed to have gone on hunger strike against God after an angel had appeared to inform him that his demands were extravagant. Patrick fasted for forty-five days until the Divinity changed His mind. In 1861, the Indian Government had to ban what was known as 'dharna' – death by sitting down and refusing food. Mahatma Gandhi fasted no less than seventeen times in his combats with the British Raj. Thomas Ashe, then leader of the IRB (Irish Republican Brotherhood), died after being force-fed while in custody in Mountjoy jail in 1917. In 1920 Terence MacSwiney, then Lord Mayor of Cork, died after seventy-four days of fasting in Brixton Prison; the event received massive media attention. MacSwiney was a poet, a philosopher and a playwright. In mid-June 1972, over thirty Republican prisoners at Crumlin Road jail went on strike to secure political status.

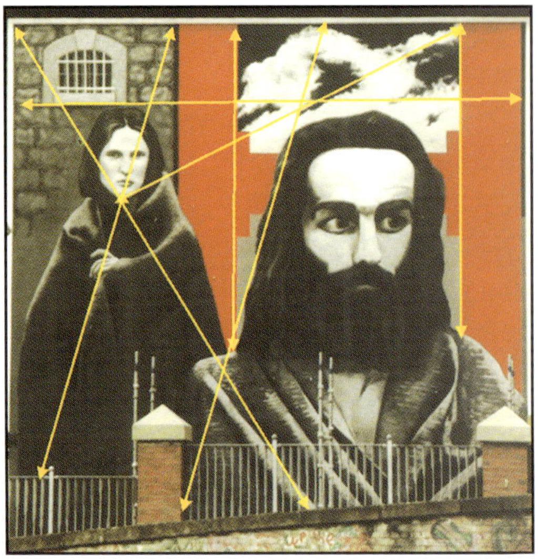

In a government statement on 5 November 1975, it was announced that there would be no entitlement to special category status for prisoners committing crimes after 1 March 1976. This was a devastating blow for the inmates of the Long Kesh prison. On 15 September 1976, Kieran Nugent refused to don prison garb and draped himself in a blanket. Thus began the 'blanket protests' that led eventually to the hunger strikes of 1980/81. The protest brought to the attention of the public the treatment of prisoners in the camps.

On Monday 27 October 1980, the strike began in the H-Blocks with seven volunteers, among them Raymond McCartney from Derry. They demanded political status, because none believed they would have ended up in prison in the first place had the politics of the state not driven them to it. They demanded the right to wear civilian clothes at all times: free association within the prison blocks; educational and recreational facilities; restoration of remission of sentence and the right to refuse prison work. This strike officially ended on 18 December after fifty-three days, but twenty-three additional prisoners were soon to join the protest.

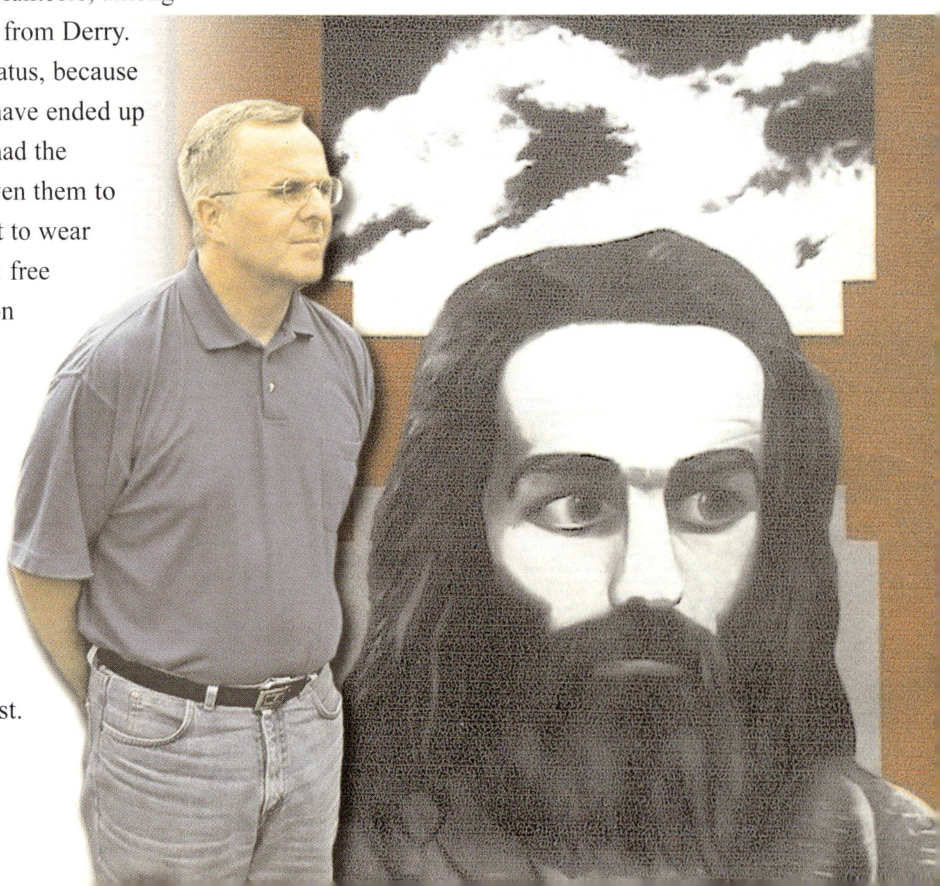

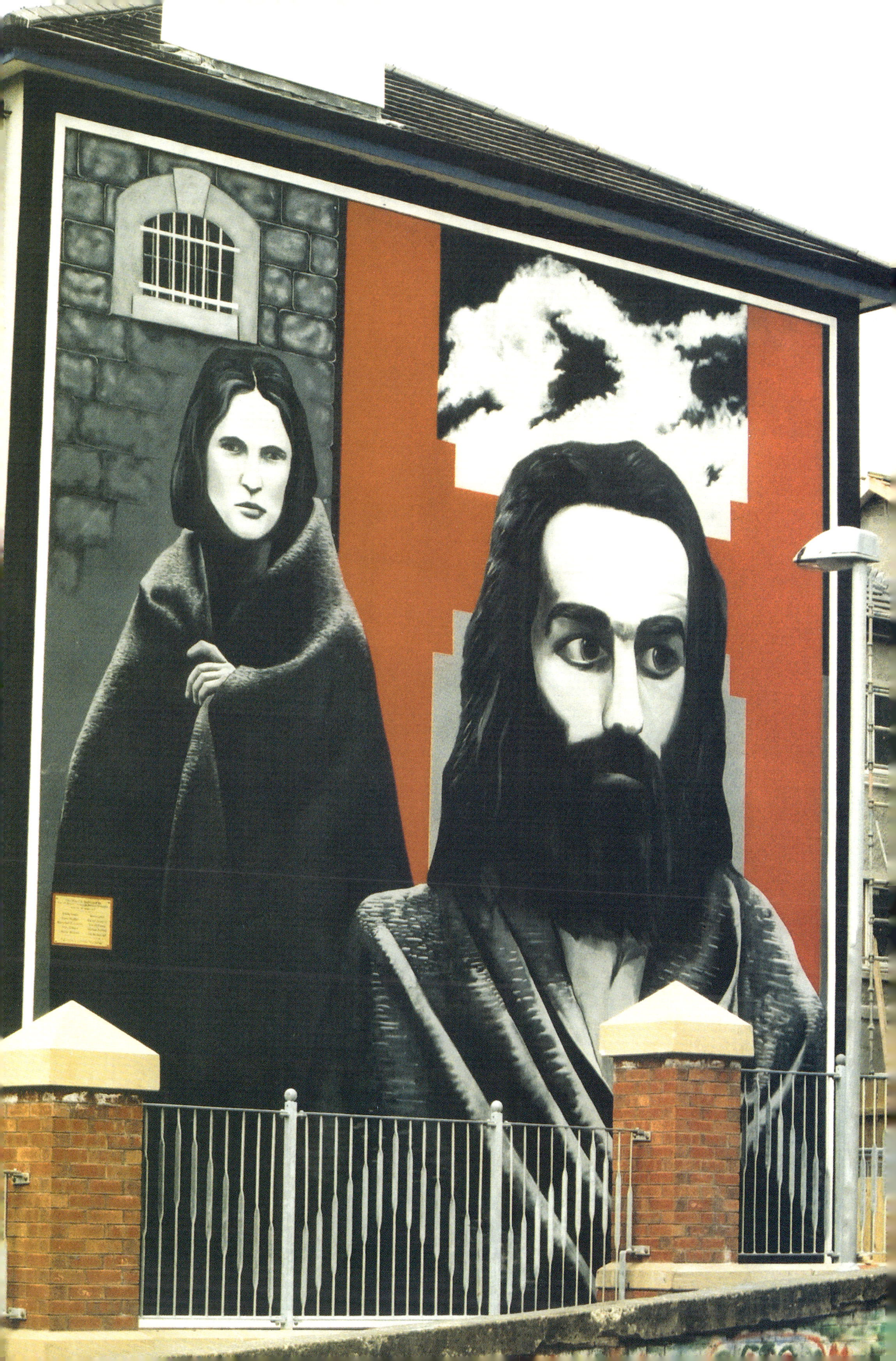

The IRA leadership outside the prison was not in favour of a further strike; nevertheless, a second strike was called and ended on 3 October 1981, largely due to the growing resolve by the strikers' families to seek medical intervention for the volunteers whenever they lost consciousness. By then, ten prisoners had died and 16,656 plastic bullets had been fired during the month of May – over 3,000 of them in Derry.

On 6 October, Northern Ireland Secretary of State James Prior announced measures that virtually satisfied all of the prisoners' demands. The events had received vast media attention; it was a propaganda victory over the British Government that would have far reaching consequences in the political sphere. Westminster's attempt to safeguard electoral support for the SDLP as the main Catholic Nationalist party led to the Anglo-Irish Agreement of 15 November 1985.

Bobby Sands, then leader of the IRA in prison, had begun his strike on 1 March 1981. His election to Westminster, as a result of the unexpected death of the MP for Fermanagh/South Tyrone, Frank Maguire, was a turning point in Sinn Féin's political strategy. By June 1983, they had obtained 13.4 per cent of the vote in the North and were gaining support in the South and now trailed the SDLP by only 4.5 per cent. Since then, Sinn Féin's support has continued to grow, much to the alarm of both the SDLP and the Unionists. After all, the Anglo-Irish Agreement was a concerted attempt to siphon off whatever electoral support SF had hoped to gain so that they would remain well in the background with only a minor (if any) role to look forward to in the forthcoming power-sharing executive. That too was a gamble, and one that did not pay off. The Hunger Strikes would go down in history as *the* watershed in the Nationalist struggle.

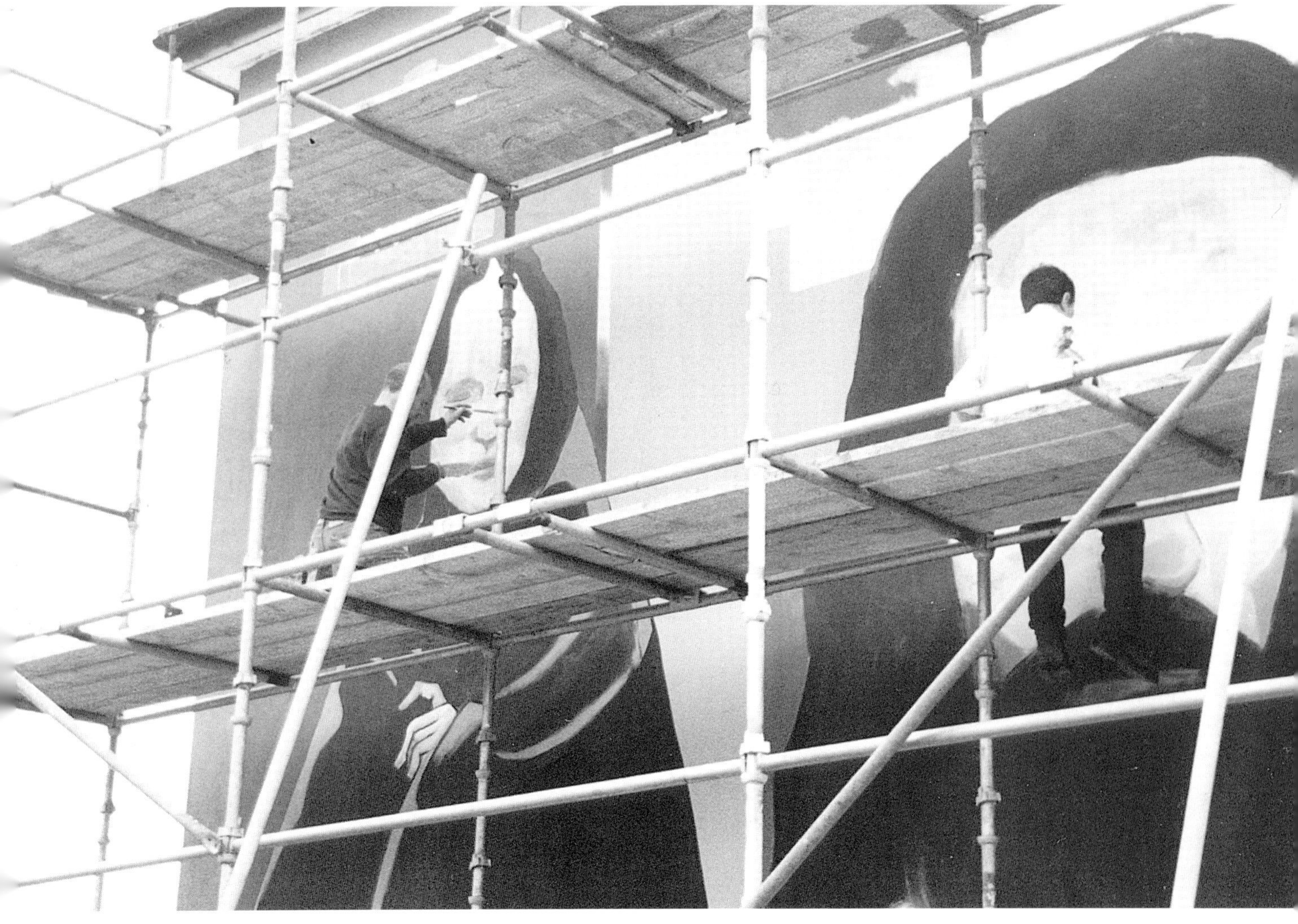

HUNGER STRIKE MURAL

We chose Raymond McCartney's face for the main figure in this mural, because this particular photo, taken of him during the strike and smuggled out of prison, was the archetypal one of the period. To get our bearings, we went to see him at his home and so were able to get a full insight into the hopeless despair the strikers had to live through. His account of the daily routine of meals being brought to his cell and left on the floor for him to contemplate and the effects of prolonged starvation on the senses were poignantly recalled.

'The most noticeable thing when you are on hunger strike is your sense of smell; that goes sky-high. They give you salt to put in your water and after maybe thirty days on hunger strike, and you take the cap of the water bottle, the smell of the water would knock you out.'

His account of the unshakeable belief among the strikers in the rightness of their cause, and the frightening experience of the gradual loss of eyesight that Sands himself has written about in some detail, made us very aware of the suffering of all those caught up in the protest.

'If you are going to hunger strike because of faith, it was a faith in what you were doing rather than a religious faith,' he said. McCartney laid particular importance on the role played by the women of Armagh prison in support of the strike. All of this helped us to see how we might best represent the whole saga in visual form.

In our approach to the *Hunger Strike* mural, we originally decided on a monochromatic image of an empty bed in a cell in Long Kesh, the iron door ajar to reveal the cell and, beside the bed, a vase with a dying rose in it. The rose would be the only point of colour in an otherwise grey and black painting. It was a poignant image, we felt at the time, but, after days of reflection and reconsidering the visual alternatives, we had to admit that it verged on sentimentality – and for that reason was abandoned.

The image we next arrived at fared no better: this depicted the faces of all the ten men who died. We eventually decided this would be too much like the one we painted for Bloody Sunday. Then we figured to return to something symbolical with *time* as the theme. The solution finally came in the form of what is now in place. The red of the rose became the colour of the H-Block, and the dramatic lighting we envisioned for the empty bed in the prison became the storm clouds between the H's uprights. In other words, nothing from two of the preceding solutions was lost in the final image. What we did leave out was the image of a clock from the symbolical version. It would have been a telling element and one, moreover, that would have registered with the local population who had lived through those dreadful months, hour by hour, way back in 1980/81.

For one must bear in mind that when painting a mural the artist is engaged in a sort of visual oratory. For a start, he is addressing a community rather than an individual. He has elected to perform a service and, in doing so, he has distanced himself quite deliberately from the egocentric self-indulgence that still informs the culture of his age. The mural has its arcane and mysterious birth right there in the public gaze. The passer-by enters into a relation with it even while it is being created. A huge wall painting demands to be taken notice of because of its size and in the case of most of our murals and, especially that of the Hunger Striker, because of its sheer effrontery. So the interaction between it and the viewer takes on a character very different from that which prevails in

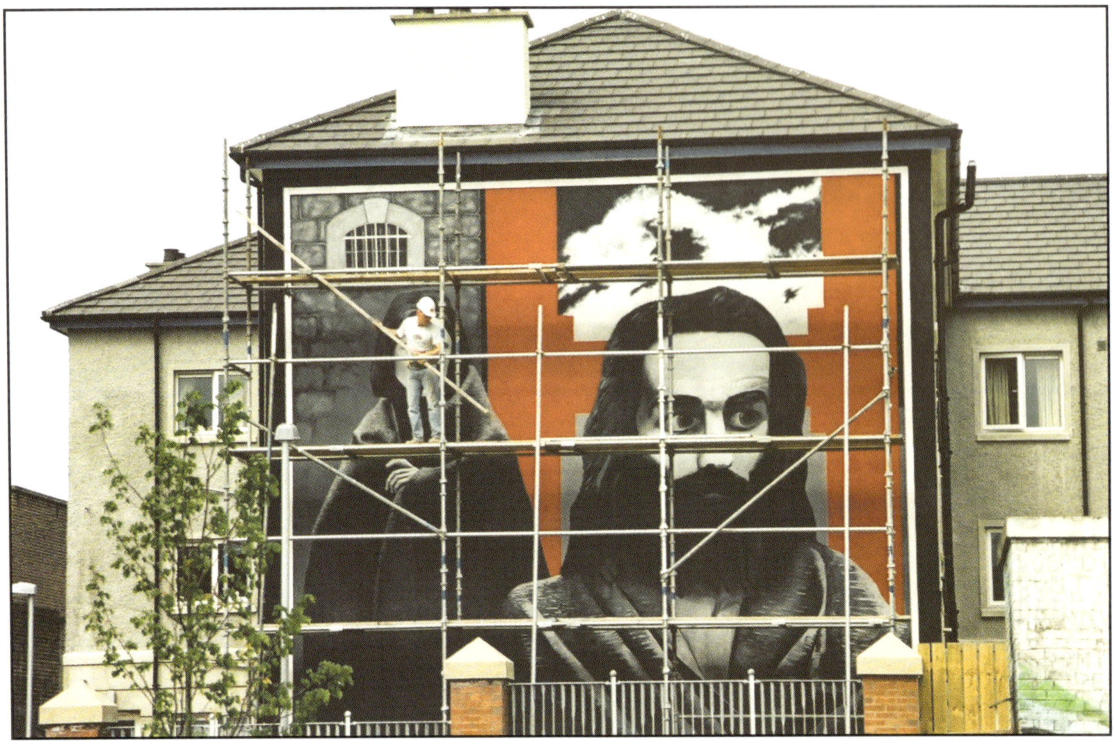

the cosy enclosed space of an art gallery. Besides that, the muralist himself is confronted with a whole set of problems that the easel painter is spared. The muralist must be an acrobat, a public relations man, a craftsman, a visionary, a designer, a sociologist and a whole heap of other things besides. He must be prepared to work for nothing. Moreover, he must labour in the full consciousness that those who disapprove of his work, for whatever reason, are ever ready to mask his final creation with banners, to vandalise it, to hide it from the public gaze with trees or walls, or to encourage the people for whom it was painted to turn against it. Envy, like violence, takes many 'righteous' forms.

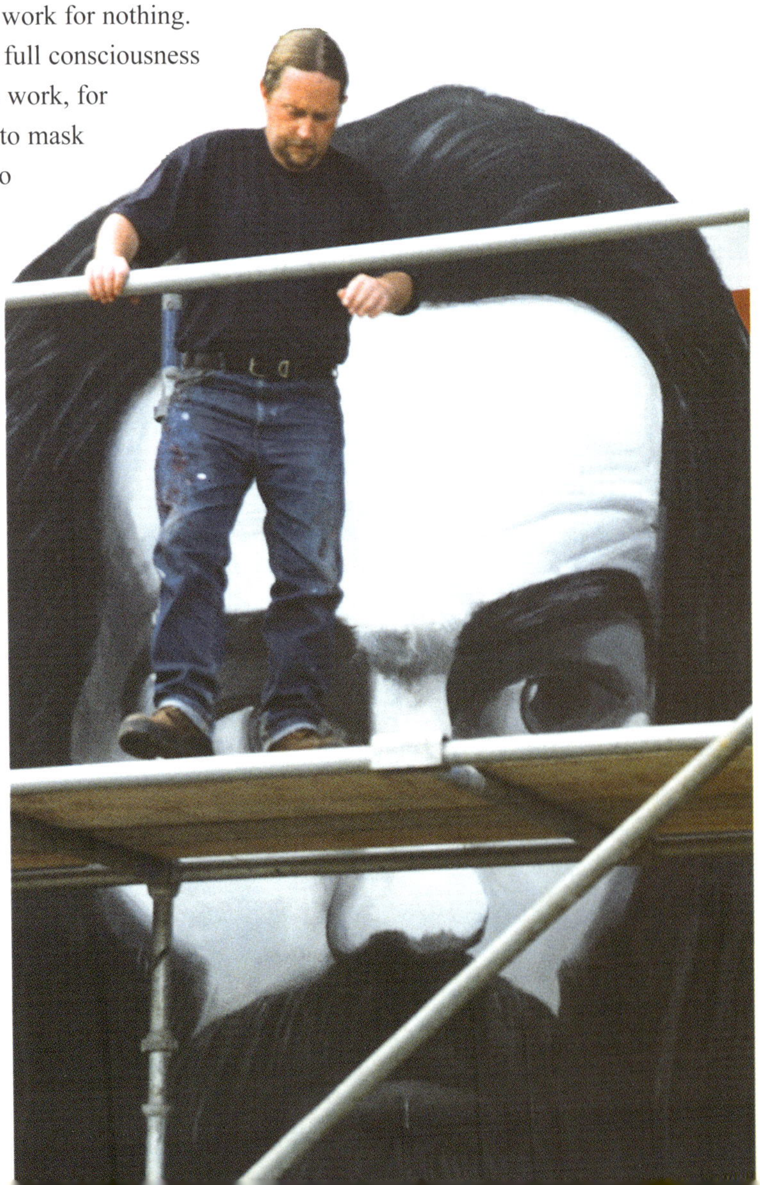

Despite all that, the mural, if it is left alone, marches on. It grafts itself gracefully onto the public consciousness where it blooms perpetually in easy accord. It sports an aura of public approval. It enters people's lives. If you want to know what the Bogside would be without these murals, think of Anne Franck without her diary.

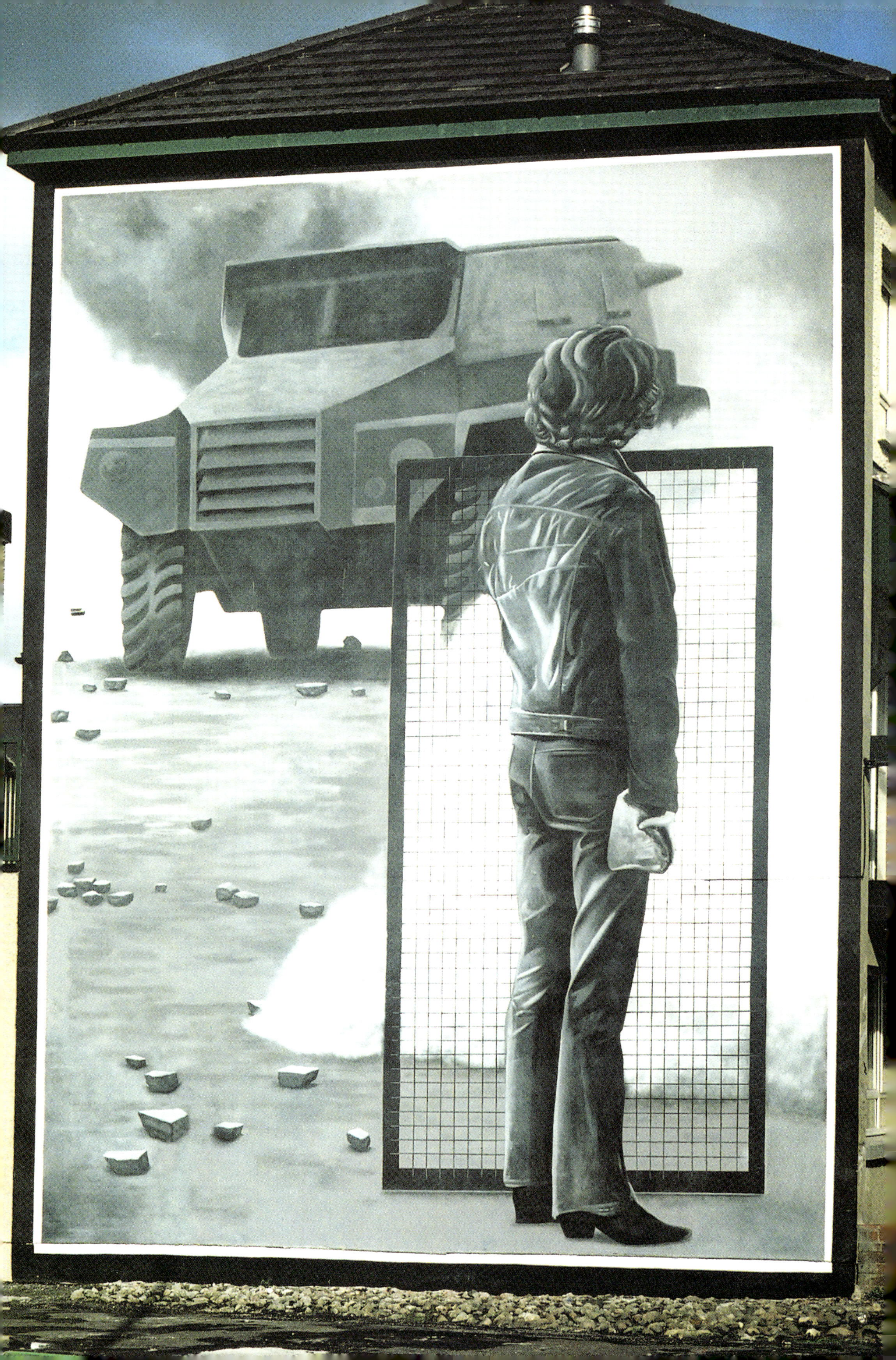

THE RIOTER

The mural called *The Rioter* is often referred to locally as the 'Saturday Matinée'. In those early days, Saturday was always the favoured day for a showdown with the roaming RUC police force, because people would be off work and kids free from school. The confrontations were regarded – especially by the young – as a game, a dangerous game for sure, but one unlikely to result in fatalities. That was before the issue of life and death got stamped on the script.

The matinées became the modus operandi after 12 August 1969 in what became known as the *Battle of the Bogside,* described elsewhere in this book. After the creation of Free Derry and the erections of barricades throughout the Bogside, there followed numerous riots between the citizens and the RUC; and later, the British army. CS gas and water cannon were used extensively during these battles. From 12 August on, no-go areas became a feature of Nationalist enclaves in towns throughout the North West. On 14 August, the Prince of Wales' Own Regiment arrived to take up duty in Derry. Many consider this to have been the worst decision Downing Street ever made with regard to Northern Ireland. Home Secretary James Callaghan, by way of exonerating himself and his government, explained later, in so many words, that they didn't know what else they could do. The dissolution of Stormont was not then on the agenda.

The attitude of the British Government was that extensive reform was essential. Even back then, they were suggesting a restructuring of the police force and had set up the Hunt Committee to look into it. Their recommendations led to the establishment of the Ulster Defence Regiment, which was really only the old B-Specials dressed up in another uniform. The UDR were to play a principal role in the forthcoming war of attrition. The Cameron report, published in September of that year, made the validity of Catholic grievances abundantly clear – even to Unionists. Its recommendations led to two nights of rioting by Loyalists in Belfast, during which the first RUC constable, Victor Arbuckle, was shot and killed.

The tidal wave, which had begun in earnest in late 1968, had been gathering momentum. It is estimated that in the three months after June 1969, 5.3 per cent of all Catholic families and 0.4 per cent of Protestants were forced to move. And by February 1973, some 60,000 people in Belfast, almost 10 per cent of the entire population, had been driven from their homes; most of these were Catholics from the North and East of the city. Rioting would become a daily feature of many people's lives. The thing about the matinée was that it was always sure to come around. By the end of 1969, the IRA had decisively split into the Provisionals and the Officials.

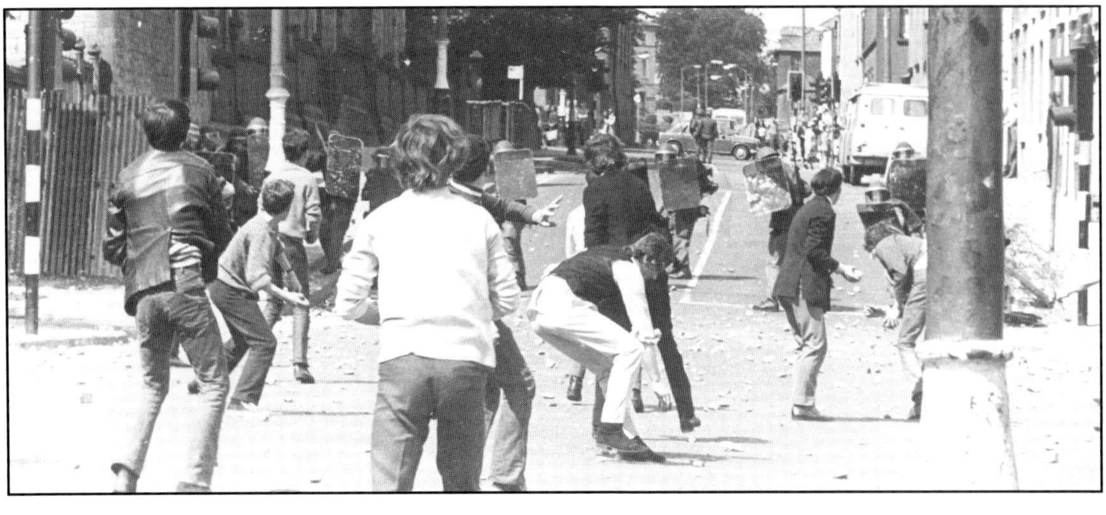

THE RIOTER MURAL

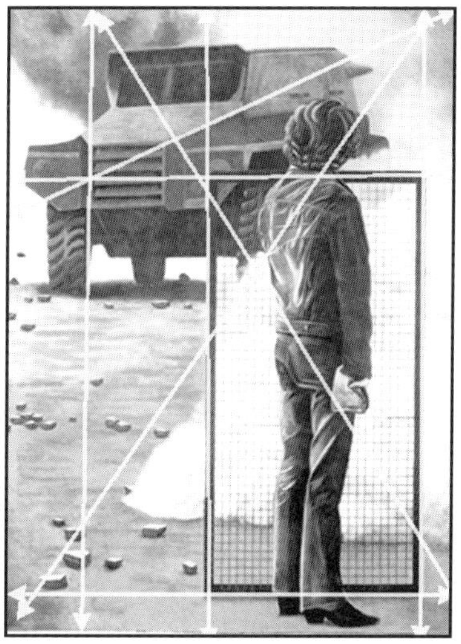

Following our tried and trusted method of economy of expression, we used the main figure from the photo. From our point of view, the figure itself required little embellishment; we merely heightened the contrast between shadows and lights and increased the size of the stone in his hand. The wire mesh that he used as a shield was probably formerly used to guard a window. The wire interstices were carefully painted, and the CS gas was shaped and rendered as accurately as possible. CS gas is very white in colour, but, as a rule, pure white in any painting is to be avoided. Our challenge was to confine ourselves entirely to the broad range of tones between white and black, relying for the bigger areas on the black and white of ordinary outdoor emulsions. We carried, in this instance, the whole notion of simplicity of expression into simplicity of means as well.

For the lighter areas in the figure, we introduced acrylic white and Mars black, just as we did with the preceding *Soldier* mural. For the Saracen armoured vehicle, we introduced a little brown so that it would not blend with the broad range of cooler greys that surrounded it; the vehicle we discovered in the library archives. We skewed the wheels a little to give the sense of a vehicle swerving around to face its quarry. It is these contrasts that make the figure stand out. Nothing of the drama of the moment was therefore lost, and the turning vehicle gives the moment the tension it needed. We then had our rioter facing what we knew to be a very typical event during the *Battle of the Bogside.*

Now he looks for all the world like a matador facing a charging bull. This feeling of intent, on the part of the driver of the vehicle, is strengthened by the straight line that runs from the edge of the windscreen to the rock. Like all of our murals, this one is easily discerned from a distance. And, like all of our murals, it seeks to transcend its merely parochial significance. Its connection with a similar event in Beijing during the massive June demonstrations of 1989, when over a million Chinese took to the streets demanding democratic liberalisation, can hardly be missed. Our rioter echoes unavoidably the image of a lone man confronting a convoy of tanks making its way to Tiananmen Square.

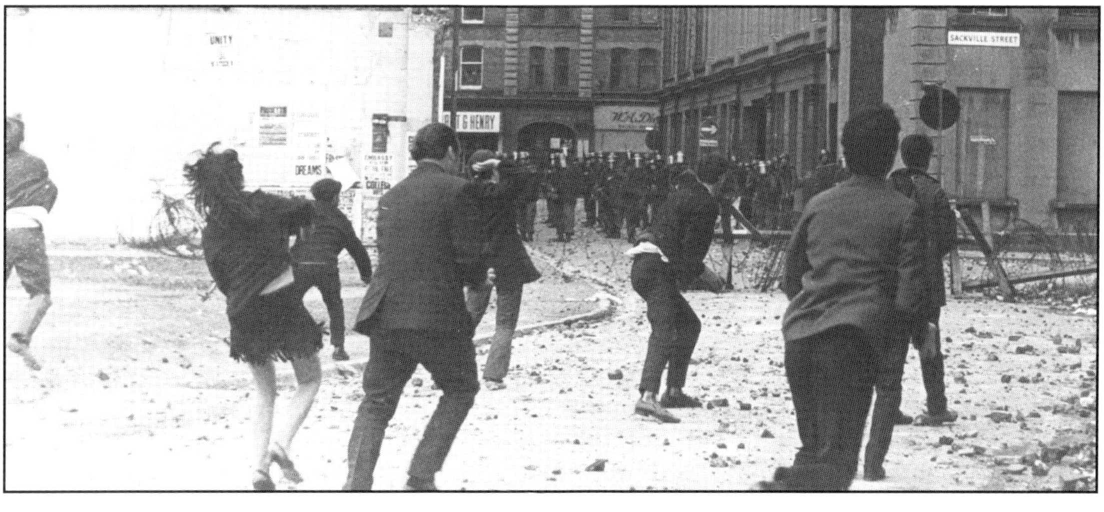

THE BLOODY SUNDAY COMMEMORATION MURAL

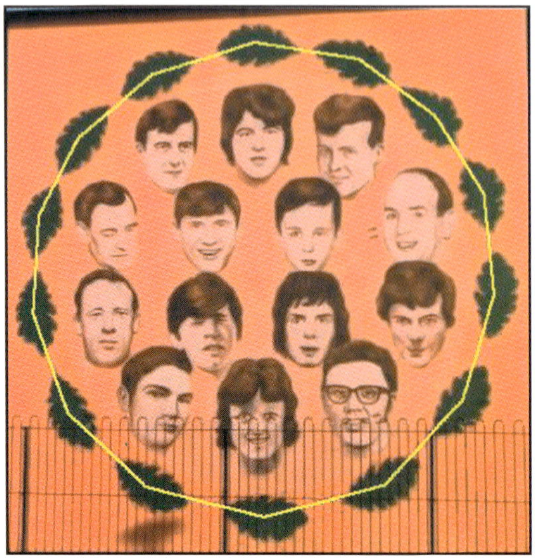

This mural was painted in October 1997 to commemorate the twenty-fifth anniversary of the Bloody Sunday Massacre. We were approached on this occasion by the Bloody Sunday Campaign for Justice committee. No stipulations as to how we would do it were given, as it is well understood that we always paint what they think is appropriate, as any worthwhile artist must.

The design is simple, the circle being the format we agreed on early in the design process as the one that would effectively encapsulate all fourteen portraits of the victims. The portraits were first of all done out on large pages after area calculations had been done on the appropriate size of circle and the total area coverage the faces would occupy if they were to be seen at their best. The faces were then strategically placed and drawn out, the youngest being given special prominence whereas the older faces surround them hinting at parental concern.

The colour, which is a shade of red, proved to be the most precarious part, as too loud or too chromatic would have had an effect opposite to what we intended. We wanted a red that was soft and mellow – in a word, sad. The painting would be defined by its reference to Bloody Sunday. We believe that we achieved just that. In evening light, with the sun shining directly on it, it can be unbearably moving.

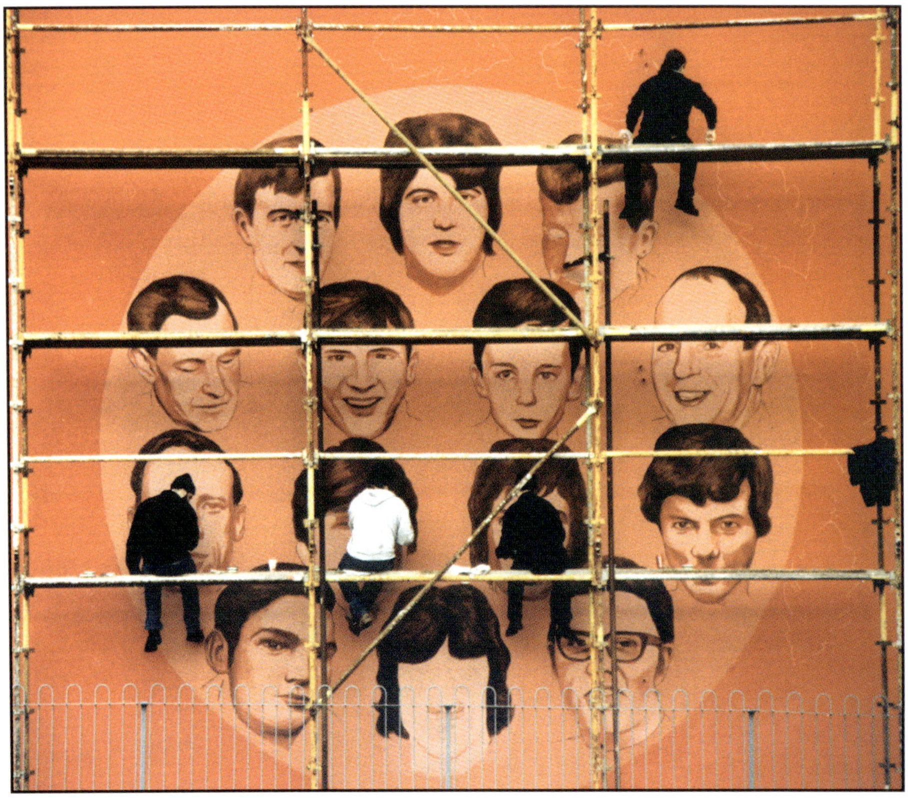

This painting is right in the heart of the Bogside in every sense. A plaque is planned for a mural bearing the names of the victims:

Gerard Donaghy (17)
John Duddy (17)
Hugh Gilmore (17)
Michael Kelly (17)
Kevin McElhinney (17)
John Young (17)
William Nash (19)
Michael McDaid (20)
James Wray (22)
William McKinney (27)
Patrick Doherty (31)
James McKinney (34)
Bernard McGuigan (41)
John Johnston (59)

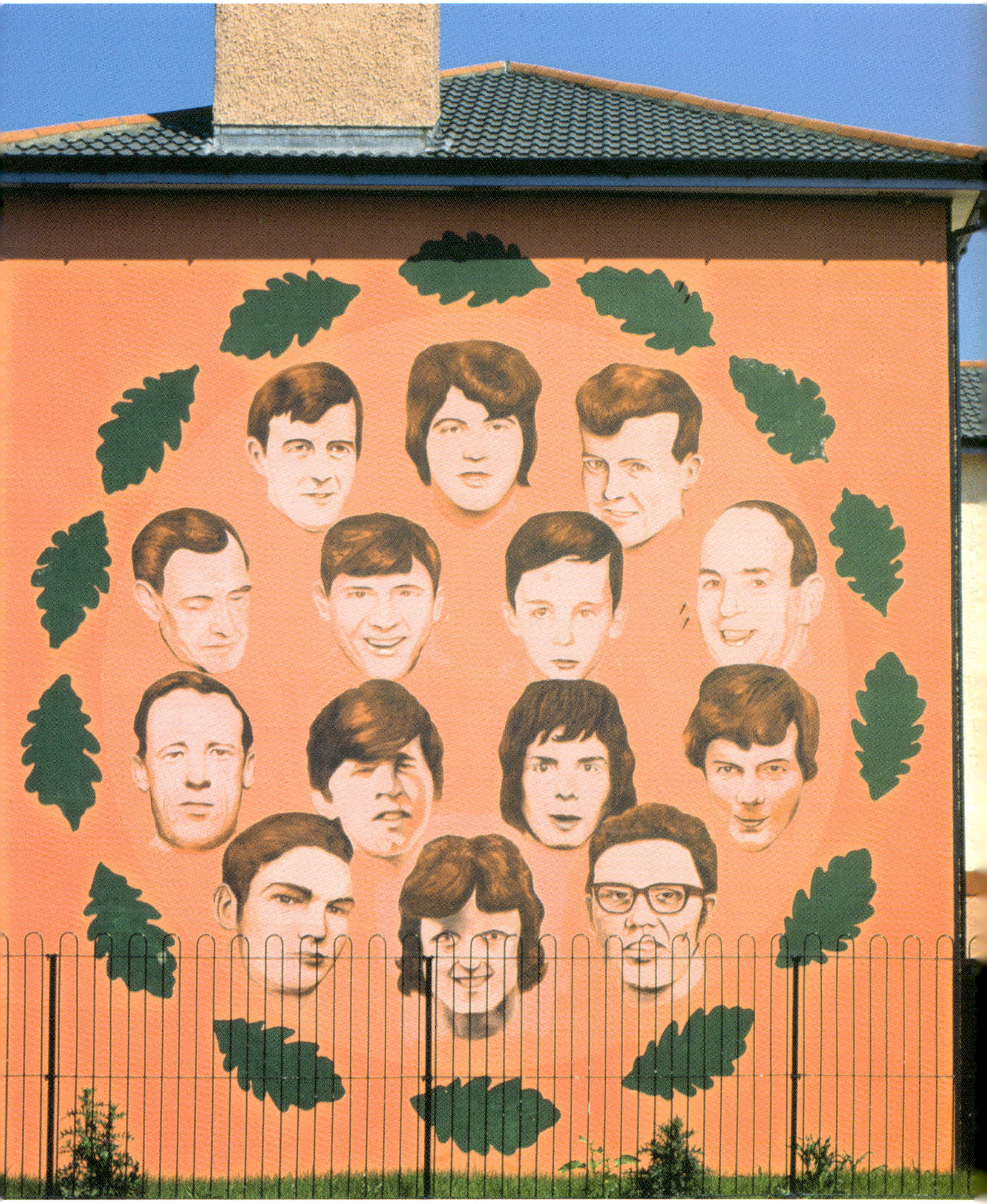

THE DEATH OF INNOCENCE MURAL

Our intention for this particular gable wall, which faces directly onto the Derry Walls, was to do a painting of Operation Motorman, one of the most violent and massive incursions by the British Army into Free Derry and other Nationalist no-go areas in July 1972. But, given the political situation at the time, we felt that such an image would be irresponsible. We decided that something supportive of the peace process, then in a delicate state, would be more appropriate.

As the issue of disarmament was the basic stumbling block to an agreement to form a government at the time, we decided we would incorporate this aspect into the work. Our thinking was that *all guns* are deadly.

We wanted the figure to stand out boldly from the background. We also wanted her *innocence* to radiate against the chaos of the world she was born into. The idea of *a shrine* was in our minds from the beginning. It resonated with our feeling that innocence is a sacred thing and possibly the most divine aspect of any of us. Innocence is the thing that is most vulnerable when men go to war. We understood innocence to mean harmless: with no intent to harm or give offence; with no will to hurt; playful, free, spontaneously human, child-like; what we essentially are, and why the crimes we commit against each other appal all of us into gibbering incomprehension. To those who knew her (and she was Kevin's full-cousin), Annette McGavigan was innocence incarnate.

We did a preparatory painting showing a table with a crucifix and a single rose, and, in the background, the storm clouds of conflict. On the right-hand side of the table was a family photo of the child in a simple frame. Because a mural deals in massive shapes, we felt that the point would be lost once this image was transferred to the gable. The idea of a shrine, however, stayed with as we searched around for a solution. The image of chaos, first rendered in the storm clouds, was also with us, for we recollected that 1972 was a very bad year of the *Troubles*. So, we made a shrine for

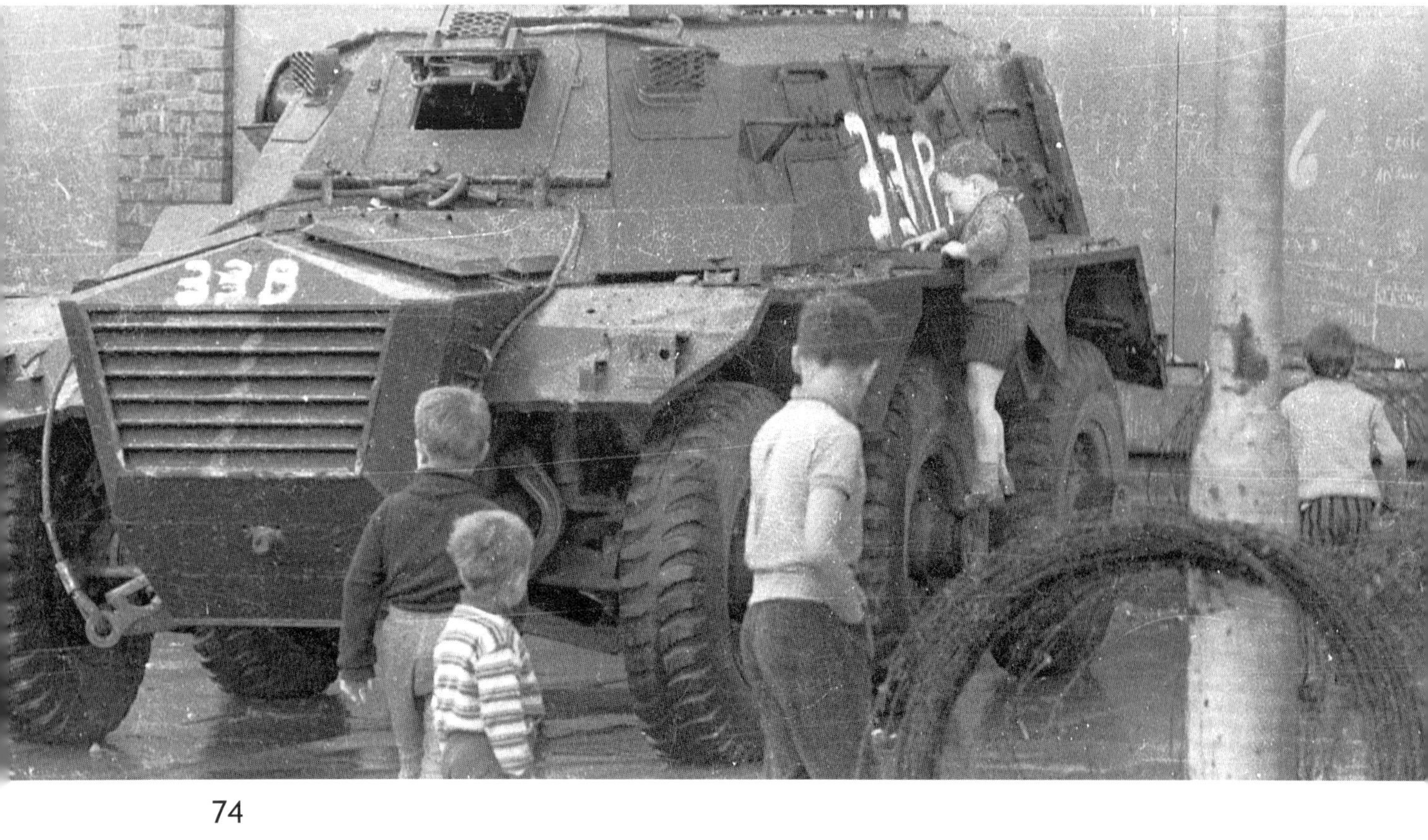

her from a rendition of the havoc that might result from a bomb explosion. One other interesting thing in this painting is that it was the first time we ever mixed black into our colours. We realised we needed a tonal contrast to the background that would lift the figure out of the wall and breathe life into it. This suggested itself to us as the best way to do it.

We then found a girl from the same school to adopt the pose that would communicate that innocence. In this way, her hands became a focal point. Our question was: how do you take such a heartrending event as the brutal death of a young girl and make it the vehicle of a plea for peace and sanity? That's why we gave it the title it has, because the death of this little girl lets us know, in no uncertain way, that in the high places where power is wielded, nobody's life amounts to anything.

Given our views on the crime, the title – *The Death of Innocence* – was, in fact, the very first element of the painting we were all agreed upon from the first, because that's what Annette's death meant to us at the time.

Much of our subsequent BBC documentary was given over to the problems we faced with this mural. The other question of how to paint it, without pointing up the absurdity of her death, or leaving the people of the Bogside with an image they would find it impossible to live with, was also one we could not shirk. Innocence must triumph eventually and we knew that was the road we had to travel.

The gun, which takes up the entire length of the left-hand side of the wall, was painted upside down. Like a monstrous serpent, it has been de-fanged; it points nowhere but to the ground and yet is closely enough associated with the main figure as to make the connection all the more moving by its subtlety. The work is literally correct in that sense. The original crucifix reappears in the right hand corner. This time, it alludes not so much to the sufferings of the 'Lamb', but to the Resurrection – as does the butterfly. The butterfly, in fact, is left unfinished, deliberately. It seemed to us, at the time, that the peace process had no guarantee it would succeed; and our feelings were far from optimistic. The colour of the butterfly is to suggest peace and wisdom. When peace is established we will finish it with a rising sun to denote a new beginning for us all.

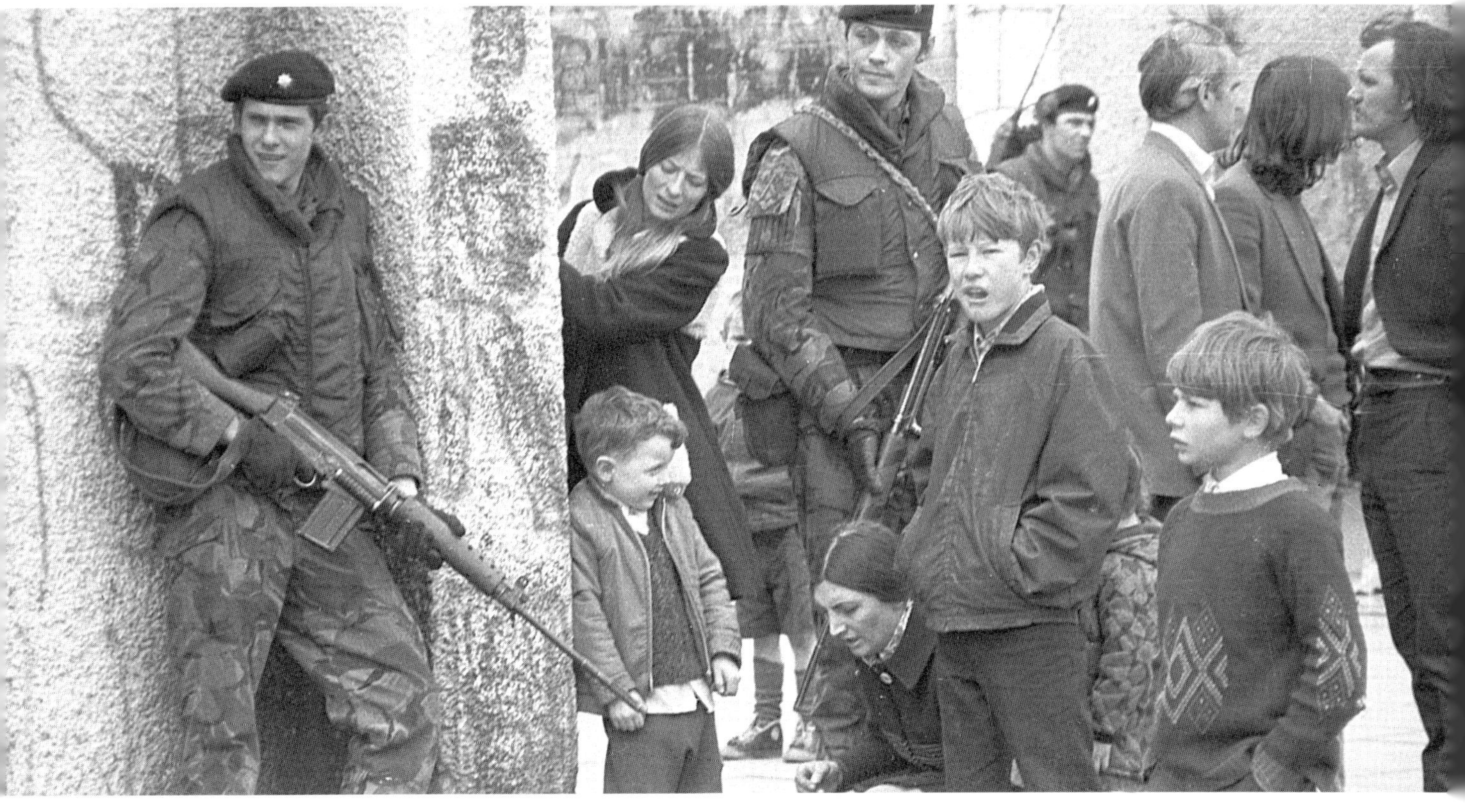

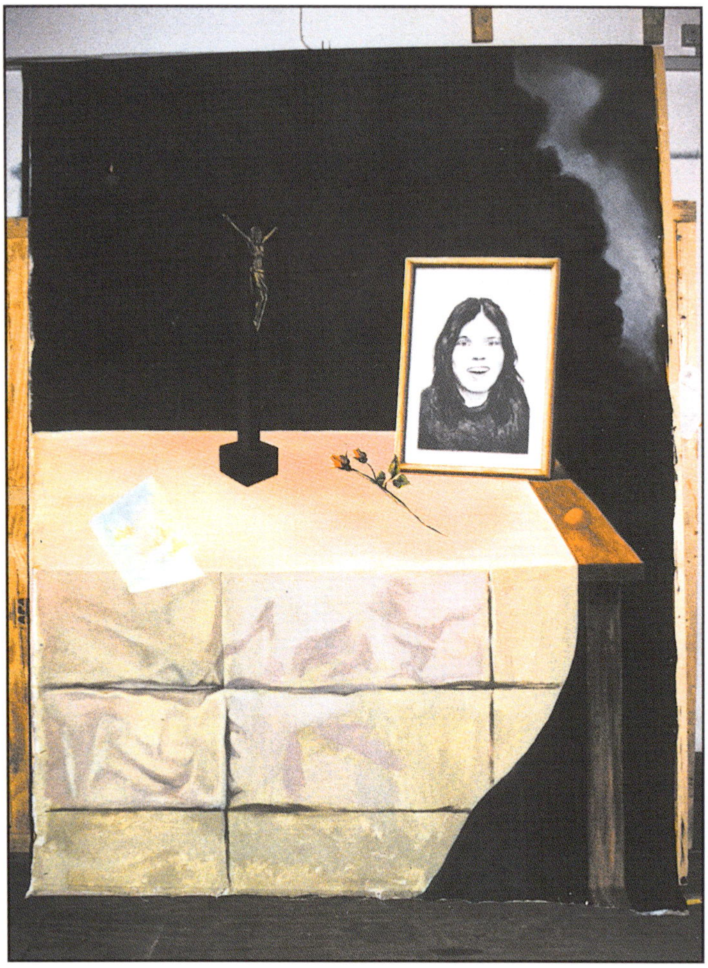

Preliminary sketch on canvas, not used in final image.

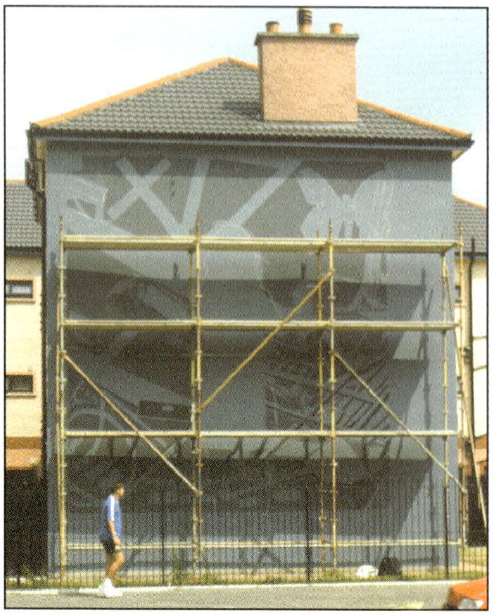

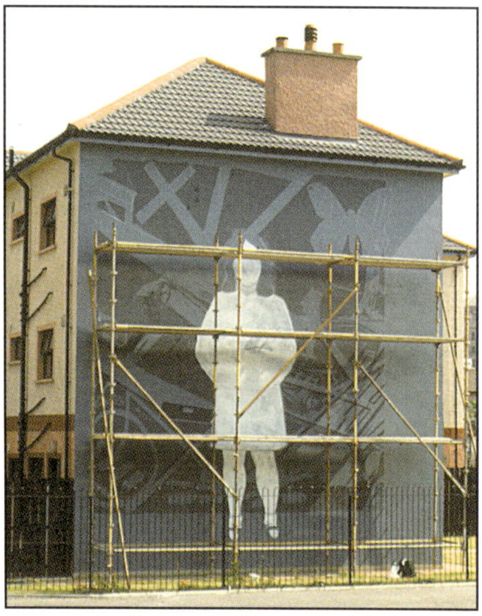

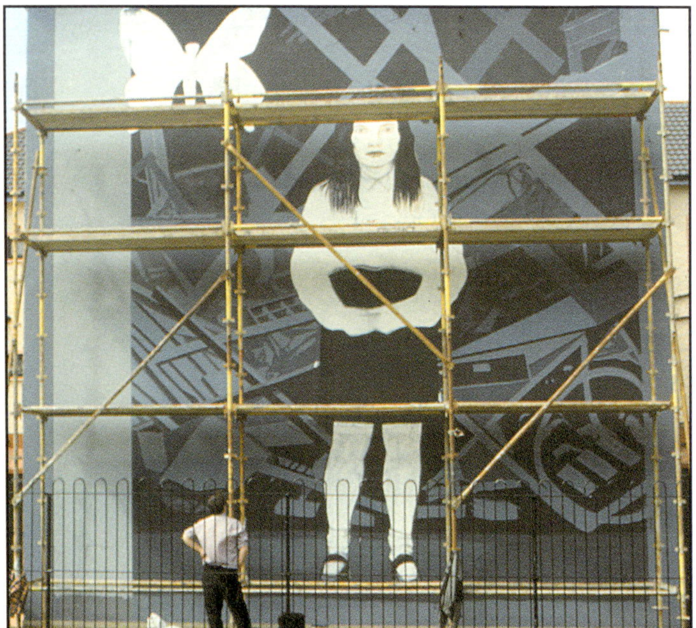

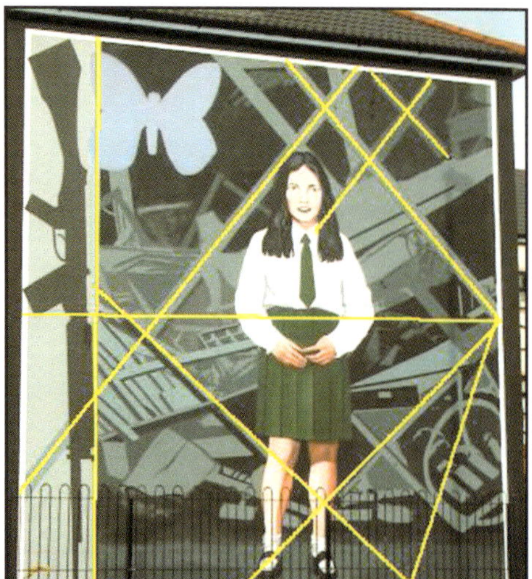

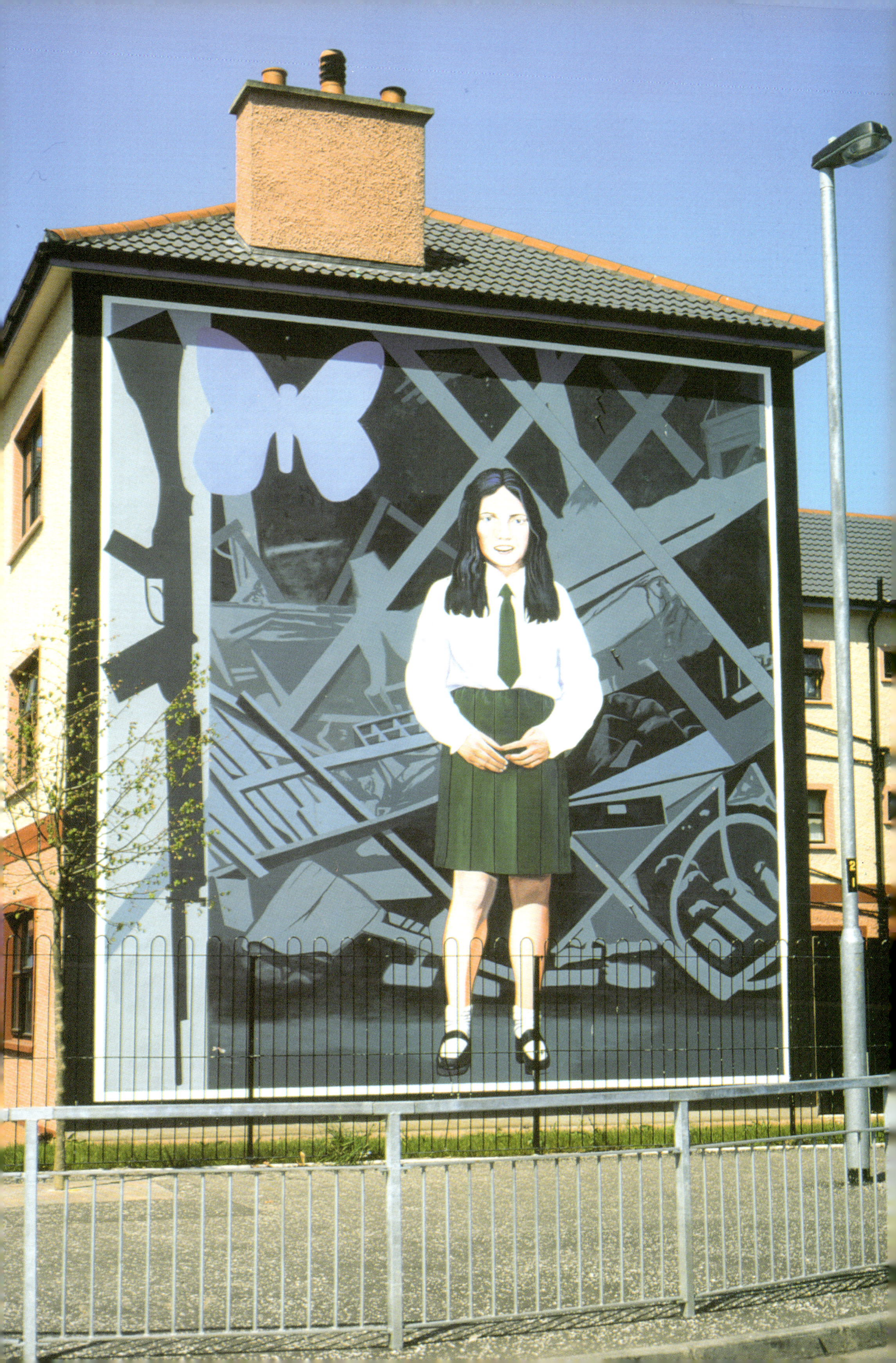

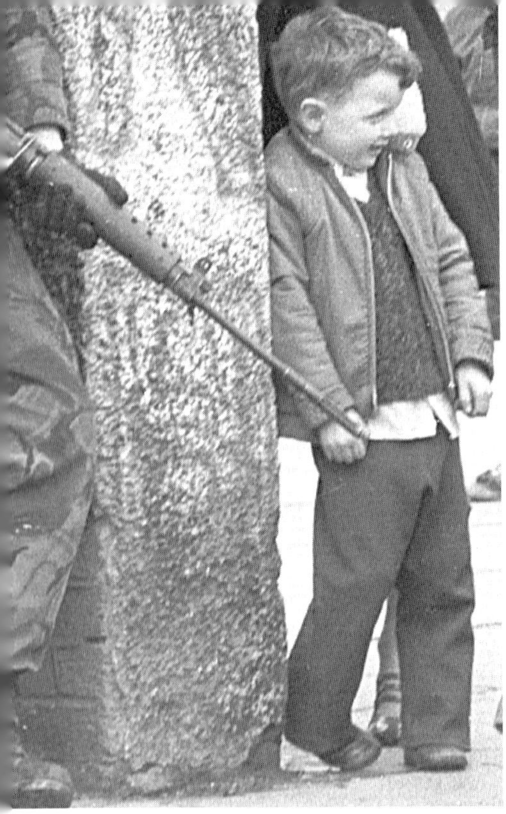

CHILDREN

Since the introduction of baton rounds to the North of Ireland, seventeen people, eight of them schoolchildren, have been killed; sixteen of them were Catholic. Both the European Parliament and the United Nations have passed resolutions calling on them to be banned.

The old-style plastic bullets, which killed fourteen of the seventeen victims, were made of steel-hard polyvinyl chloride (PVC), weighed four and three-quarter ounces and measured four inches in length by one and a half inches in diameter. They left the barrel of the gun at a velocity 160–170mph. Its predecessor, the rubber bullet, was used to kill the other three victims. The original baton round, made of teak with a metal core, was first used by the British in Hong Kong during the 1960s, where a 14-year-old schoolgirl was killed.

Since their introduction in February 1973, more than 60,000 plastic bullets have been fired. Apart from the seventeen deaths, thousands of people have been seriously injured, including two people who have been permanently blinded. Other serious injuries caused by baton rounds include brain damage, deafness, internal haemorrhaging and a range of serious bone fractures. The latest version of the baton round, the L21A1 introduced in June 2001, is lighter than its predecessor, but leaves the barrel at a much higher speed. Tests have shown it has the capacity to lodge in a person's skull, and the US military found it to be twice as deadly as its forerunner.

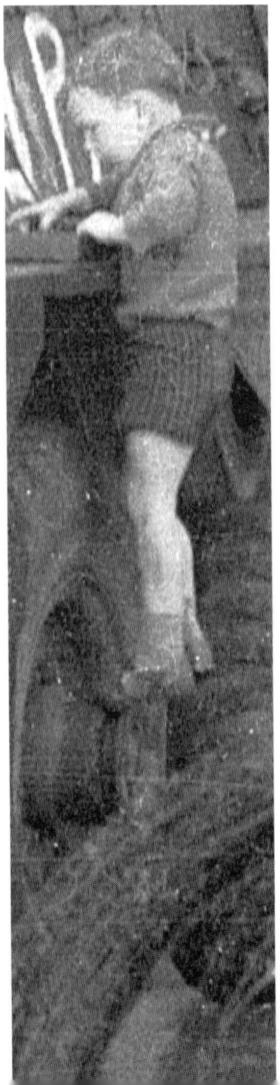

The baton rounds were developed at Porton Down, the MoD's research labs – a maze of forbidding buildings located on over 7,000 acres near Salisbury. It is the proud possessor of the world's longest running programme of chemical warfare experiments on humans. Its germ warfare products are said to be linked to Saddam Hussein.

The RUC and the British Army have consistently ignored guidelines for the use of plastic bullets. Among other stipulations, it is mandatory to fire the weapon from a standing position and at a minimum distance of twenty metres, and only at selected individuals, and never into a crowd of people. The bullet must also be aimed at the lower part of the body. Less than twenty metres is permissible, but only if someone's life is clearly in danger. Most of the seventeen fatalities have resulted from point-blank shooting at the upper part of the body. Most of the victims were proven not to have been involved in rioting when they were killed. The security forces fire not only indiscriminately at crowds, but also with immunity from the law. No RUC officer or soldier has ever been convicted in relation to any of the seventeen deaths caused by baton rounds. It has been observed that eight times as many plastic bullets were fired in three and a half days of Nationalist protest in the aftermath of Drumcree 1996 as were fired during four and a half days of Unionist rioting. This clearly demonstrates the sectarian bias in their use. There are a number of murals in Belfast commemorating those who have been killed by plastic bullets.

Stephen McConomy

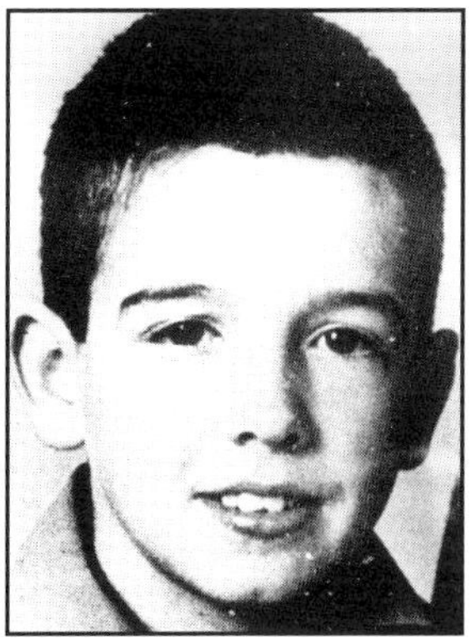

On the evening of 16 April 1982, stationed at the top of Fahan Street that runs steeply from Butcher Gate down into the Bogside, there was a British Army Saracen, known locally as a 'Pig'. It was manned by members of the Royal Anglian regiment. Above it, on the Walls, RUC police milled about. They had been alerted by a bomb scare. As was usual then, if not inevitable, a group of four or five young boys aged between ten and thirteen picked up small rocks and pelted the heavily armoured vehicle; looking on was 11-year-old Stephen McConomy. As the dreaded plastic bullet gun appeared at an opened latch, the boys turned to scarper. As Stephen mounted the footpath opposite the 'Pig' with his hands in his pockets, the gun was fired. He was hit on the back of the head and taken clean off his feet with the impact. He had been shot at a range of 4 metres. He died three days later at the Royal Victoria Hospital in Belfast after being transferred from Altnagelvin. He did not regain consciousness.

Statements given later by eyewitnesses to Fathers Raymond Murray and Denis Faul corroborated that the boy had not been involved in any of the stone throwing, that at no stage was anybody's life in danger, that he had been walking away at the time and that those who tried to help him were warned off by the gunman so that it took a full three minutes before they could reach him. This action is a classic example of the arbitrary contravention of all the rules of practice laid down for the use of the plastic bullet. It transpired later that not only did the soldier responsible have to pull the trigger twice, as the gun was faulty, but he apparently knew nothing about the rules governing the use of plastic bullets. No charges have been brought against him or anybody else involved.

Paul Whitters

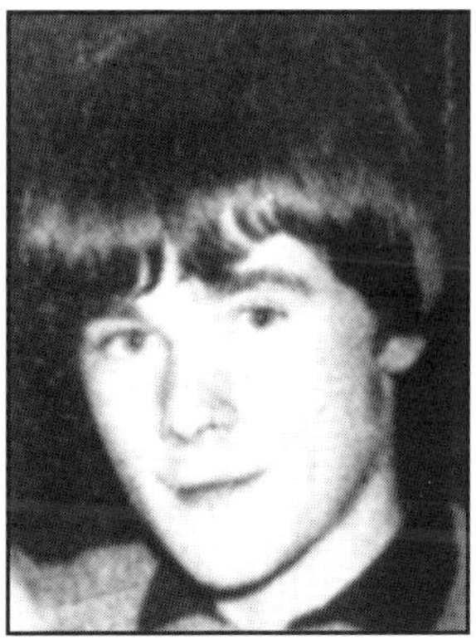

Paul Whitters, aged fifteen, was hit on the head by a plastic bullet fired by an RUC man on 15 April 1981. He was born in Scotland and had lived there for eleven years prior to moving to Derry where his parents came from.

That afternoon, he had been involved in some stone throwing with a group of youths in Great James Street. Eyewitnesses say that a policeman, one of several who had been the focus of attention, fired at the boy as the gang dispersed, leaving Paul on his own. Statements submitted later give the distance as either 15–16 ft or 20–21 ft. In any case, it was not possible to miss the boy from that range and no attempt was made either to fire to injure or to arrest him. When the boy fell to the ground, two policemen appeared from the bakery, where they had taken refuge, to haul his body inside. He died ten days later at the Royal Victoria Belfast, the third teenage fatality in Derry in less than two weeks. All witnesses agree that the policeman fired directly at the boy's head.

At the inquest, the officer responsible claimed to have fired from a distance of 20–25 yards. He was neither charged nor even disciplined in relation to the boy's death and the jury accepted the RUC's contradictory versions of events. The cause of death was given as severe brain damage. Such a lethal weapon can in no way be taken as the deployment of 'minimum, reasonable force' – the rule adopted by police forces in any part of the world. The boy's father described the inquest as a 'cosmetic exercise' and the verdict as no surprise.

Annette McGavigan

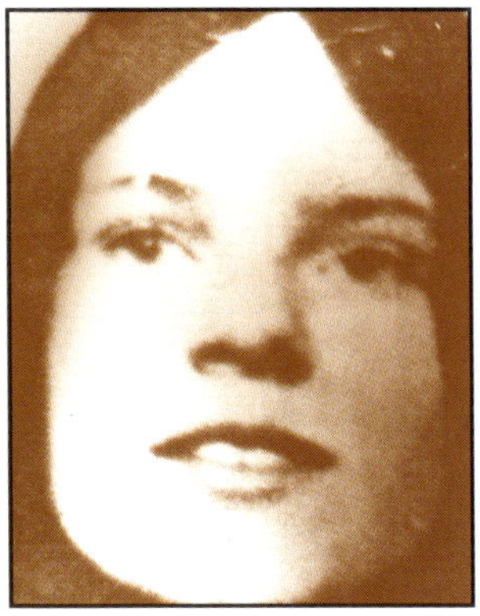

On 6 September 1971, trouble flared up in the vicinity of Abbey Street. Two nail bombs were thrown at troops. The British Army claimed afterwards that three separate shooting incidents took place five minutes later. They alleged that nine shots had been fired from the area of Eglinton Place and Blucher Street. The official army statement declared that soldiers returned fire only on identification of individual gunmen. A 14-year-old schoolgirl, Annette McGavigan, lay dead. That much was true. The IRA said they did not fire the fatal shot. A subsequent publication, *Shoot to Kill*, edited by Kader Asmal, stated that a soldier fired the fatal round. This was corroborated by the statements of locals. Annette's mission that day was to try to retrieve a rubber bullet for her collection of riot souvenirs. She was a pupil of St Cecilia's Secondary School and the 100th victim of the *Troubles*. The family is still trying to come to terms with the tragedy. The effect of this particular killing on Bogsiders was profound and unforgettable. Annette was, in the words of her mother, 'an angel'.

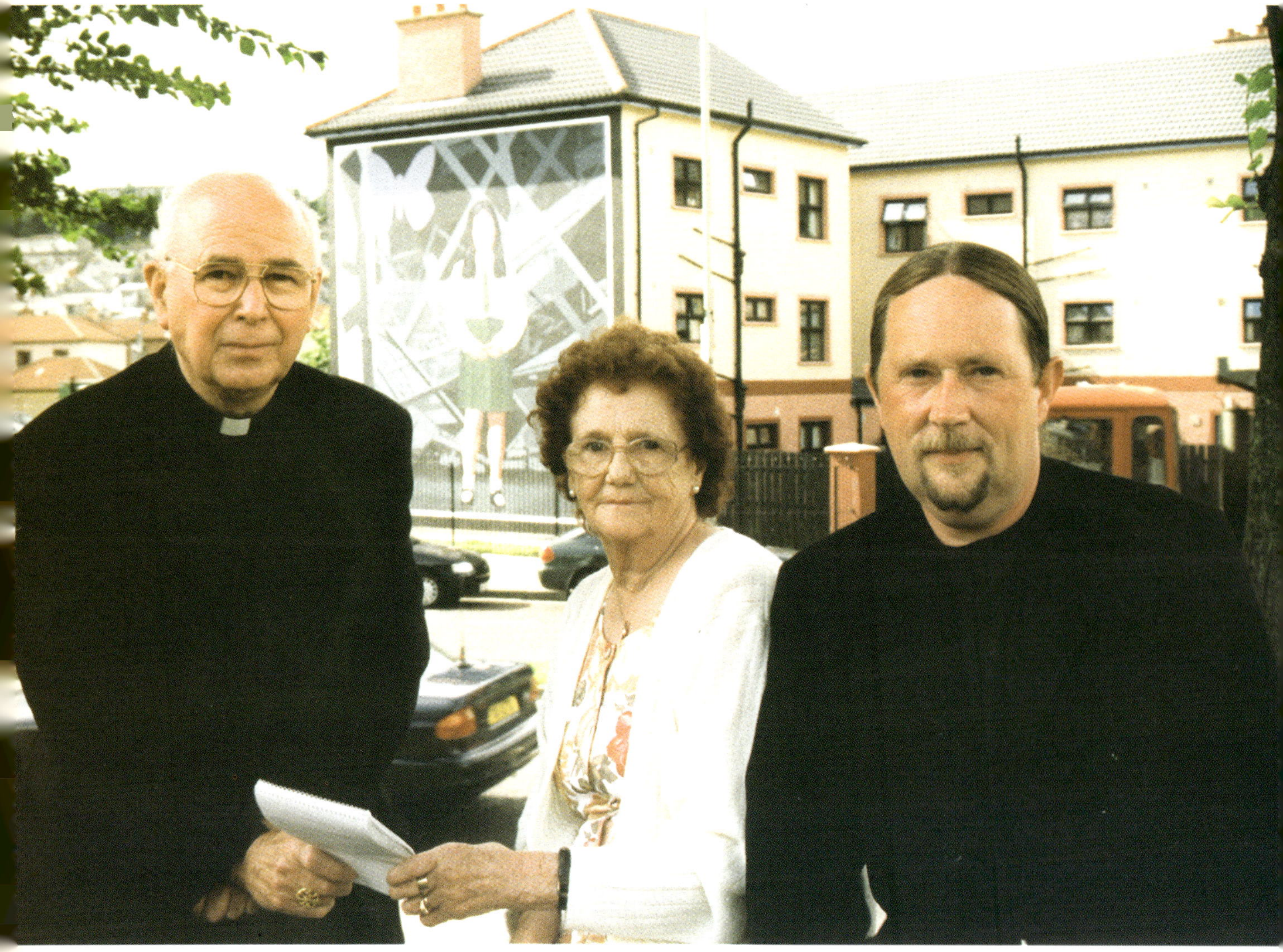

Annie McGavigan pictured with Most Rev Dr Edward Daly, retired Bishop of Derry on left, and Tom Kelly.

Manus Deery

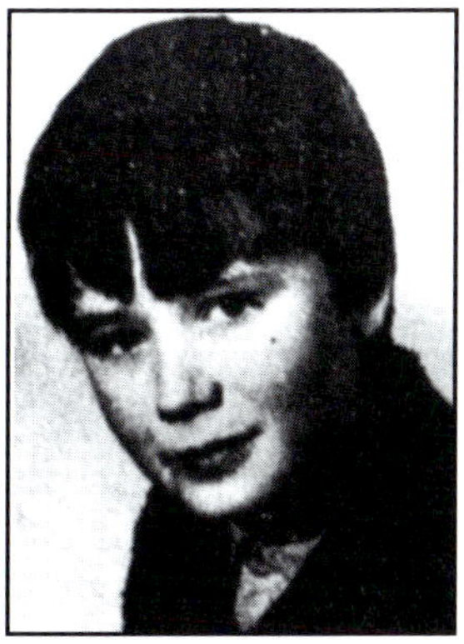

Manus lived with his parents in Limewood Street in the Bogside. Although just fifteen, he had joined the workforce of the Thomas French factory in Springtown and had been so employed for just two weeks. The day of receiving his first wage packet was also the day of his death.

That day, 19 May 1972, he came home from work around 5.00pm in a jubilant mood and had tea with his family. He watched television until 9.15pm when he decided to go down to the 'chippy' situated in the shopping precinct adjacent to the Bogside Inn. En route he would call in to see his cousin Tom Kelly in order to swap comics. On his way there, he bumped into his older brother Mickey who warned him to be careful, as two soldiers had been injured earlier in a car-bomb explosion in Queen Street and soldiers were known at that time, and especially on such occasions, to open fire on civilians from the city Walls that overlooked the Bogside.

Around 9.30pm he met up with pals. They decided to hang around the garages at the back of the Bogside Inn, their usual meeting ground. Shortly after 10.00pm, a shot rang out and a tracer bullet ricocheted off a wall and hit Manus on the head. Another friend was injured and a third passed out in shock.

In Altnagelvin Hospital, Manus Deery was pronounced dead at 11.10pm. No adequate investigation was carried out into his murder. A jury, predictably, returned an open verdict. Copies of soldiers' depositions at the 'inquest' that were later given to the Pat Finucane Centre are illegible. There is no evidence that the RUC ever conducted an investigation into Manus' death, although they did submit a false and contrived text to the Director of Public Prosecutions, which was accepted, even though it contained witness statements that the people involved denied ever having given; and with good reason, as they lived in the Bogside, which at that time was strictly a no-go area for the RUC.

Inadequate or non-investigations of which there have been quite a few to date, contravene Article 11 of the European Convention of Human Rights. As with Annette and the other child victims, none of the family ever fully recovered from the trauma. They must look now to a recent European Court judgement on the practice of 'non-investigation'. The words of Manus' sister best communicate the depth of feeling and loss that still persists and will continue to persist when all the evidence is finally totted up and all the pedantic findings dispensed to the public.

For Manus

We remember so well the night you died,
The unbearable pain and the hurt inside:
We felt numbed and stunned, we just stood there and cried.
And with you, Manus, part of us all died.
Twenty-nine years on, we still feel the same;
The hurt, the anger, and the unbearable pain.
And yet we still have no reason as to why.
A British soldier chose you to die.
But if we live until we are a hundred years old,
We promise you Manu: we'll make sure the truth is told.

You see, it's only now we're not afraid to speak:
The army and government we're not afraid to meet.
It's only a matter of time before we finish our quest
For Justice, so we can finally lay you to rest.

Helen Deery

OUR WORKSHOPS

Since 1995, the Bogside Artists have been giving cross-community workshops in Derry. Tom has been engaged in this work since 1984. They have given talks and seminars in places such as Limerick, Belfast, Sydney and Boston. Their work has become of considerable interest to a wide range of schools, community groups, students of many disciplines and especially students of art, sociology, Irish culture and history. Tom, drawing on over twenty years tutoring in community art in a reconciliatory capacity, has, alongside William and Kevin, developed a pioneering model for workshops in the city. These are built around the framework of a guided tour. Young Catholics and Protestants are taken by coach to the sites of Nationalist and Loyalist murals. This informal setting allows for the free flow of views and ideas. By the time they reach the Bogside, they will have a feel for their own responses and also an insight into what constitutes sectarian and propagandist art and what constitutes commemorative and historical painting. By then, they will be able to see the differences between tribal beliefs, historical fact and authentic individual responses to those facts.

They come to see that self-belief is the foundation of creative endeavour, that the material of that expression has no boundaries and that the will to express is a priceless democratic right, however difficult it may be in practice. The group then returns to their base for a general discussion on what they have learned. At this point, there may be a slide show to raise the debate from the merely parochial to a general discussion on the subject of art history. The rest of the workshop consists of addressing the practical problems of mural art with hands-on experience.

The Bogside Artists have worked with the homeless, children with special needs, students and unemployed from all over the city. They have worked with the Restorative Justice Campaign, a group set up by volunteers who see the need to channel the negative energies of disaffected youth living in the bigger housing estates to more positive goals. They have worked consistently with

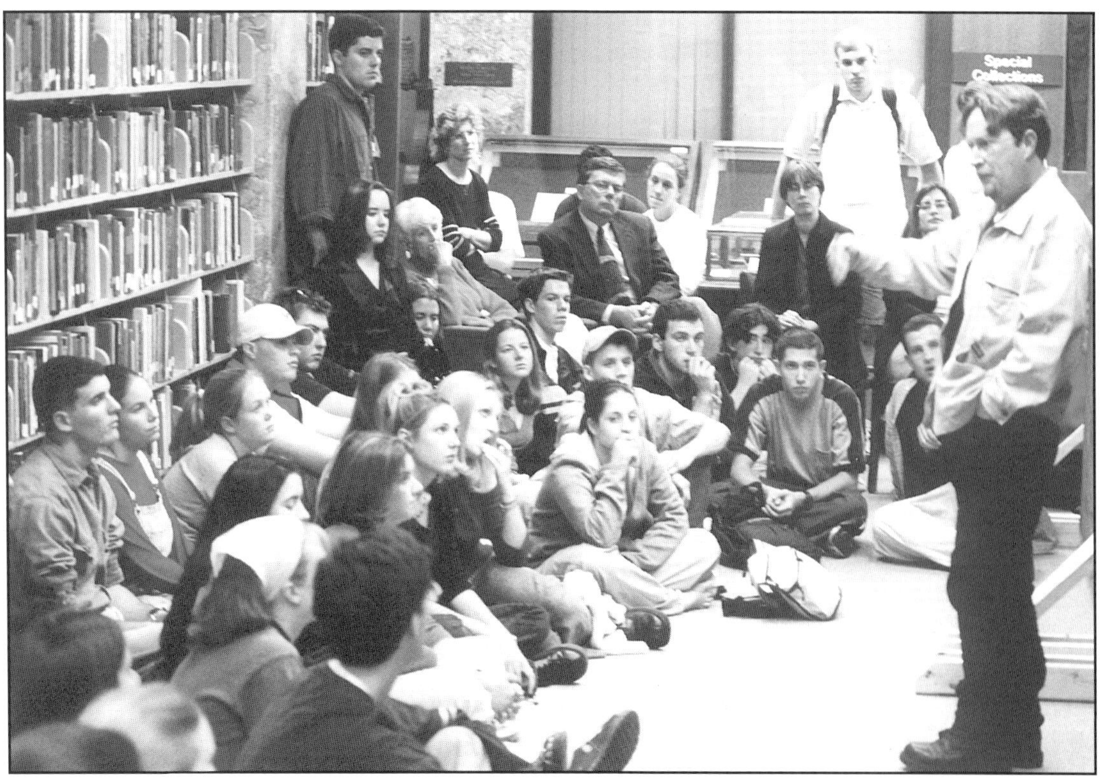

Villanova University, Philadelphia, USA.

secondary-school pupils. Recently, they have contributed to the Festival of Hope. Tom, who is the principal organiser and facilitator of these workshops, explains the mission clearly:

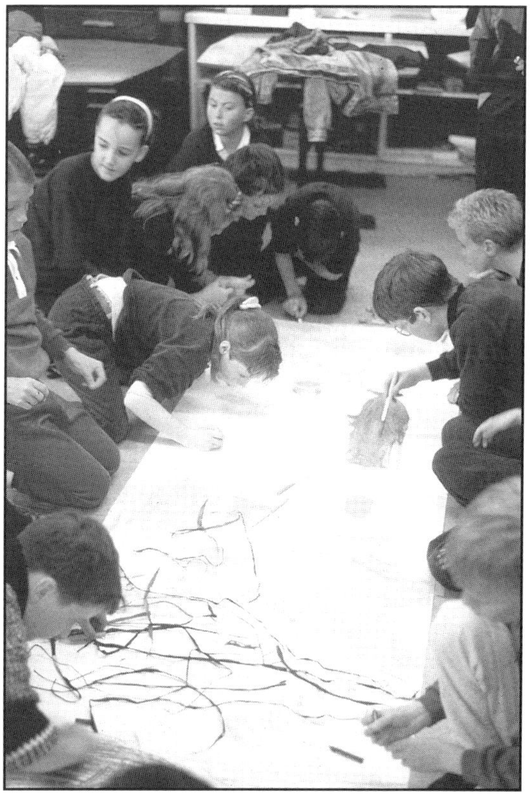

In our workshops, Protestant and Catholic youth are brought together to examine their various backgrounds and to look at the way art is used in both its negative role as propaganda and in its authentic role of self-expression. The artists pay particular attention to what the young, who have experienced so much of the pain and grief of a fragmented society, have to say. Annette McGavigan's mural in particular owes much to their input. As with the collective as well as the individual, the understanding of the past is imperative if one is to be empowered to go beyond it. In the early days, we had a studio at the Calgach Centre, but, unable to secure help with the rent from the various funding bodies, we had to let it go. These workshops and talks are largely educational and cross community and are never confrontational. Ideas of a cultural or social nature are freely discussed and the role of art in articulating these ideas is focused on. Both sides are led into the awareness of equal rights in the domain of free expression. Both sides are enabled to respect differing views, however much they may disagree with them. They come to understand what is meant by free expression.

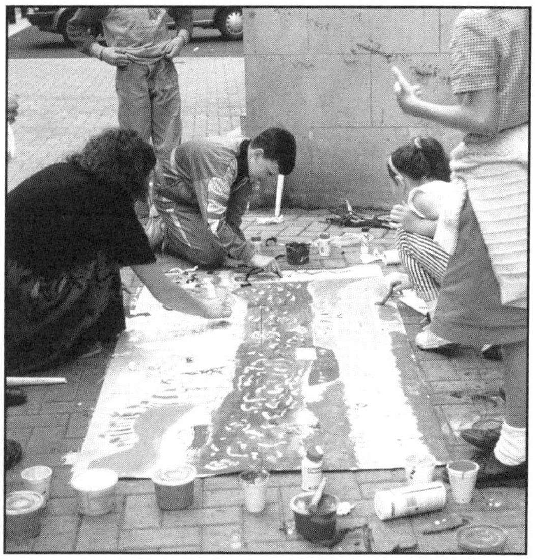

Those who come to the workshops are given the chance to see and examine the different backgrounds and conditioning that can influence opinions. These activities indeed formed a significant part of their BBC documentary.

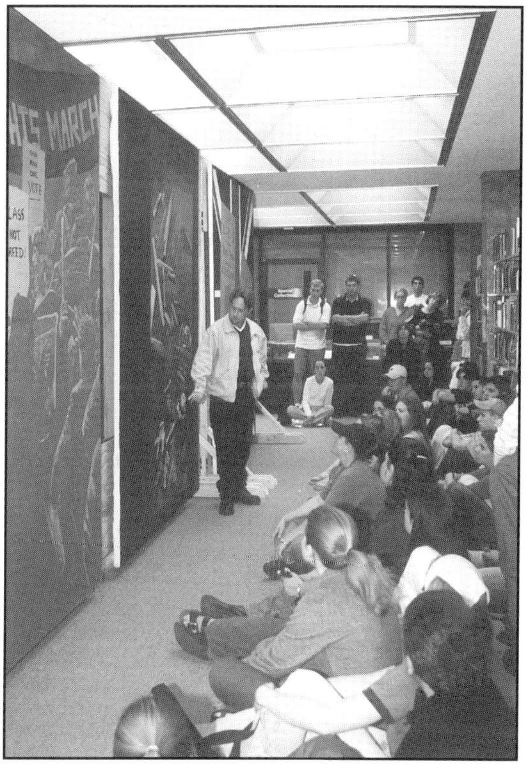

Other workshops we have conducted involve direct hands-on experience of the business of being an artist. These are run in collaboration with the schools and colleges of the city. They are instructive, encouraging, and extremely successful. *At no stage, let me stress, do we tell kids what to paint or how they are 'supposed' to paint.* That is simply the complete reverse of what we are about. During these discussions and workshops, we ourselves get a chance to evaluate whatever visual ideas *we* have been working on in the light of the views young people express. We will continue with these talks and workshops for the foreseeable future, because we think they do some good in an area where good is most urgently required.

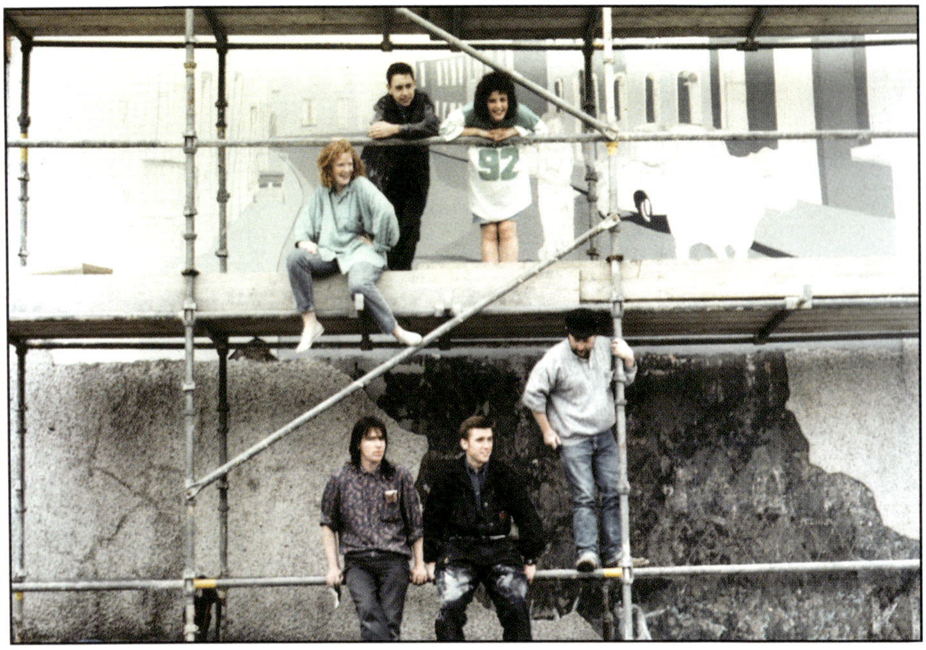

Gobnascale, 1987.

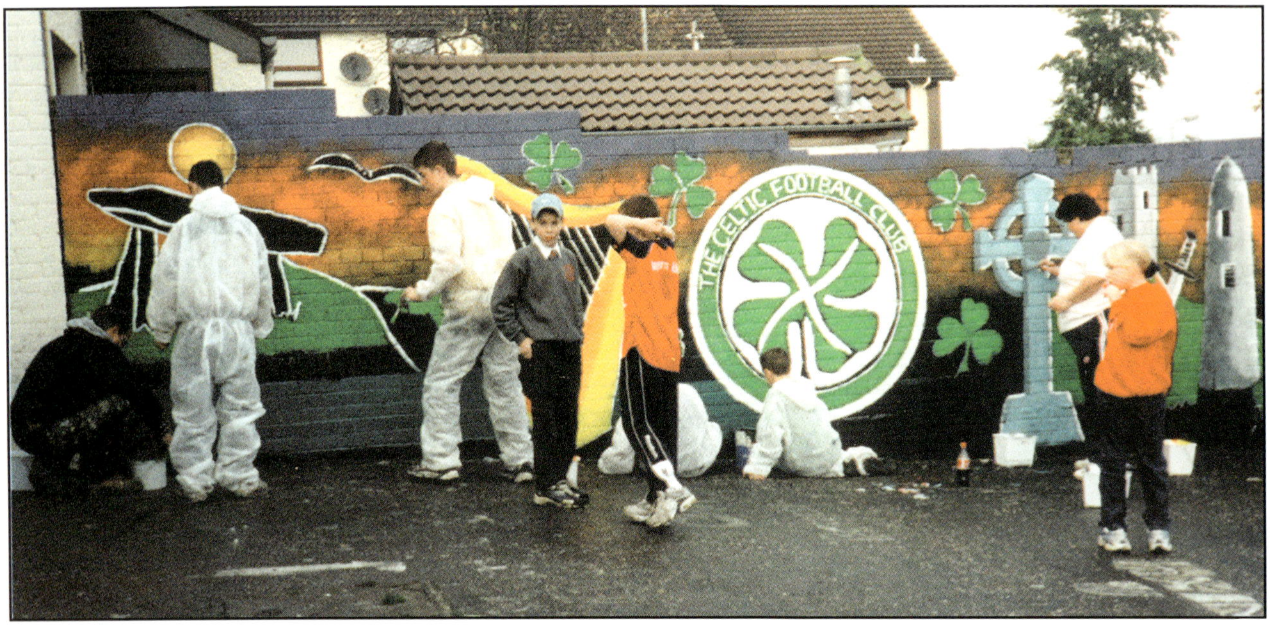

Community Restorative Justice, Ballymagroarty, 2001.

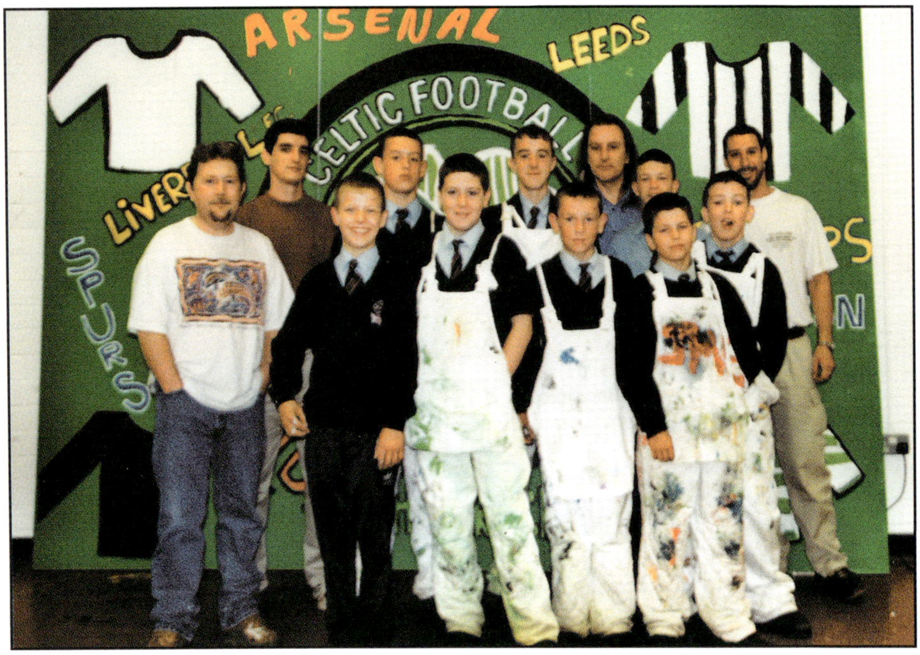

St Peter's Secondary School workshop.

THE MURALS IN CONTEXT

The abstract notion of 'society', much touted by politicians, is, of course, a shibboleth. Society is the *sum total* of human relationships, including those we designate as 'role playing'. Man is a social being and his life is, by definition, contextual. How he relates to himself, his work, his friends, his past, his present, his future, his family and the world in general, determines his life and defines him. From the wastelands of the social pariah to the 'pillar of the establishment' is a broad

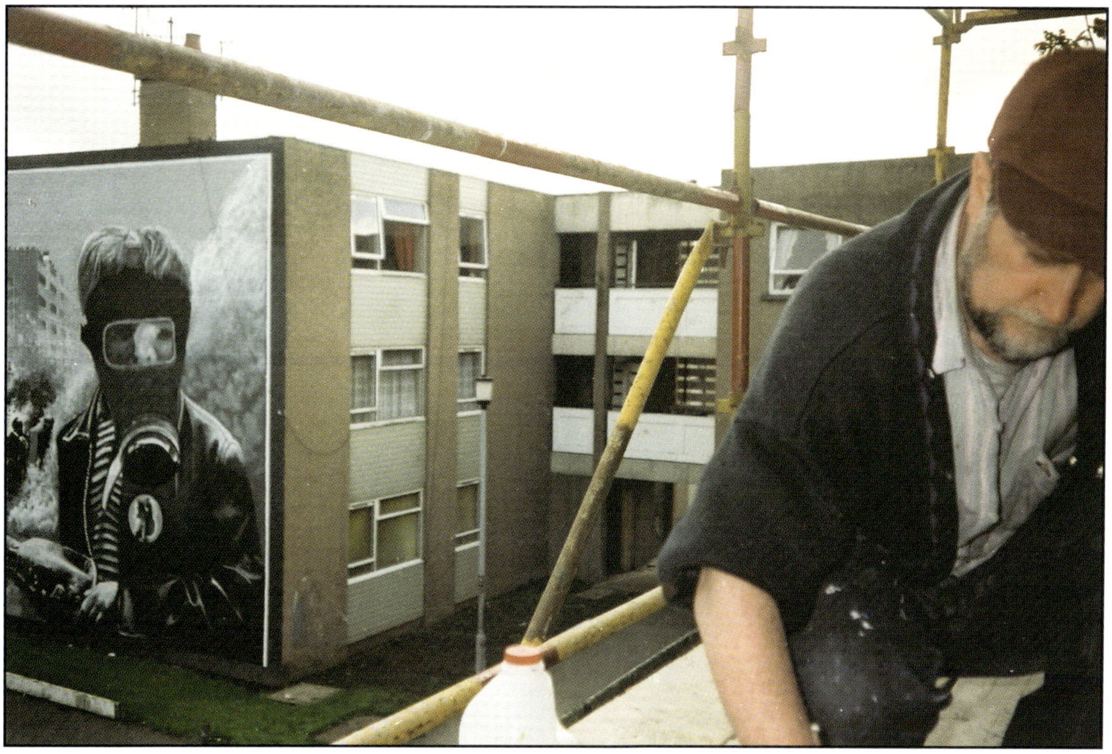

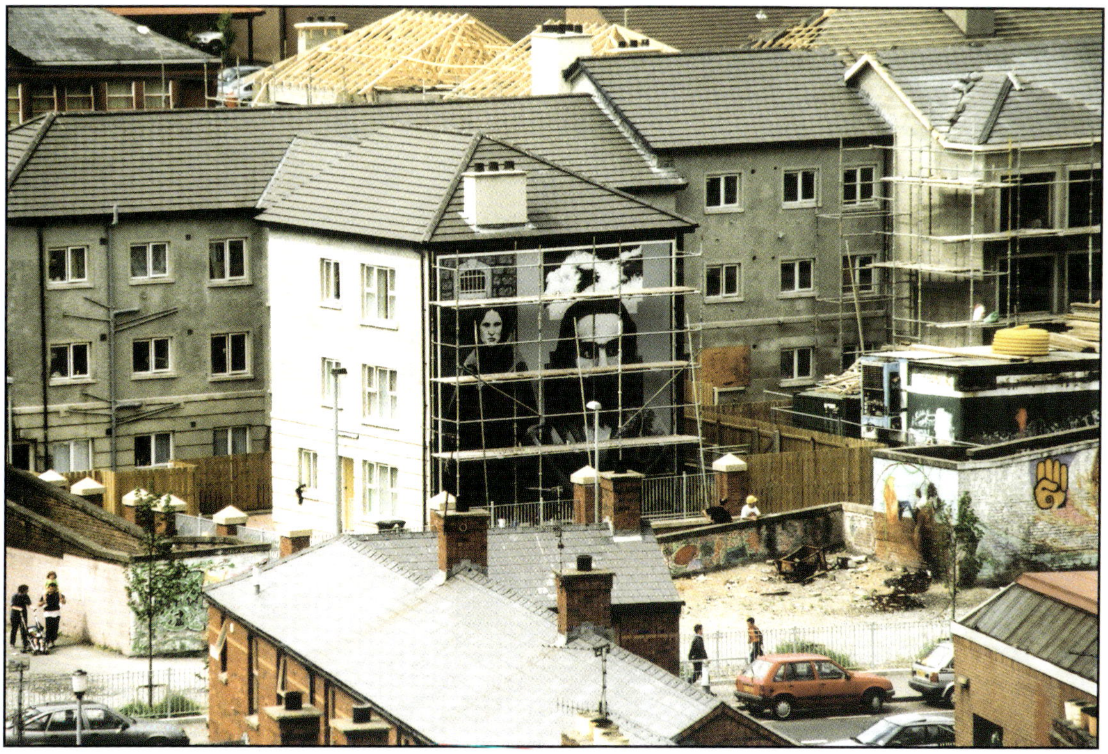

spectrum indeed. It is a spectrum explored by the satirists in general and is the inescapable focus of the theatre everywhere. The theatre deals expressly with all aspects of social relationships. Is theatrical expression political? How can it not be? The theatre, in fact, has had a profound influence on the history of painting.

Painting deals with context quite consciously. Context is as much a theme of Manet's *Dejeuner Sur L'herbe* as it is of Beckett's *En Attendant Godot.* It is as much exemplified in Picasso's *Guernica* as it is in the work of Surrealists like Magritte and De Chirico. All art is *social.* All art is, therefore, political in essence. Whether it becomes overtly political or covertly political has as much to do with context as it has to do with the artist himself. A portrait of Hitler would be a revered object in a Neo-Nazi's lair, but to a Jew, in any context, it would be something else entirely. However well painted it may be, it is still negated by its own content – its meaning.

Careerists in the art world manipulate context in order to win maximum attention for themselves. Advertisers too, like Benetton, have not been slow to learn the trick. Therefore, to label certain artists as 'political' is simply to say they are 'overtly' political in the same way as a pickpocket is conspicuously a thief, whereas the club owner who charges kids a quarter of their wages for the privilege of spending what they might have left on his overpriced booze, is merely a 'businessman'. Both are playing the same game. The word is not the thing.

How we relate to things will have a lot to say about the choices we make. After all, bigotry itself, and its extreme manifestation racism, is at heart a *relationship* problem. 'Us Good – You Bad', is a passionate belief for many people face to face with those not like themselves. The 'Other' is ever the enemy, until his conversion – or elimination. Afterwards, he may be canonised.

In art, the antithesis of the ugly (bad) and the beautiful (good) is primarily a contextual problem whose parameters are always shifting. It is here that the artist holds sway and serves to mould public perception. In the same way, standards fluctuate in art, even if an accepted base of aesthetic principle survives. Consequently, modern art critics, bereft of any normative frame of reference in our time, are all at sea as to what constitutes 'good' art and what 'bad'. Wily collectors and unscrupulous curators everywhere are ever ready to capitalise on public ignorance, whereas novelty for its own sake holds sway. They are not alone. All advertisers, whether or not they own a gallery, have a vested interest in brainwashing the gullible.

This by itself would, paradoxically, make our work very reflective of where modern art is headed at the moment, for it has long been an embarrassing fact to many curators that the gallery itself provides a false context for the viewing of art. The gallery, in effect, becomes a mediator between the viewer, for whom the work is intended, and the artist. It therefore officiates at the corresponding alienation of the work from the public and so disguises its social character and relevance. Art galleries, therefore, look wistfully at community art and the work of muralists like ourselves. They establish 'Outreach Programmes' in the hope of redressing the balance. Performance artists, let us not forget, came into being explicitly to fill this gap.

Since the 'scandalous' arrival of Duchamp's urinal, the use of context has become a favourite weapon in the artist's armoury. From that point of view, there is really nothing new about contemporary work. It's just that its pretensions have got grander. Surrealism, as a movement outside of its psychological pretensions, was pragmatically an investigation into context in order to arrive at new contexts and thereby a new art.

In the case of the Bogside Artists, the context was given. We were born into it. The site we chose to paint our murals, the Bogside, was a familiar part of our own habitat. It was a daily fact of our existence, where we had lived and played. It was our history. In January 1972, it was drenched in blood. That too became our history.

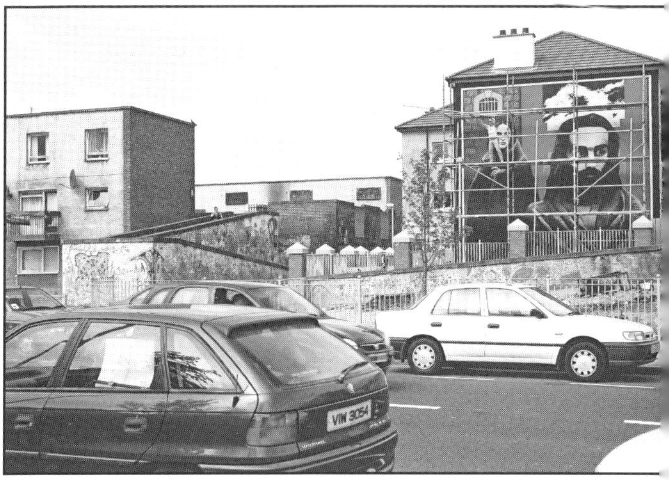

The modus operandi of the careerist artist, whose will is to challenge the viewer on the presupposition that the viewer is actually blind and stupid, would nakedly contradict the context in which the muralist seeks to work. The wall painter's first remit is to *communicate*; else he would not have chosen a public site in the first place. He is willingly addressing public context, public mind, public belief, public perceptions, in all their variety and contradictions. He is not appealing to the dilettante or the culture vulture. He knows full well the criteria that once guided them in their diagnosis of what was 'good' and 'bad' in art are all shot to pieces. Money, power and media control constitute the Yellow Brick Road to fame and fortune. And if fame and fortune is what you want then The Yellow Brick Road of the gallery circuit is what you have to travel.

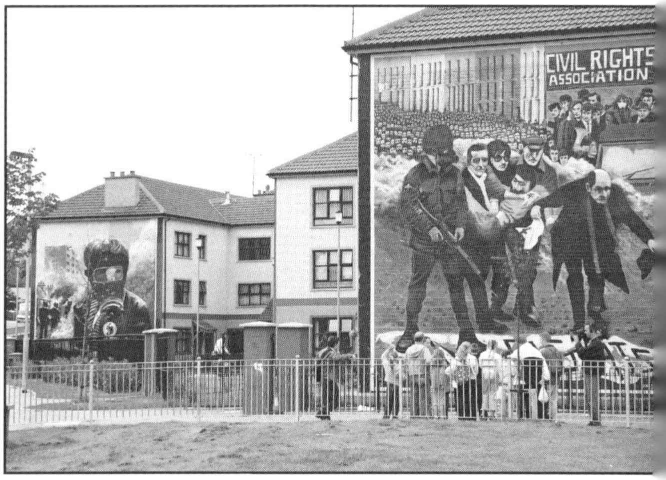

This will explain why the muralist is a rebel, painting with passion, because he knows that true art is poetry. And poetry is not the proper arena for the cult of careerism that rightfully belongs to the market place. He is appealing, first and foremost, to the man in the street on the assumption that the man in the street is *neither* blind *nor* stupid.

This is the context in which the muralist places himself. It can be thin ice to walk upon, as the experiences of the Bogside Artists will readily testify; because it involves the *whole* social context. There are political currents to avoid and cultural rapids to negotiate. There is antipathy, envy and exclusion to overcome. We seek to honour the context we have been given, not to abuse it in the name of a juvenile delusion of licence masquerading as 'freedom', which alone characterises much of what passes for so-called 'modern art'. That, of course, doesn't prevent funding bodies from shelling out huge sums for examples of the latter while the humble practitioner with something genuine to say is swiftly passed over. These, of course, are the same people who will tell you that art is not 'political', if you will believe them. Neither too is education.

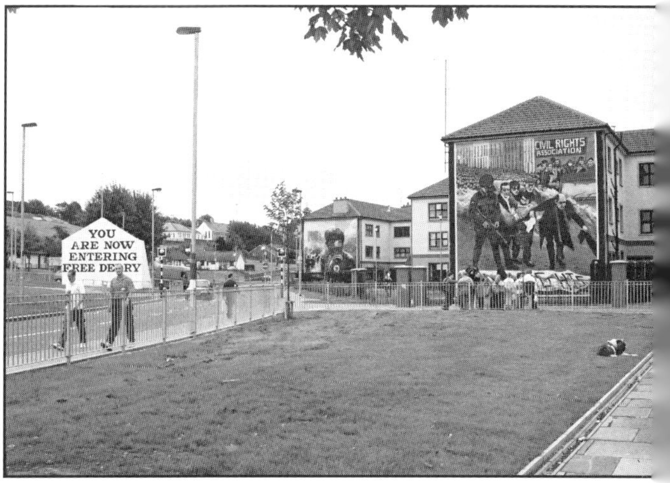

the Documents of HELL

Man knows what hurts;
Knows how to apply what hurts;
How long you will last
In a tiny space,
Deprived of this, deprived of that.
Knows what charge to use:
How strong the knot,
How long the drop,
Where precisely to fix the prop.
Plots your hidden points,
Maps your weakest joints.
Man *knows* what hurts.

Tracks your habits, likes and hates,
Your trembling dependencies,
Your rooted attachments,
Your playground dreads,
Your cradle fears,
Your brain, your nerves, your heart,
The plan, the chart,
Of your inner street,
The house to where you run for cover,
The room wherein you hide and cower,
Your sacred places of retreat.

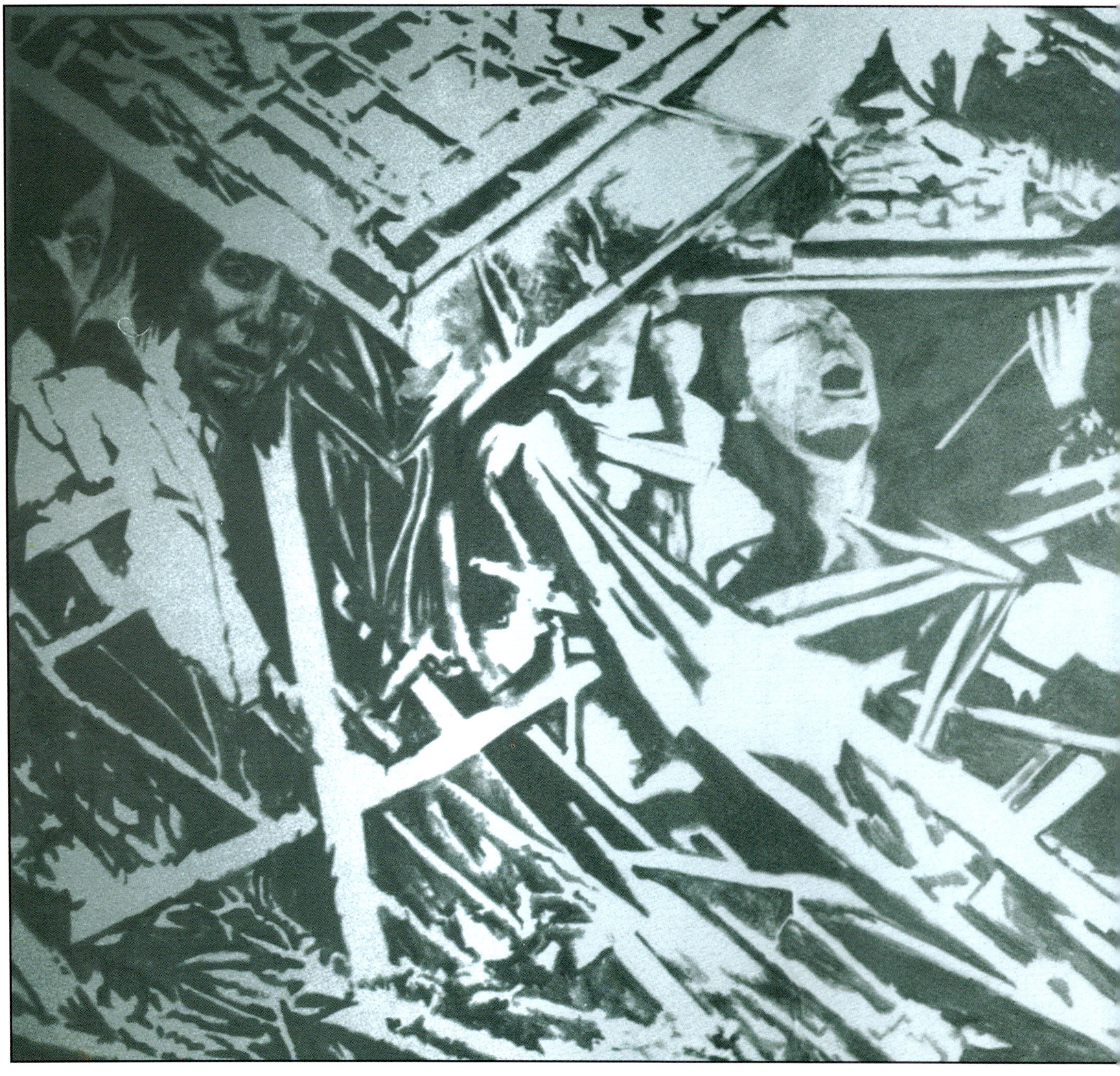

Man knows all this and more,
Has quarried deep,
Clawing out the lore.
Such priceless stuff!
Trawled from lakes of blood and pain,
Ciphered down in compact books
As mind springs loose from brain,
And heart explodes.
Numbers, symbols, letters writ,
Before the child's small hands
Cease snatching at the poisoned air.

Time *its* eyelids close!

Neatly phrased, typed up and indexed,
Dated, filed, labelled, wrapped,
Stashed away in rust-proof boxes,
Or neatly digitised in stacks;
Behold the measured archives of evil.
Click on the documents of hell.

William Kelly

Caught Up. Triptych, 8ft x 21ft, acrylic on canvas.

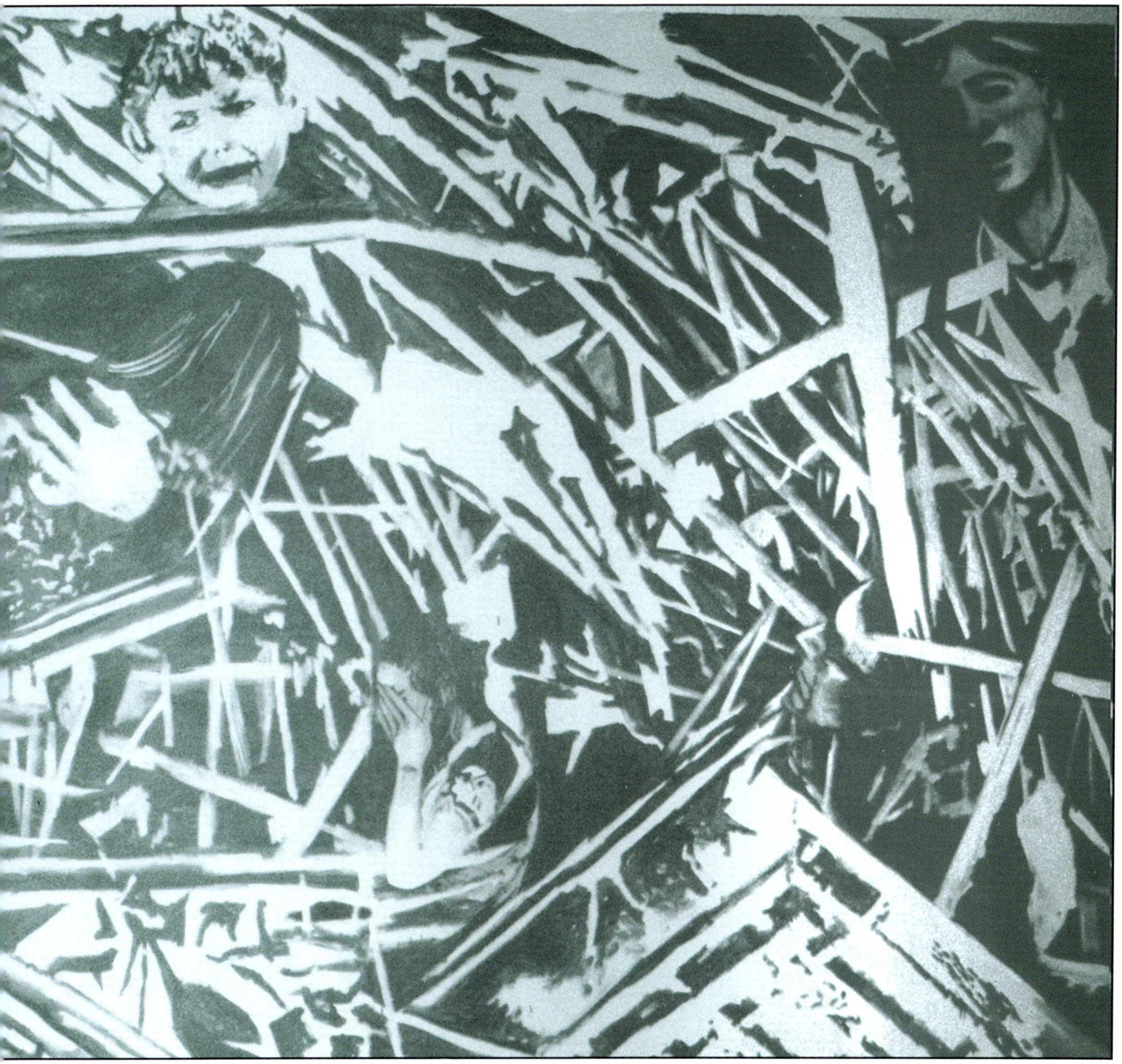

EXHIBITIONS ABROAD

Due to the enormous success of their 1997 art tour of Australia, the Bogside Artists, Tom Kelly, William Kelly and Kevin Hasson, were invited by the Arts Centre at Mildura to launch a millennium-touring exhibition that would take in the principal cities in Australia. This tour, begun in January 2000, has so far visited Mildura again, as well as the Red House Gallery, Adelaide, the Perth International Festival, the Onkaparinga Arts Centre, the Fountain Gallery at Port Douglas, Ballarat campus of the ACU University, St Patrick's Campus of the ACU Melbourne, the Fine Arts Gallery of Newcastle University, St Mary's Campus of the ACU Sydney and the McAuley Campus of the ACU Brisbane. It was last seen at the Queensland Irish Association, Brisbane.

President Patrick Brennan declared the exhibition to be 'really marvellous and deeply moving'. Dr Lindsay Farrell, who helped present the show and also spoke at the opening, said the work was 'unique of its kind in contemporary art'. The show at St Mary's, under the auspices of Judith Carroll, was opened by the Mayor, Councillor Virginia Judge. From an Irish family herself, she described the work as 'deeply moving'. Other venues planned include Brisbane and Canberra.

Many talks, interviews to radio and the press, and lectures have been given that have served to highlight the issues facing artists in the North of Ireland in their efforts to articulate their experience via the medium of visual expression.

This exhibition of the artists' work, the most comprehensive exhibition ever to have come out of Ireland concerning the *Troubles*, was split between the John Moore Art College Gallery and the Leavy Gallery of Villanova University. Tom Kelly represented the work there and spoke to over 700 students about the marginalisation of the artists and about his hometown, paying particular reference to the enormous creative potential Derry has in all aspects of the arts. His talks and slide shows there excited much debate and interest in all things Irish. Professor James Klingler, who hosted the show at Villanova, described the work as an 'awakening'. He said he could not begin to measure the immense benefit it had brought to the departments of sociology, modern history, Irish studies and art. Jim Murphy, who opened the exhibition at the John Moore, stated that he was specially honoured to do so because he was witnessing the work, not so much of 'a victimised people or victimised artists, but of a surviving people and surviving artists.' At Villanova, Tom was fortunate to make the acquaintance of Dr Anthony Compolo, the renowned Christian sociologist who has written many books on the subject, in one of which devoted a chapter to Tom highlighting his dedication to the use of art as a way of reconciliation between Protestant and Catholic. As a result, Dr Compolo, on Tom's invitation, has expressed an interest in visiting Derry whenever the opportunity presents itself.

The artists, meanwhile, will continue to work towards the completion of their major project, begun in '94, which is nothing less than a complete chronicle, in the form of murals, of the key events of the last thirty years. Once completed, it will transform the Rossville Street area of the Bogside into an open-air art gallery – a people's gallery, made for the people, by the people and through the people. 'The Bogside Modern', as the artists like to call it, will be an artistic and historical statement unique in the world. It will enable the people of Derry to appropriate their own story in a way that is enlightening, edifying and commemorative, thereby setting an example for other artists from economically and socially oppressed areas to give power and visual expression to their quests for justice. The group can be contacted via its website address (http://cain.ulst.ac.uk/bogsideartists).

THE BOSTON STATE HOUSE

Senator Steven A Tolman Calls the Bogside Artists' State-House Exhibition 'A Rousing Success'.

(Matthew Irish, secretary to the Senator, Boston State House.)

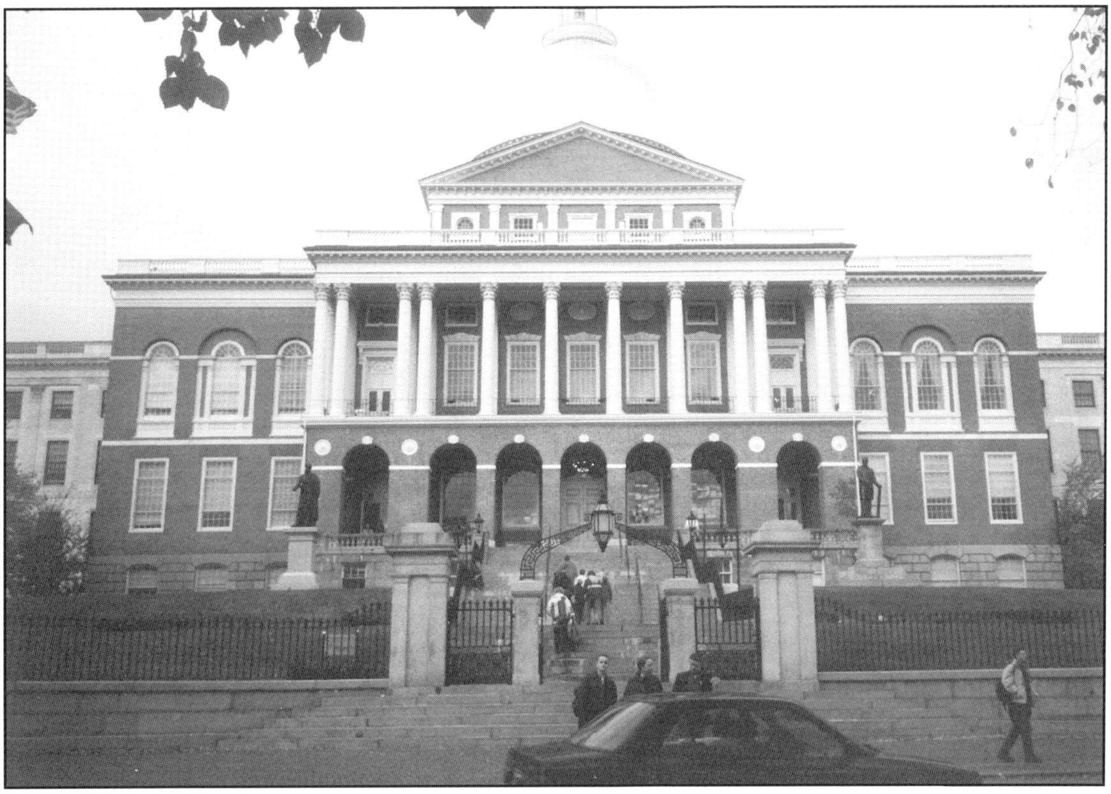

Boston – State Senator Steven A Tolman (D–Boston) announced the success of the Bogside Artists' art exhibition at the Massachusetts State House. The exhibition was opened by Senator Tolman on Thursday 3 June, in the course of which he was presented with a plaque by the artists on behalf of the people of Derry. The public exhibition attracted a great number of visitors as well as state legislators and their colleagues.

The exhibition has already completed a tour of Australia where it was a great success. In addition to opening the exhibition in the State House's famous Doric Hall, the artists were also introduced before a full House of Representatives during a formal session. *They received a standing ovation.* Senator Tolman and Representative David Donnelly subsequently introduced House and Senate resolutions recognising the work of the Bogside Artists and officially proclaiming their exhibition as belonging to the historical annals of the State House.

Senator Tolman stated: 'I am proud to have been able to sponsor the Bogside Artists on the State-House leg of their American tour. In my five years in the building, I have never seen so many people excited by an art exhibition. We actually had Senators and Representatives asking to have the duration of the exhibition extended. I am especially happy to see the exhibition being so warmly received in Boston which, as we all know, is Derry's sister city.'

OTHER WORK

The following is a sample of other work we have done. Apart from the mural, most of these constitute the bulk of our exhibitions on tour.

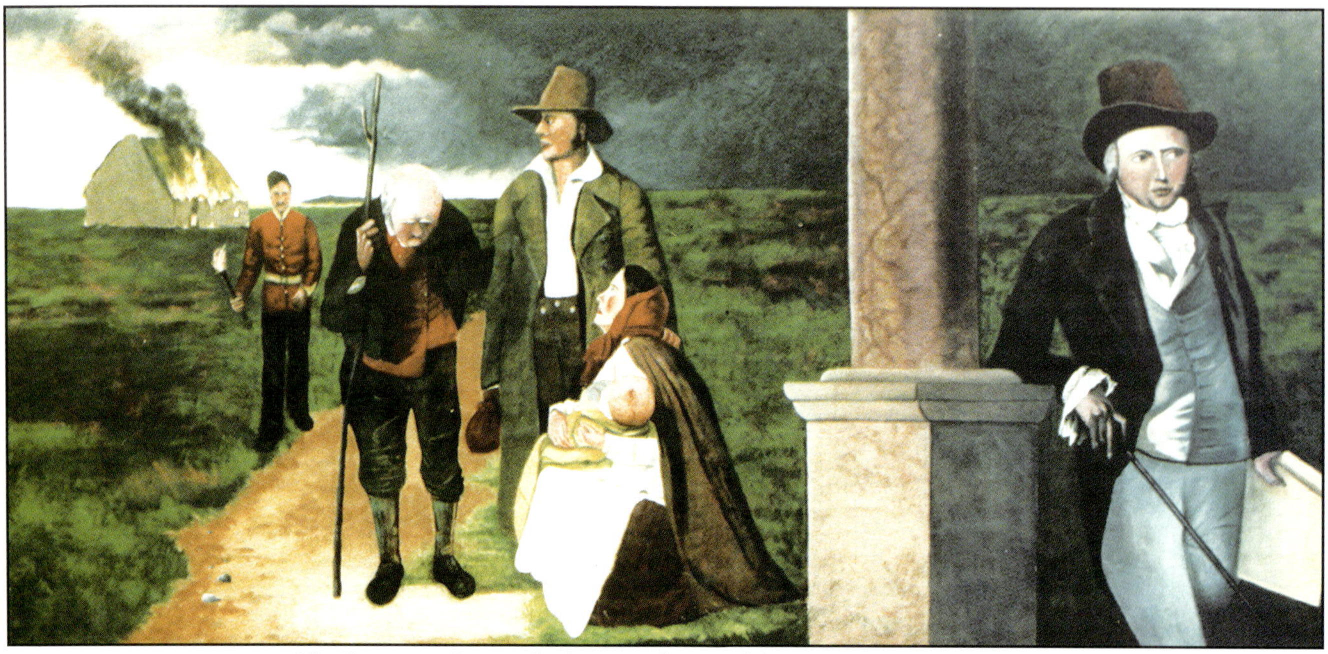

The Evictions, Donegal – large scale mural (see opposite, bottom left).

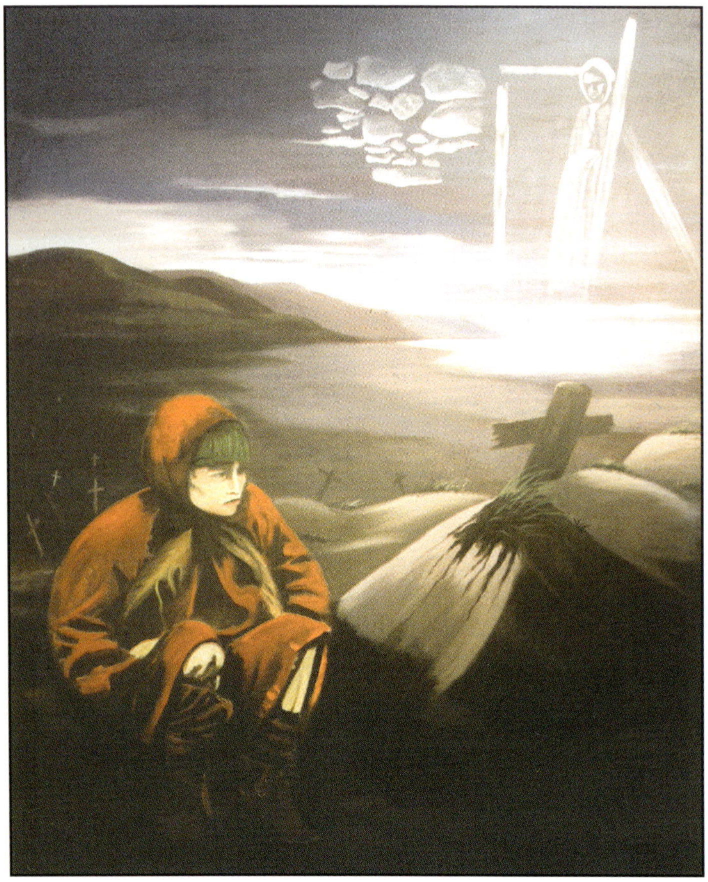

The Famine, acrylic on canvas, 7ft x 6ft.

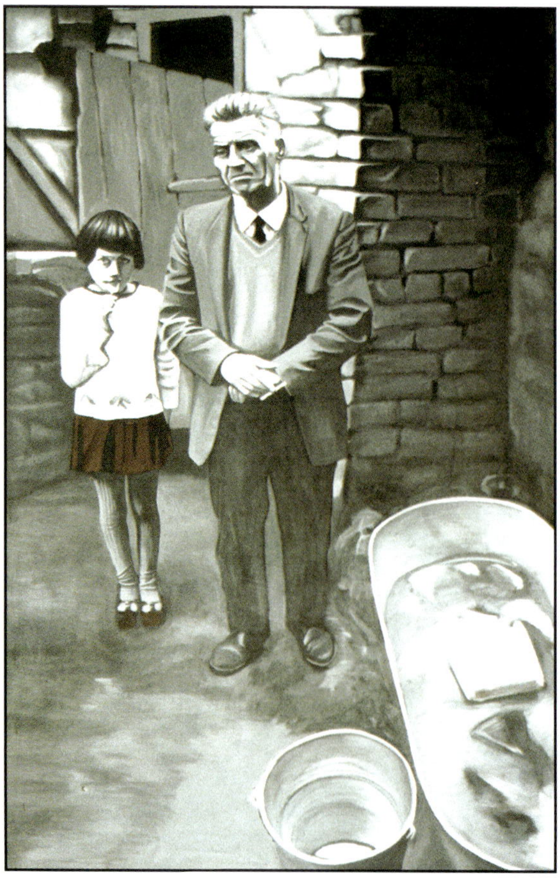

Gerrymandering, acrylic on canvas.

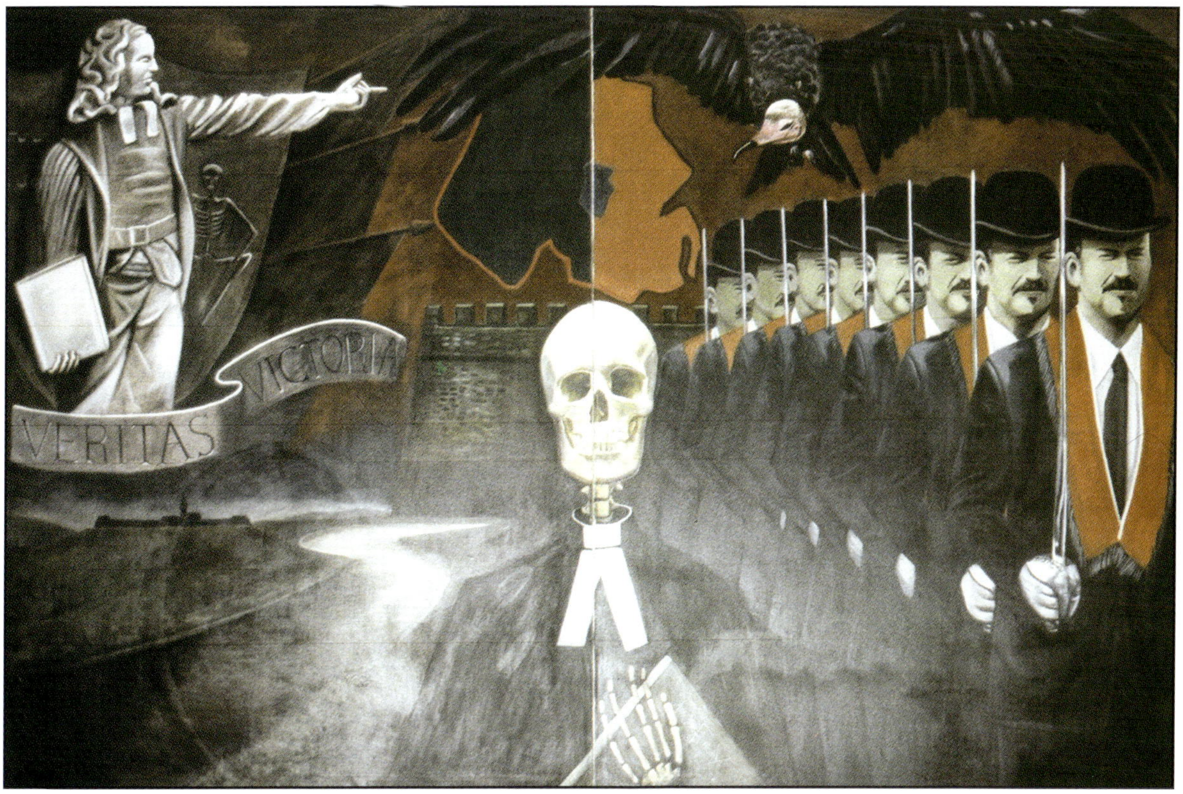

Above and below left, The State, triptych (each panel 7ft x 5ft), below right, Sectarianism.

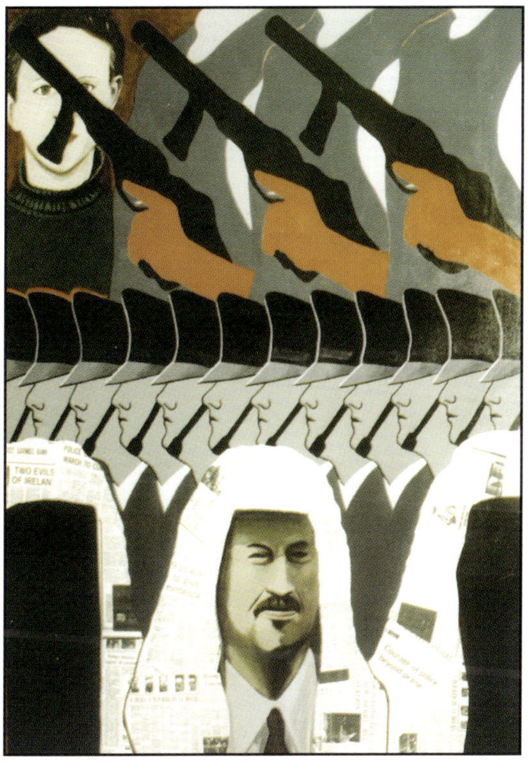

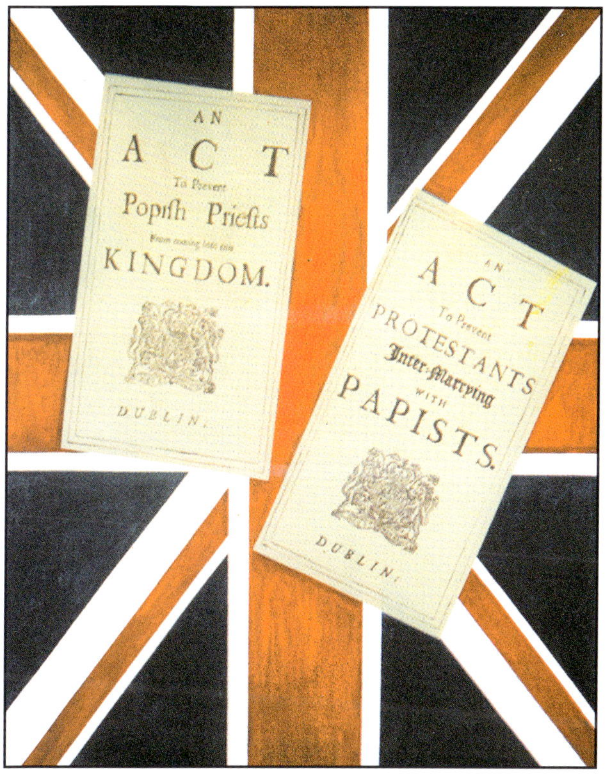

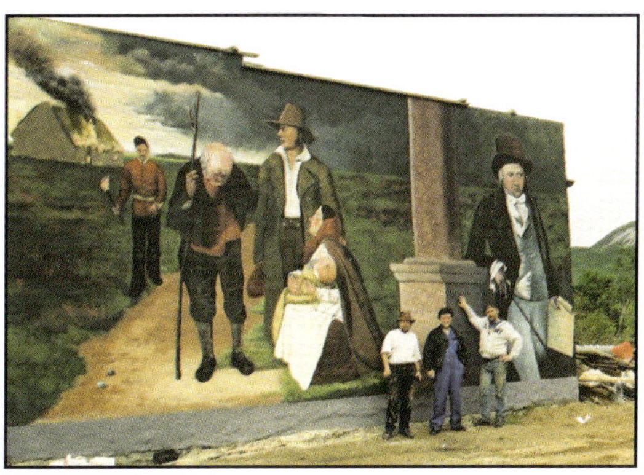

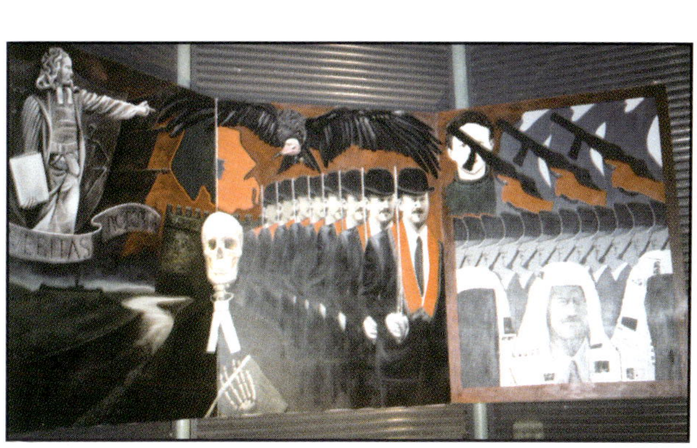

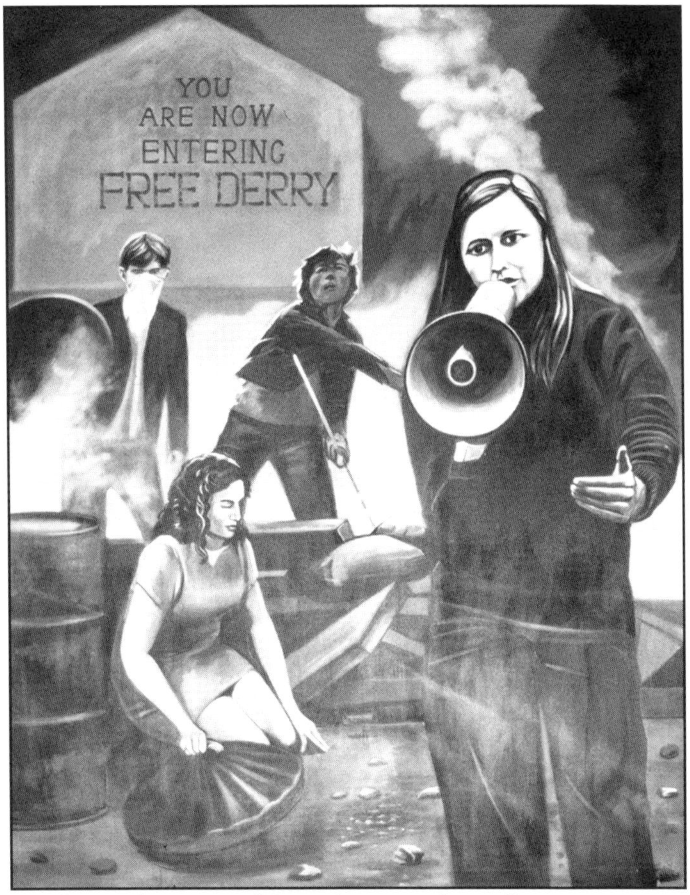

Original cartoon of Bernadette mural, acrylic on canvas.

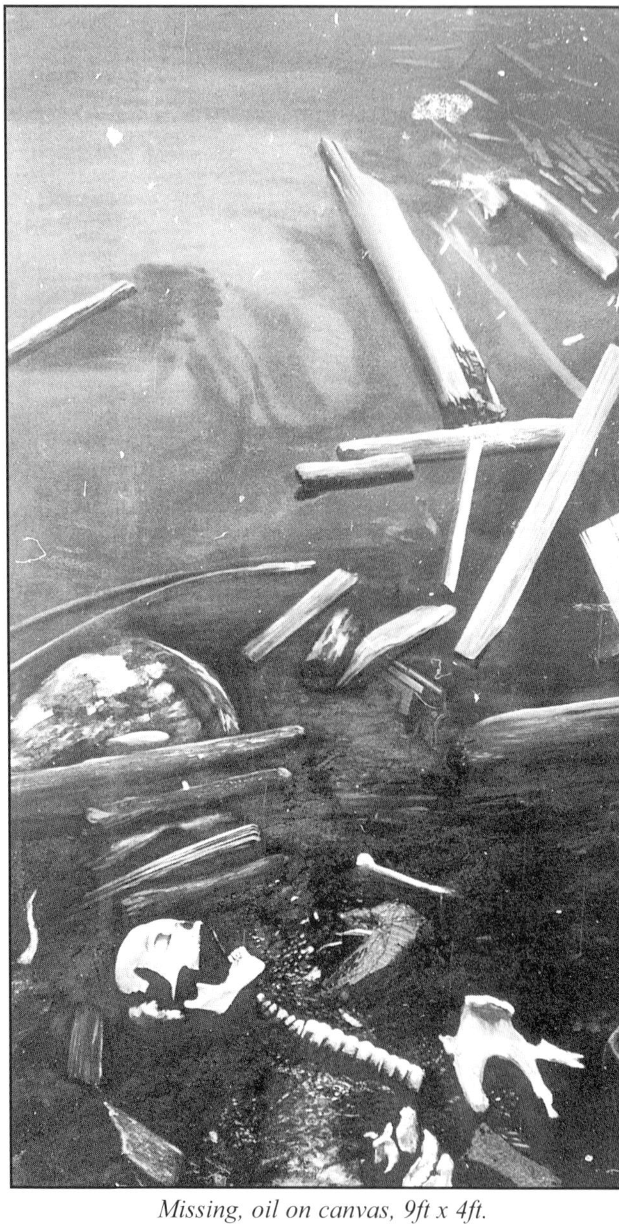
Missing, oil on canvas, 9ft x 4ft.

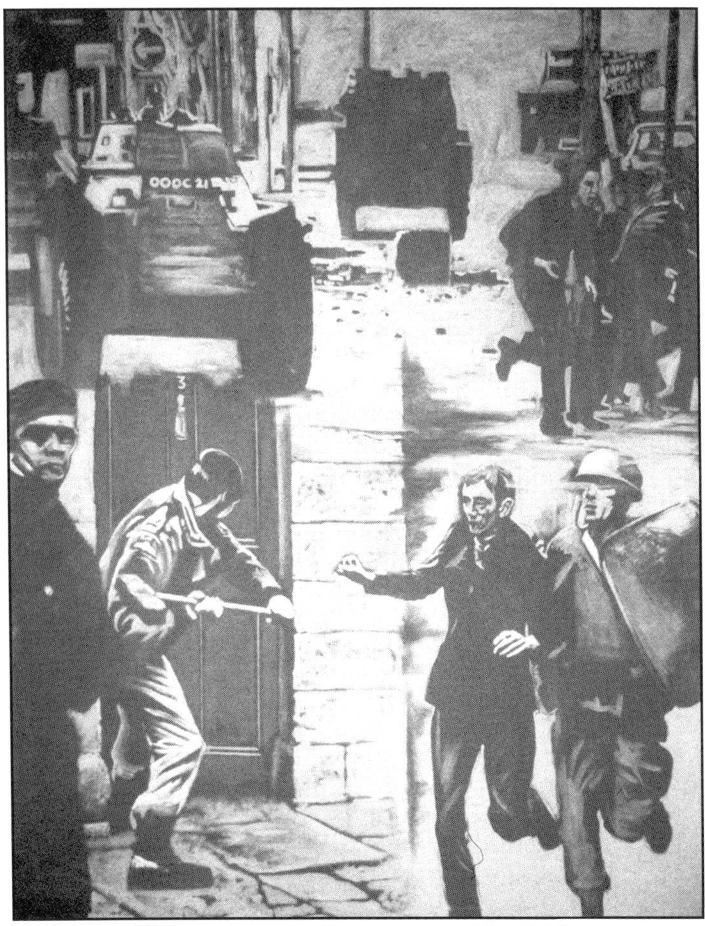
Internment, acrylic on canvas, 7ft x 5.5ft.

THE PAINTING: *LET THE LIGHT SHINE*

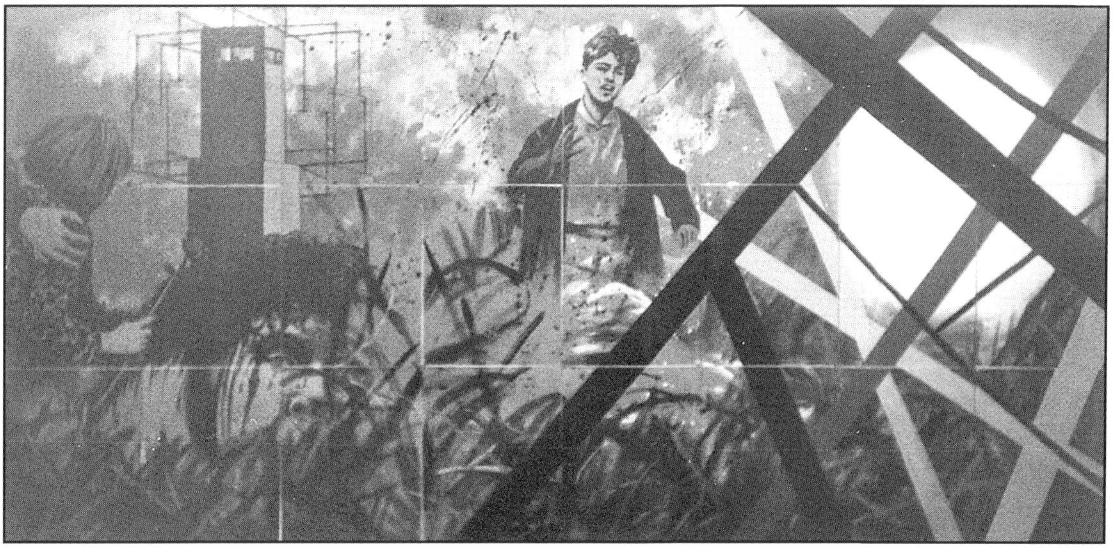

It is made up of twenty-four canvases, each measuring 2.5ft by 3ft. They are numbered on back and are arranged, L to R, 1–8, 9–16, and 17–24. That is, there are three rows that together depict the image.

It gives a depressing but typical view of Derry. The yellow orb depicting the light of sanity that political trouble obliterates. The painting can be divided in two with the yellow orb able to stand independently. In that event, the left-hand panel would be entitled *The Watchtower,* while the right would retain the original title.

In addition we have twenty pages of A4 size laminated text. These are contained in ten frames measuring about 2ft by 1ft. Two pages per frame. These frames are without either glass or Perspex and are by no means obligatory in terms of displaying text.

A video of ourselves made by the BBC and lasting forty minutes runs with the show.

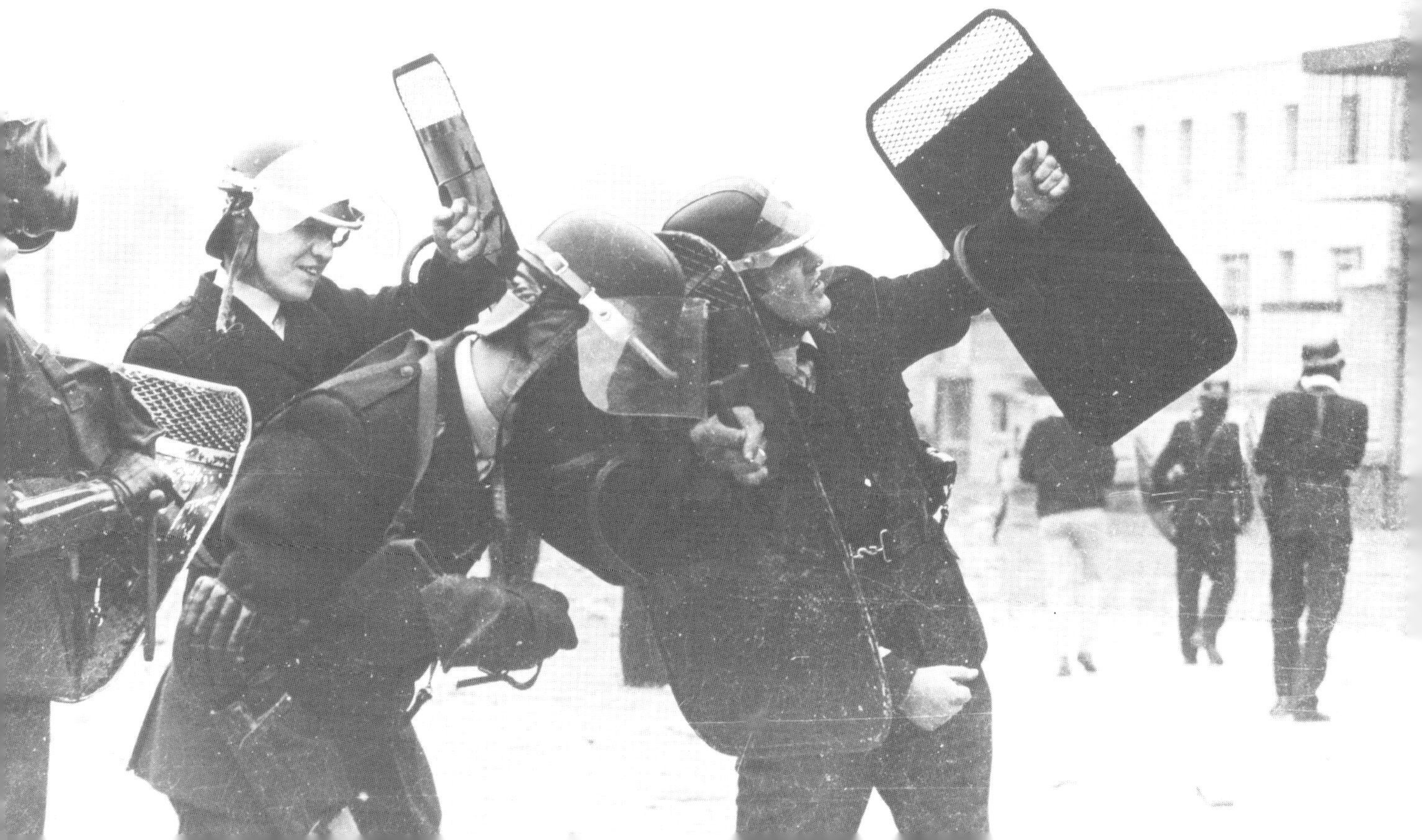

TECHNIQUE AND PERCEPTIONS

First published in *Exhibita* Magazine, Issue 5

The [Bogside] artists have an ideology, and a strong one at that. They do not wish to follow the well-worn ruts of the gallery circuit, because they believe that good art will find its own way without the trumpeting of either critics or curators. Had they not been so thoroughly marginalised

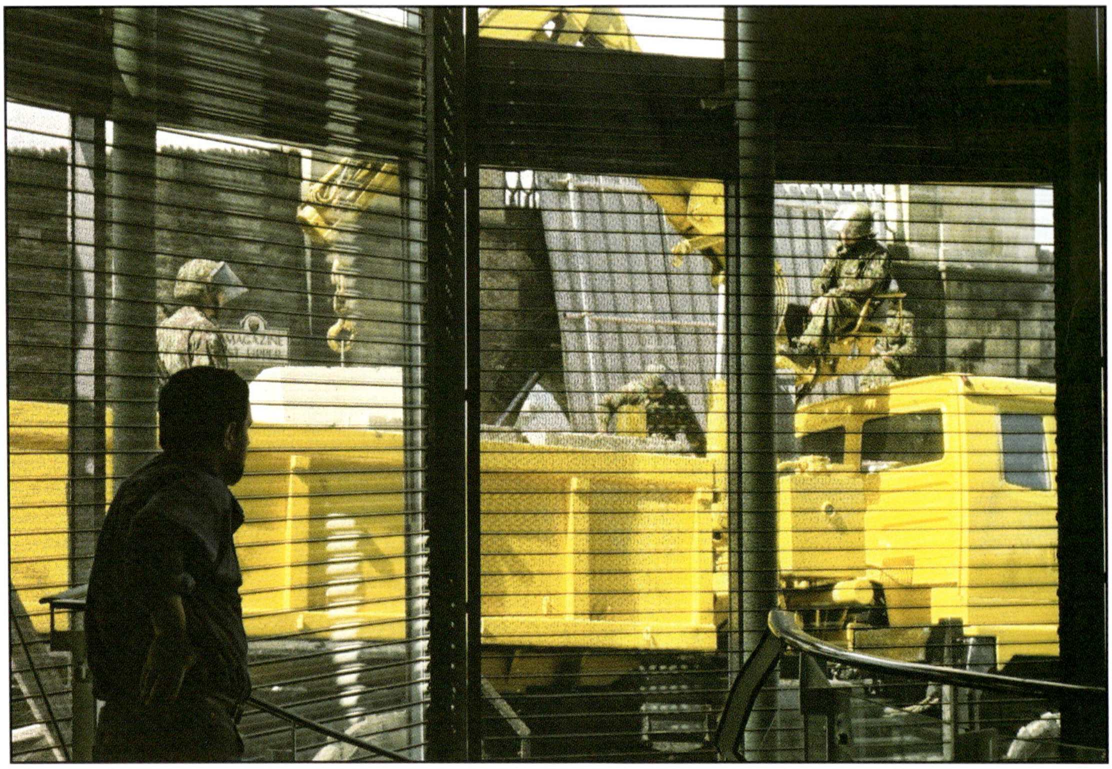

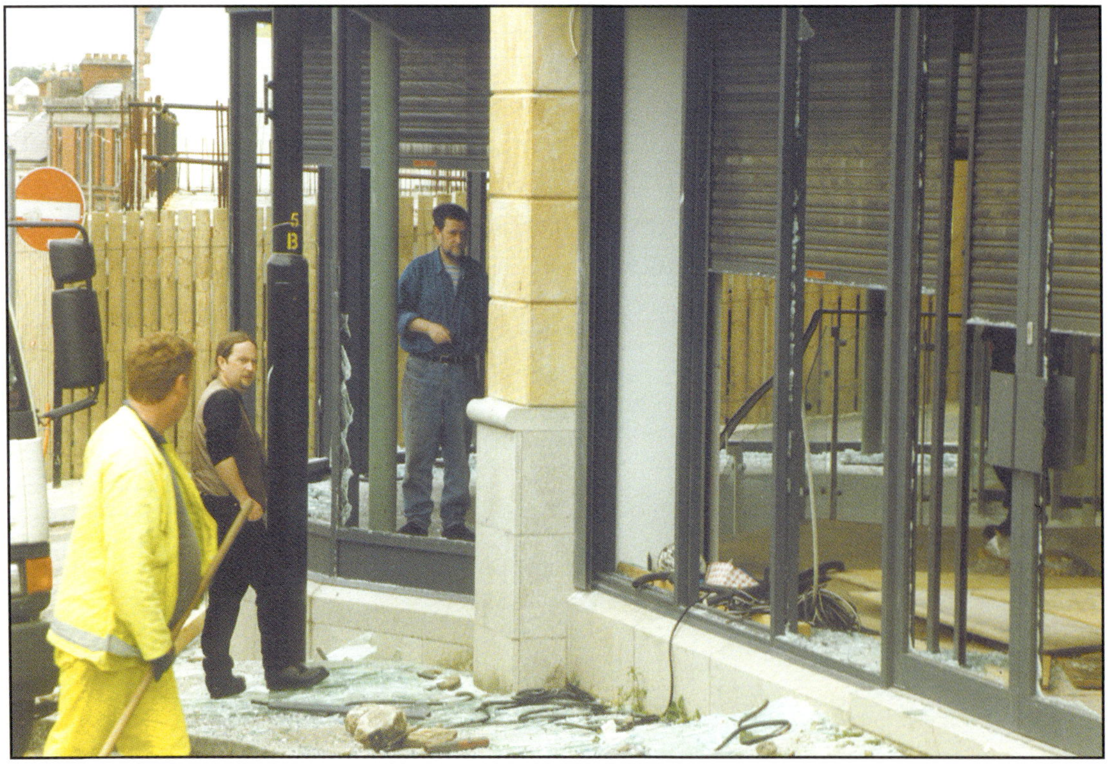

The artists' studio after the Twelfth.

from the beginning by the Irish and UK art funding bodies, ostensibly set up to help them, they might have thought otherwise. While artists of independent means are consistently blessed by the arts councils year after year, so that they can boast not one catalogue but many, the Bogside Artists are only now presenting their first. For this they are indebted to the Community Relations Council and Derry City Council. They have let their views of the UK gallery system be known from Sydney to Boston.

They are three individuals with differing points of view. In their endeavour to communicate a shared truth, they discuss at length what has to be expressed before going on to a more rigorous investigation that involves collecting images and ideas. There follows an incubation period during which the essence of the solution crystallises. They know that, as a team, it is quite redundant to operate in any fashion other than the democratic one, where each voice has equal weight. It is in this way that they begin to put a structure to the final image. The same method is used with regard to their work on canvas. Throughout this process (which is by no means peculiar to image production), respect is given to the facts. The clear intention is to 'tell it like it was' by filtering out any emotional bias as far as possible. This is the toughest part. It has to be said that most major difficulties they have so far experienced have been encountered at this stage.

The populist press usually prefers factoids to facts and is generally hip with tribal perceptions at every level from the football terrace to the polling station. Its reportage of the events in the Six Counties had a profoundly demoralising effect on a people already suffering more than they could be expected to endure. It was left to the artists of Derry and Belfast to re-establish the human dimension that the press tried to vilify and negate.

What the artists have also to take on board are the people who have to live with the finished mural and the place where the mural is situated. These are important considerations that go beyond the merely aesthetic. 'There is simply no room for self-indulgence or stylistic tap dancing in the type of realism we are engaged in.'

In the construction of their work, particularly the large murals, there is a deliberate emphasis on design. Lines of force are carefully mapped out: assonance and alliterations are established; focal points and contrasts fixed etc – long before a brush is lifted. A careful balancing of forms is sought for along the tried and tested schemas of pictorial construction that go all the way back to the Renaissance and beyond. This method concurs with the artists' shared aesthetic, and, more importantly, with the nature of the material they are working with and the affects they seek. They want their paintings to appear solid and so are as dependent on simple but powerful structures.

The triangle in fact, which is the very essence of this stability, is a favourite motif that is used extensively for this reason. This is the primary substructure of *The Petrol Bomber* and later the Bernadette Devlin portrait. For a people caught up in 1994 in a dangerous and anxiety-ridden environment, it became a spiritual imperative for the artists to present something solid, secure, reassuring and permanent. In this way, the work would reflect the unbreakable spirit of the people. These considerations are there embedded in the walls and are as transparent to all who would care to look as a fly in amber. That's why the murals of the Bogside Artists are quite unique in Northern Ireland's political iconography. They are works of art, as distinct from sectarian manipulation or territorial marking for its own sake. They are poetry and are meant to be poetry. It is their contention that ' . . . only from the truthful state of mind can good art be brought forth.'

They believe that sectarian or racist art, however cleverly it may be done, does not qualify as true art any more than does the anti-Semitic posters of the Third Reich. They feel that it would be profoundly disrespectful to those on both sides who have paid the price for democratic justice, to fix in the public eye anything other than works that seek to edify a people whose long suffering demands redemption through meaning.

'People who come to see our work in Derry expect to see a frenzy of expressionism. They are surprised to find that we pay very careful attention to problems of design and meaning. We eschew expressionist technique in the main, because we consider it to be merely a *registering* of emotion and not its depiction. It affixes, but it does not describe. The angry slash is a corpse mocking the vitality it once had. It is a trace left behind by an emotion, not the emotion itself. It is stillborn. What the muralist is seeking is not to be found here. Would that it were, for expressionism is *easy*. You don't even need to know how to paint.

Confronted with despair, and the sort of existentialist vacuum that injustice always visits on its victims, you are obligated to seek an expression that will at least *reassure*. In times of turmoil, the victims do not need a mirror in which to view their misery, or their anger for that matter. What they need most then is an antidote. Our murals look as they do, because that is what we have tried to give – a feeling that however frightening and uncertain the flux of events we were all caught up in, we were not entirely cast adrift. We were not completely without inner resources. And that is why we looked to the old classical canons of pictorial construction. They had endured, just like ourselves. And they would go on too, just like ourselves.

Art that is bereft of poetry, of meaning, and mature meaning at that, defeats its own communicative purposes. "He who has a *why* to live for, can bear almost any *how,*" said Nietzsche. Poetry is the *why* of art. In the absence of it, mere technique by itself will not save the day. There are many fine realistic painters around, but few of them would rise to the poetic power of a Vermeer. Many people can play the piano or guitar brilliantly, but how many can compose well for either? The vocabulary used by Bob Dylan is not beyond most 12-year-olds, but how many poets of Dylan's stature are there? Art critics, those soothsayers and interpreters of the holy scripture of art, have forfeited, in the name of 'modernity', whatever criteria they once had by which to separate the good from the bad, the sensational from the merely insulting, the good object from the neurotically fragmented. Novelty rules. Who even bothers anymore to look for Rembrandt's compassion in a painting? They would seek in vain, for it is competitive ambition of the worst kind that informs the art of our time. As the ancient Greeks admired the cunning of an Odysseus, so modern capitalism seeks its own self-flattering reflection in the knavery of contemporary art. This is a spiritual crisis, make no mistake. *Loss of meaning* is what we suffer from. And no computer program, however slick its mimicry of creative technique, is going to make good the deficit.

Our preparations for the making of a mural take place long in advance. There was a time when we had a studio where we could do this in peace. That was in the Calgach Centre in Butcher Street where we first showed the exhibition of paintings and photographs that is currently on tour in the USA. We were not in situ on the evening of 12 August 1999 when the left flank of a rioting mob swept through the premises smashing windows and making off with our tools, paints and brushes. Their creative output was visible next morning. There are contemporary critics who might have waxed lyrical at the surrounding graffiti with its expressionistic flair and judicious choice of effects. But we, skint as always, found little to admire as we surveyed the chaos that had once been our workplace and haven. Not long afterwards, not having the wherewithal to pay our rent, we were 'let go' by the landlord.

Mural painters, particularly 'political' mural painters, suffer from a prevalent misperception on the part of the 'guardians of culture'. Critical writing in art is a commodity like any other and so, like the latest fashion, is falsified in its contents with respect to the class or set whose values it supports and often informs. Those who lack self-insight do this unconsciously. The rest, who consider themselves 'experts', call the shots. To these, we, as artists from the 'residual class', the 'sans culottes', belong irretrievably to a set, the set of 'semi-talented, propagandists' who exist somewhere between the Orang-utan and the ex-Vietnam psycho so skilfully portrayed by De Niro in 'Taxi Driver'. We are perceived to be tele addicts or dredging the tabloids for ideas to paint on some poor unfortunate's wall with a manic view to stirring things up. When nobody is looking, we climb down from our trees just before dawn to furtively splash paint on a gable end. Inspiration, don't you know, comes with half-a-dozen pints of Guinness and our first idea is *always* our best. If stirring things up was what we were really about, we would assuredly pass for 'modern artists', because that is what modern artists do and that is what is expected of the modern artist, don't you think?

To the 'thinkers', we also belong to the subset called '*political* wall painters'. These same 'thinkers', and there are quite a few of them in the North of Ireland, would spit phlegm at the notion that Michelangelo was also a 'political wall painter' – as were Raphael and Picasso. Contradictions are the weft and weave of pain . . . and humour. The idea that we might actually *know* what we are about, and are professional enough to be able to do it, is too much for them to accept. Our studio at the Calgach Centre, where we used to give our cross-community workshops, is now a clothes shop.

Nowadays, our symposium takes place in Tom's gaff in the Bogside. It is an appropriate venue, because Tom holds his Christian meetings there and we always think that, in terms of interior décor, it is light years ahead of its time. One wall of the box is yellow, one lime-green, one blue and one red. After a couple of cups of coffee, you are in a strange place, believe me, and even if you are not 'talking in tongues' you soon feel you are 'thinking in eyes'. Here, the nuts and bolts of what we have to do are considered from all angles. As we each have our own viewpoint, and each has something important to say, we usually find ourselves all at sea; three men thrashing around looking for a black raft in a thick fog . . . at night. Often the raft isn't even there. As a result of talking to people both younger and older on the possibilities the theme affords, certain elements suggest themselves right at the beginning. That is stage one. Stage two usually takes place via phone calls and subsequent meetings, as each of us is inspired by either an alternative or an additional element. Stage three is when we meet up for the first time at the library. It is by dint of asking the right questions that we arrive at an interim decision as to the probable content of the mural.

Here, we begin the laborious business of unearthing visual data concerning the 'final' image. I say final, because we maintain total flexibility throughout. At any stage, the original image may be tossed out altogether as a better one suggests itself. We expect to have to change our mural while we paint it, as things that look great on paper often fail miserably when they are enlarged a thousandfold.

We always sacrifice visual interest to *meaning,* because there is great power in simplicity. We aim for *poetry,* because feelings are the magma out of which the solid idea crystallises. The nature of our work, of course, does not allow for showing off, a preoccupation best left to the fantasists in the trade who dream of being whisked off by some well-connected curator to the halls of fame where gullible dilettantes wander aimlessly about like deer fixated by headlights and with open cheque books in their hands.

Once the scaffolding is up, the work itself goes on effortlessly. The gable surface is first primed and then an undercoat is put on. Next, the wall is squared up and the image fixed. The basic tones are placed with some care and the mid-tones follow. Highlights and lighter passages are left until last. 'Who paints what' is simply a matter of who *wants* to paint what. If one man can improve on the work done by the chap above him or below him, he will usually do so. Ego is left aside with respect to the final image. We have never had a row or a falling out, let alone a falling down, an ever-present possibility when one is swaying around on dodgy scaffolding in a stiff breeze wafting in from the Foyle. All in all, we are a testament to the fact that, given a worthwhile project, people can work well in harmony, despite their different beliefs. The chance encounters that we are privilege to, more than pays for the grief.

For instance, it was while working on the Bernadette mural that we met the World War II U-boat commander. He was an elegant chap; white hair, and good Mediterranean tan by all accounts.

"I commanded a U-boat during the vor," he announced gallantly as Kevin searched for a cigarette end he had buried somewhere in his overalls. "Yes, for sure,' he went on. "We sank der Englishers in the Atlantic.' He paused to adjust his cap as he turned to go. "No regrets!" he cried suddenly, wagging a Reichian finger. "No regrets!" His assumption was of course, that we, as 'political wall painters' were anti-Englisher to a man. We could have told him that the whole anti-Jewish bullshit, so beloved by him and his buddies, had its intellectual roots in the work of Englishers like Robert Knox whose diatribe *The Races of Men* emerged in 1850 to great acclaim and continued for the rest of the century. A book by another Englisher, Charles Darwin, with his 'survival of the fittest' cant, effectively gave a green light to all aspirations for world supremacy on the part of the mythic master race, to which destiny the Germans elected themselves, having first dumped God to facilitate matters. The Germans out-Englished the Englishers by a street and have been paying for it ever since.

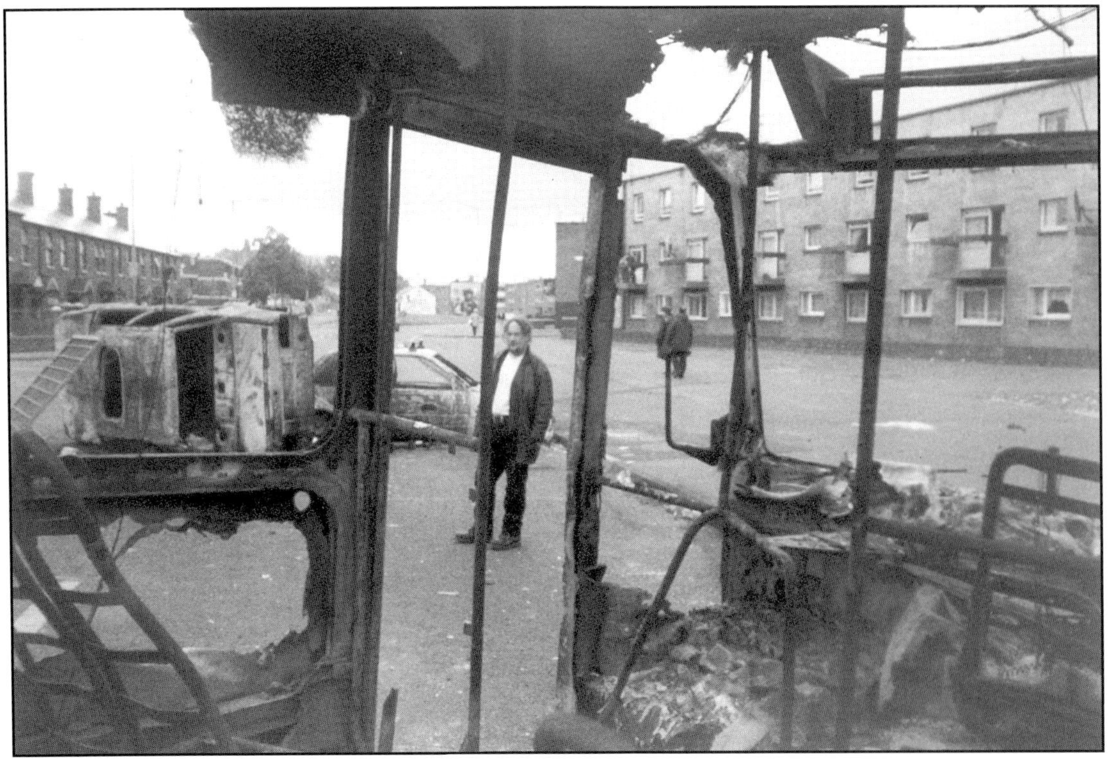

Then, there was the chance encounter with America's Cultural Ambassador, Jean Kennedy-Smith. This much-revered sister of John F Kennedy just happened to be strolling around Dunlewey at the time we were painting our mural there. The wall we had been given overlooked a tranquil lake of great beauty. A boat takes tourists up and down the lake to view the low lying hills and the big grand mansion nestled among them, belonging, like the rest of Ireland, and not a few of its inhabitants, to the Guinness family. As you approach the lake, you cannot see the wall, which is a gable end abutting an amusement arcade of sorts for kids. Coming back from the lake, on the other hand, you cannot miss this wall, as you have to pass within inches of it to quit the shore. By then you might even want to see it more closely, as you would likely have got a glimpse of it from the boat on its return journey.

Such was the fate that befell Ambassador Jean Kennedy-Smith as she made her way up the gravel pathway from the jetty towards our mural-in-progress. When finished, our mural would depict crofters being driven off their patch to make way for sheep rearing. We depicted the burning cottage, the evicted and stranded family of grandad, son-in-law, daughter with child, a redcoat with a torch and the absentee landlord leaning with all the indifference of the morally redundant against a pillar of his colonial house. Even at this stage, it was well advanced.

She stopped and fetched us down like Snow White summoning the seven dwarfs for supper. Shaking our hands in turn she introduced herself.

'I think your work is just wonnnn-der-fall,' she intoned.

We were honoured of course. There were the Kennedy features, the intelligent eyes, the perfect teeth, and the strong jawline. It was a face that had lived the lives of ten Donegal folk – and in better weather conditions too. She had been to Derry, she told us, and was very impressed with the people there and the hospitality she received. Then, she talked at some length about the cultural life of the island, showing a special interest in theatre and dance. She shook our hands again as she left; a very nice lady, we thought. Then she strode off with her entourage, stopping very briefly to wave with her left arm, leaving us to ponder the encounter.

'Well,' said Tom, picking a fag end from behind his ear, 'Jean Kennedy won't be forgetting me in a hurry.'

Kevin and I looked at each other as we scrolled hastily through our memory banks to see what, if anything, Tom had said to the Great Lady that could be deemed of lasting impact.

'No kiddin'?' said I, defeated. Kevin was scratching his head, deep in thought.

'How can you be so sure, Tom?' he asked finally.

Tom held up the hand that had shaken the hand of Ambassador Jean Kennedy-Smith. It was covered in blue paint – bright blue.

The whole debate on how England then and now sees the Irish is a heated one, even today. It not only includes Cromwell, but Oscar Wilde, and involves not only Thatcherism and British foreign policy in general, but the conservative English press.

On the cultural level of course, the Brits still think they have it; hence the shameless promotion in New York recently of the wares of the YBA (Young British Artists) by those humble creators of 'Maggie Thatcher', Messrs Saatchi & Saatchi. Predictably, negative public reaction by sensitive New Yorkers ensured that the stock went up. There's dough to be made, no matter how you look at it, if you just give people what they want. In Ireland, art promotion is in its infancy and neither Dublin Castle nor the Royal Hibernian Academy calls the tune these days . . . but the memory *does* linger. Art in general, however, would seem to be going rapidly down the steep slopes of 'buy-one-get-one-free'.

This whole debate of identity, diplomacy and English perception of the Irish, and vice versa, has been the subject matter of much Irish writing. There have even been a few television series like *To The Manor Born* and quite a few films on the topic. It is lucidly explained in Brian Friel's plays, notably *Translations*. And, to understand how radical these perceptions can get, you have only to leaf through the past issues of the tabloid press in its coverage of the *Troubles*.

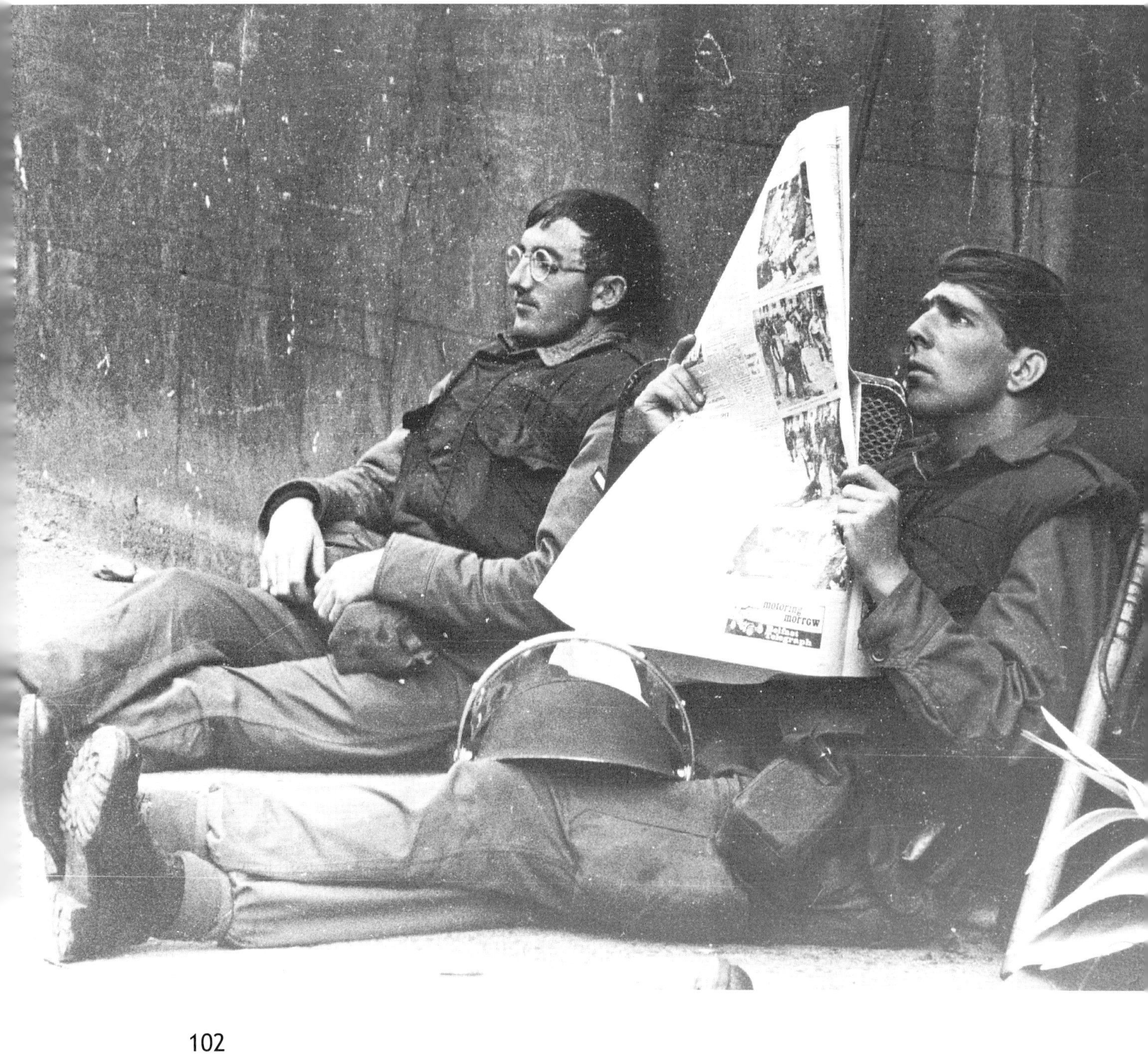

FREQUENTLY ASKED QUESTIONS

The social context in which we work is, at one and the same time, a geographical area and a psychic milieu that bristles with a heightened social and political consciousness. That is why we are asked reasonable and often difficult questions from people all over the world:

Why did you decide to form a group in the first place?

Tom had been working as a muralist since 1984 with the Outreach Programme of the Orchard Gallery. He was a pioneer in the field, seeing in art a valid and effective means of reconciliation. Tom's lifelong friend Kevin Hasson and, later, his brother William joined him in mural making in 1993 after Tom had left the Orchard Gallery. They completed their first mural together in October 1994. William had been a freelance artist who had exhibited his work throughout Ireland. For him, it was a natural transition to join the group. All three were profoundly disenchanted with the gallery circuit and how it was run. All three had grown up in the Bogside and had witnessed the worst of the *Troubles*. They agreed that it was necessary for the Bogsiders to take back their own story from the milling machine of the British media and to tell it in a way that both edified and instructed. One has to remember that the Bogside was a bleak wasteland in those days where the pallor of the 1972 atrocity hung over the place like a shroud. We felt that the biased reportage of our history, as it was relayed back to us by television, radio and newspapers, did not do justice to the abominable suffering endured by a people over such a long period. We felt this all the more keenly, as we ourselves were part of it.

What do you say to people who think your work is propagandist and inflammatory?

We are well aware of the difference between propaganda and art. It is mainly a difference of intent. We are chronicling history – no more, no less. To do otherwise would be an insult to our craft and a sin against our calling as creative witnesses. True, those who choose to see otherwise must take the integrity of our endeavour on trust. We like to think that the style of our approach makes our purpose clear. We do all we can to distance what we express and how we express it from the character of propaganda. Neither racism nor bigotry has any real place in art or any other form of communication. Also, we paint what *we* decide to paint. Freedom of expression is a fundamental democratic right for which men like Solzhenitsyn (to name but one artist out of many thousands who have been persecuted for claiming that right) paid dearly. Art, too, has its martyrs.

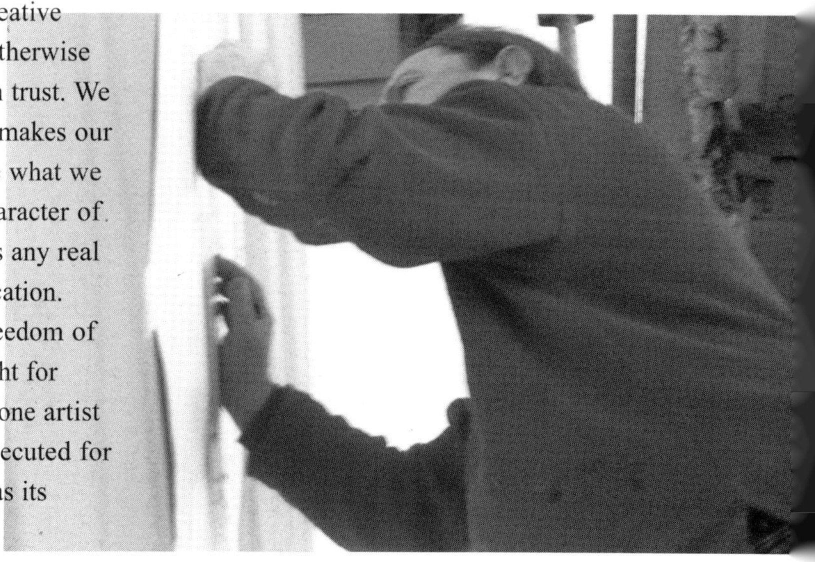

What obstacles have you encountered before, during and after you have begun work?

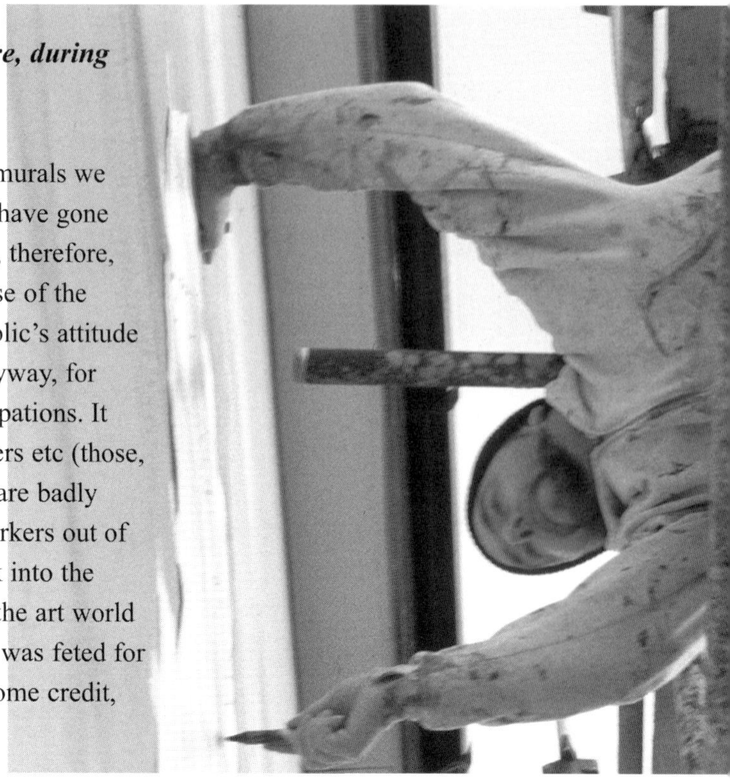

To get the money to paint each of the five murals we have completed so far for the Bogside, we have gone collecting from door to door. These murals, therefore, really do *belong* to the people in every sense of the word. We like that idea. Elsewhere, the public's attitude to artists is '. . . well, they would do it anyway, for nothing.' This is true of all vocational occupations. It explains why nurses, teachers, social workers etc (those, in fact, who help more than anybody else) are badly paid. Take the vocational and voluntary workers out of the picture and the world would crawl back into the jungle over night. Artists who 'make it' in the art world are feted in the same way as Ronnie Biggs was feted for escaping from prison. Biggs, to give him some credit, managed to escape back in.

How much local support do you receive?

The actual making of the murals has been greeted with support, even from the Protestant community, many of whom were as distressed about Bloody Sunday as were the Catholics of the Bogside. Local artists, who view themselves as hip with what is fashionable in modern art, do not consider our work 'contemporary', a fatuous argument from our point of view, insofar as our work *cannot* be other. What they mean is that we are not ordering the world to suit our purposes, which is what is in vogue in the art world at the moment. We are expected to kneel at the shrine of sensationalism and novelty as if we could inflict that nonsense on the people of the Bogside. Modern art so-called is this; you must order the world as if you were God, but you must do so for the hell of it (there being no valid reason left, presumably, for doing anything). God is capricious, chaotic and absurd, like the rest of His Creation, and closely resembles Jean Paul Sartre on a pub-crawl, and if thou wouldst walk in His likeness, thou too must be capricious chaotic, absurd etc. We have been approached by many capricious etc contemporary artists anxious to work with us so that they could hoist their neglected flags to our mast. In every case we have declined.

Do the murals serve any real purpose?

Whether you are prepared to admit it or not, these works are very popular and internationally known. They draw in large numbers of tourists, thereby keeping the tourist industry happy. Tourism in Northern Ireland employs some 34,500 people. That is a heavy investment for a place whose population numbers 1,700,000. Hotels in the city, taxi firms, restaurants, pubs, hostels and private entrepreneurs all have a stake in the popularity of our work. We state these as simple facts, since it was never our intention to create a tourist draw. It is simply a by-product of the successful fulfilment of the vision we conceived for the Bogside from as far back as 1993. Over and above the commercial benefits they may bring to Derry, the murals serve a much deeper and, to our mind, more crucial purpose. *They function as talking points for the local population.* They assist in the process of reflection on times and events lived through. In so doing, they assist in objectifying the past in a very positive sense and in this way they are curative – profoundly so. Had they been badly painted or been, as our critics demand, 'contemporary' with all the inevitable obscurantism that involves, they would have failed – and we with them. They also raise self-esteem, encourage artistic endeavour in the young, give pride to the old, and last, but not least, lend a definitive and unique character to that area of the city that is recognised the world over. The artists, for their part, are committed to completing the remaining five murals for the Bogside, which together will give a coherent and accurate chronicle of the key events of the *Troubles* that continue to shape our present.

Do you get paid?

No. All our work has been done on a voluntary basis and will continue so. The cost of an average mural, depending on scale, can cost anywhere between £600 and £1,000 bearing in mind we use only paint and brushes and not expensive spray equipment or high-power projectors. Were we in the business of showing off our skills at the expense of what we are trying to express, we might very well go down that road. All 'our' murals belong to the people and will remain in place according to their will.

How long does it take to do a mural?

Depends on the weather. We have tried painting under a tarpaulin roof, but our work suffered and so did we. A mural can take anything between two and six weeks.

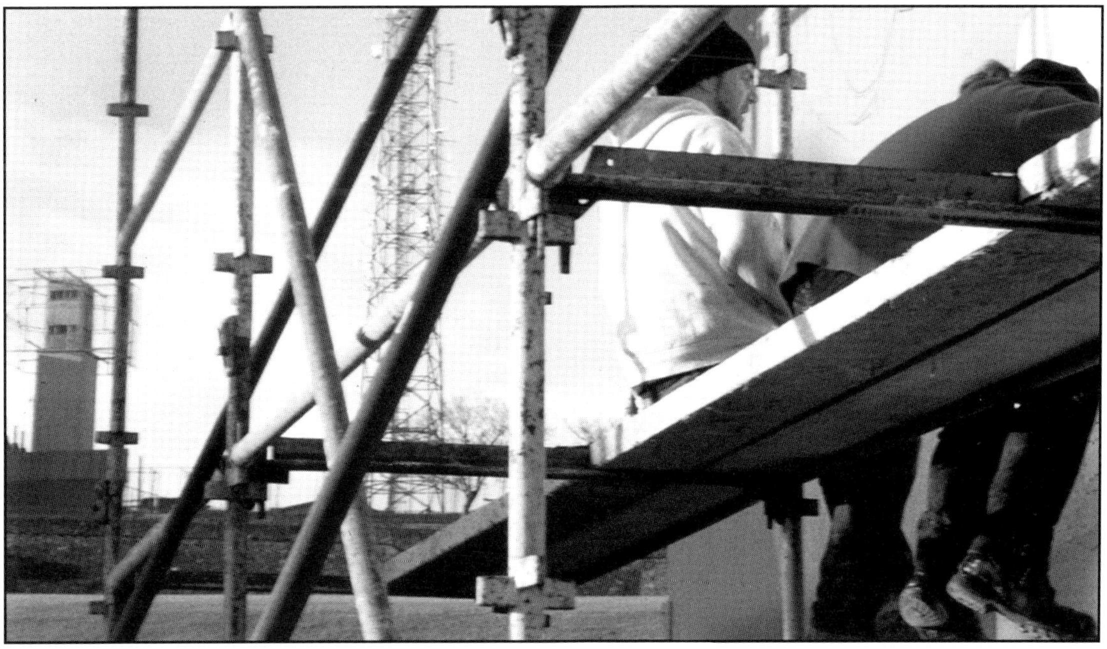

How can three different artists with three different world views manage to paint in harmony?

If there was a methodology to this, we would be happy to give it. But the fact is, we do not permit our varying views to jeopardise what we believe to be much more important, viz our friendship. The secret lies there. We are also aware of the idolatrous worship of ego that currently fuels the art world. We keep well away from it. 'Me-My-Work-and-I' is not a platform on which you can hope to express anything worthwhile. You serve the craft if you love it. If you don't love it, you should not be in it. And if you do love it, you will not abuse it, or, least of all, debase it by offering it up to the promulgation of racism, bigotry, false beliefs, demagogic worship, or any other form of the evils that afflict us.

Do you think art is over-rated?

Birds sing: men make art; it is a natural human activity; where would we be without it? Man does not live by bread alone, but where is the starving man who would not swap his Rembrandt for a loaf of bread? In other words, life itself and the respect for life is what is primarily important. Art these days is money. Is money overrated?

Do you think the work institutionalises the struggle?

No. That's like saying jazz has institutionalised the struggle for justice. What hasn't, in those terms? Jazz, as a music idiom, may be institutionalised, but not its content. Today's anti-establishment menace is tomorrow's money-spinner. And what do you mean by struggle? The class struggle? The establishment loves the rebel even before it gets rid of him. If, in his lifetime, Ché Guevara had received all the money made from his posters since his death, he would be sitting where Fidel is at the moment, only smoking bigger cigars. The day we give up creativity is the day we stop asking the arts councils to fund us and adopt the more reliable method of scratch cards.

Who have been your major influences?

Well, there have been a few. The Unemployment Bureau springs immediately to mind. Then, of course, there's the Oxfam Shop, the Salvation Army, St Vincent de Paul's, Help The Aged, Bill Gates, Al Gore, our beloved Goebbels, Jean Claude Van Damme, Salman Rushdie, Thatcher, the Hotspur Annual 1967, Les Patterson, Germaine Greer, and the very late Frank Sinatra.

THE PEACE PROCESS

There is a tide in the affairs of men,
Which, taken at the flood, leads on to fortune;
Omitted, all the voyage of their life
Is bound in shallows and in miseries.
On such a full sea are we now afloat;
And we must take the current when it serves,
Or lose our ventures.
(Brutus to Cassius in Julius Caesar: Act IV, Scene III)

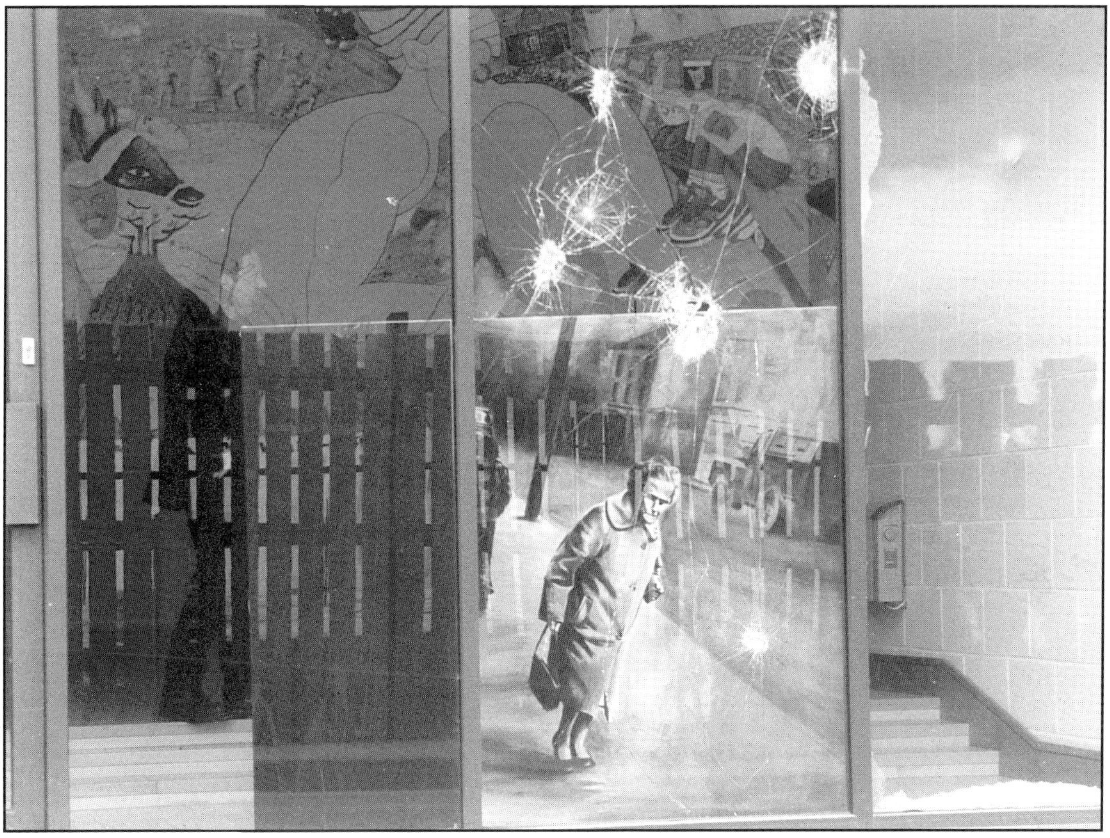

Peace in Northern Ireland is a peace-building process in which is utilised vital lessons learned from other areas of conflict in the world such as Guatemala, Yugoslavia, South Africa, Uganda, the Middle East etc. Strategies involving arbitration, facilitation, mediation and shuttle diplomacy are deployed to engage civil society with the machinery of government. These strategies involve complex guidelines: the unsung heroes from both camps, who implement them, often put themselves and their families at great risk. Funerals and parades, because they are possible flashpoints of trouble in the Six Counties of Northern Ireland, have often relied solely on one or more of these strategies for a peaceful resolution. The annual fiasco that is Drumcree is a testament to how difficult this can be. Politicians are left with the mess to clean up and to grapple once again with a restoration of faith in the peace process.

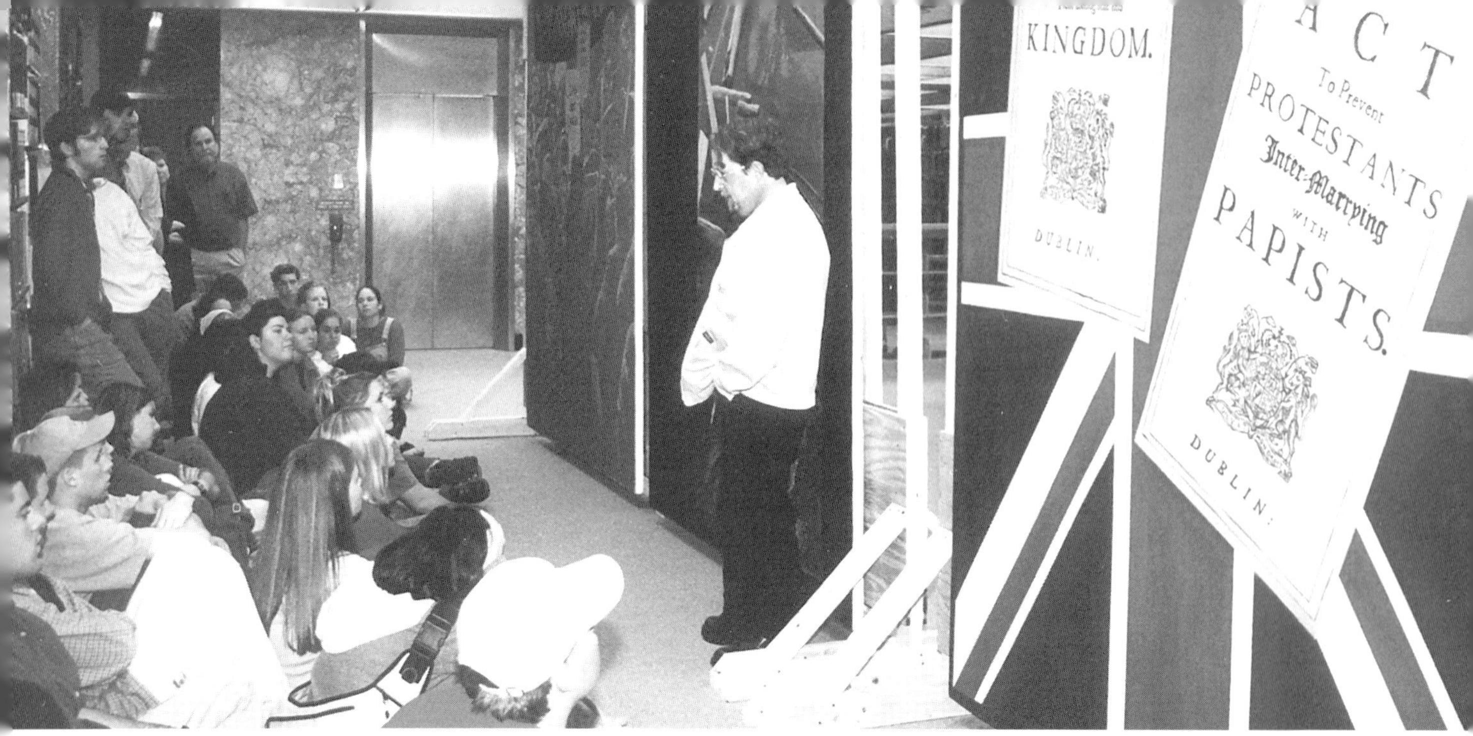

We have lived through most of the *Troubles* since 1969. Since then, some 3,800 people have been killed and many more thousands injured. Such statistics abound, but, in essence, make less sense than they promise to deliver. For a start, the total population of the Six Counties is roughly 1,700,000. Statistics are simply that . . . figures, and figures are far removed from the realities they describe. What make them important per se are the conclusions that can be drawn from them. The year of Bloody Sunday, for example, was the worst year for deaths with 479 people killed.

The cross-community workshops, talks and tours conducted by us have been part of this overall process to get two warring camps to understand each other. They are based on the premise that both sides have a story and both sides have a *right* to tell their story. As cultural expression is a democratic right, it is good and proper for those like ourselves who have a resilient sense of injustice, to ensure that all of us can avail of this right and be encouraged to implement it. Without it, there would be no art of any social relevance at all, anywhere. When we speak of art in this context, we mean art of all possible media, for visual expression is but one mode of creativity the human spirit has been gifted with. Cultural diversity is the reef from which creative expression is mined. Trouble inevitably begins

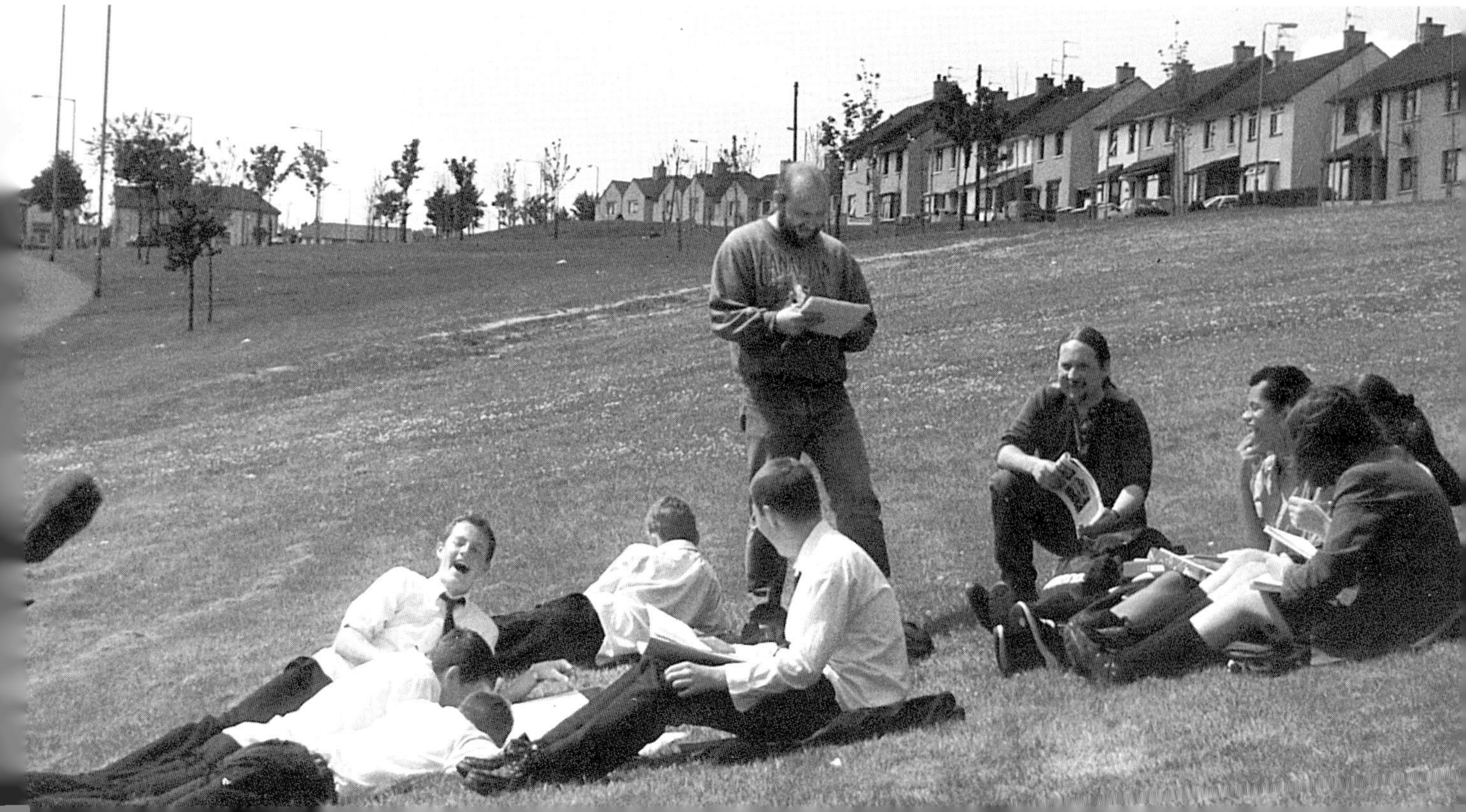

when difference takes on the crown of superiority in contempt of the fact that what joins us together is vastly more important than what keeps us apart. What is required is mutual understanding, not only of one's own conditioning, but also that of the other. The ending of the siege of Derry by the successful rescue mission of the ship called the *Mountjoy* in 1689 is as important to the Unionist as the 1916 rising is to the Nationalist.

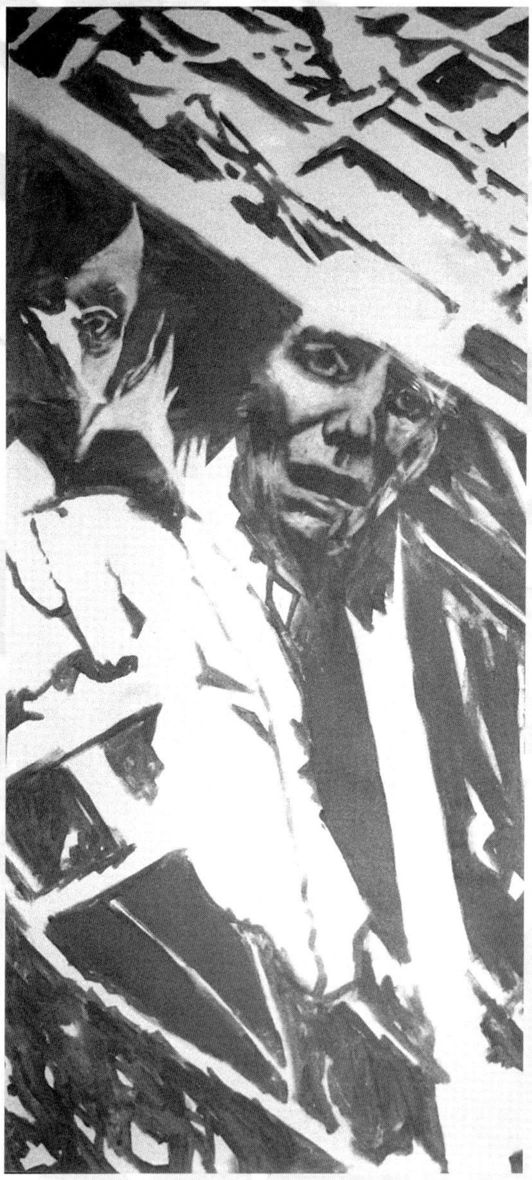

James Connolly considered it juvenile and offensive to attribute to an entire nation the crimes of a few. 'Throughout most of their history,' he wrote, 'the British people had no political existence whatever, that England was, politically and socially, terrorised by a numerically small governing class, greedy to enrich itself at the expense of defenceless men; that up to the present generation, the great majority of the English people were denied a deliberate voice in the government of their own country; that it is, therefore, manifestly unjust to charge the English people with the past crimes of their Government.'

The spiritually traumatised do not figure in the statistics – and there have been many of those. In fact, all of us, to some degree, have been affected by the *Troubles* and it will take a long time indeed before the normalcy that is enjoyed by most civilised cities returns to Derry. After the car bomb of 15 August 1998 in Omagh, when twenty-nine people were slaughtered and over 200 injured, it was clear to us, as if for the first time, that we were *all* victims.

BOGSIDE MURALS

at a glance
will arrest you
will stop you in your tracks

and search you
armed with stone and mortar

full force in the face

painting these walls must have been a fistfight

plastic bullet words

petrol bomb brushstrokes

paint stirred in the blood
with blood and smoke

there will never be a peace settlement between
mural billboard graffiti

no plaster decommissioning

when these walls start talking to you
it's time to rethink your life

Craig Czury

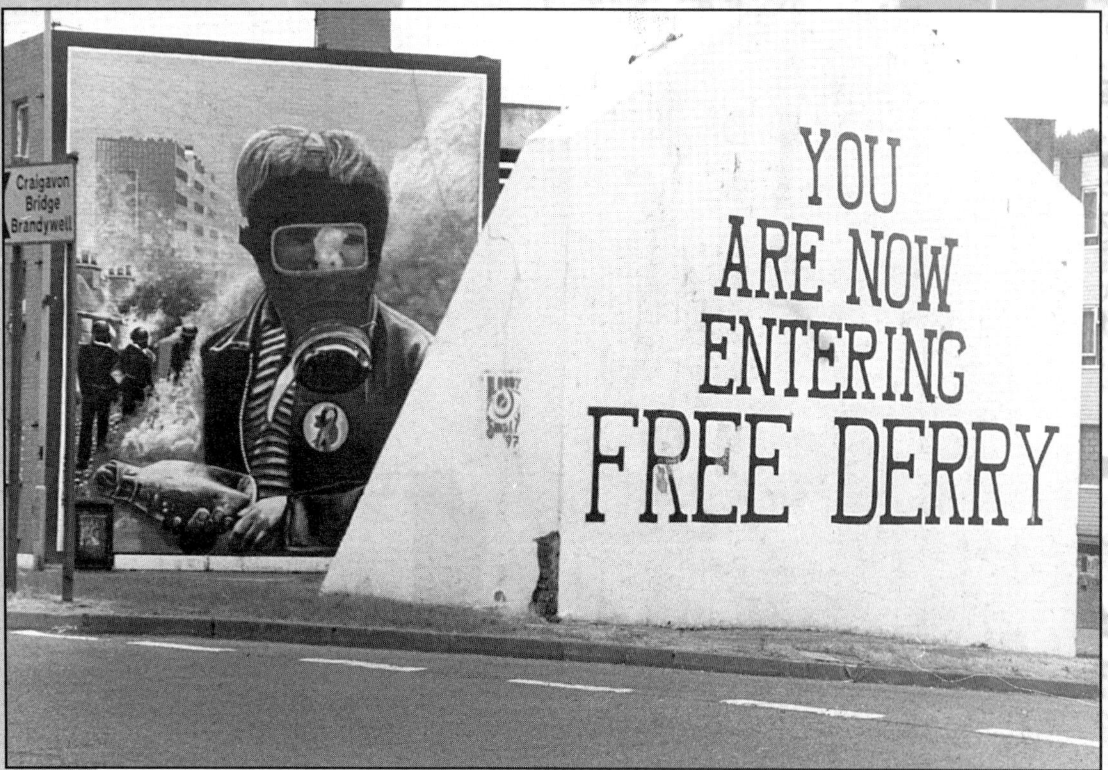

REQUIEM FOR MODERN ART

A touch of conceptual,
A sprinkling of video,
A pinch of Picasso,
Soupçons of minimal,
A dollop of Warhol,
A smidgen of reason,
Silkscreens of cows and women in season.
Colour the mood, vary the lines,
Think dialectic, remind them of time.
Paint politick. Blast a gun at the cotton!
Scrape your mark on the void unbegotten.
And, should I add my soul to the pot . . .
What say you, ten grand plus VAT, the lot?

Shadow the form, glaze it fuller:
Can there *be* an ugly colour?
Should I fence it with frame, border my pain?
Answer no questions, declare I'm insane?
What will they say? Whom will they pick?
Whose backsides will I have to lick?
Beneath the guff and beery patter
It's money, fame and sex that matter.
Who'll say what of this plagiarised rot?
Who will give bread for this, when I would not?

My grandma's garden has more art I know,
A child at play with chalk more honesty to show,
The weaver bird, the preying hawk, more care,
A lunatic cries more truth, more dare.
So, to hell with art. To hell with meaning!
There's nothing sacred in artists' dreaming.
Nothing at all in foxes scheming.
We want wealth, women, wine in the evening.

A touch of conceptual,
A sprinkling of video,
A pinch of Picasso,
A dollop of Warhol,

A smidgen of reason,
Silkscreens of cows and women in season.
Colour the mood, vary the lines.
Think dialectic. Remind them of time.
Paint politick. Blast a gun at the cotton!
Scrape your sad mark on the void unbegotten.
And, should I add my soul to the pot,
What say you . . . three grand plus VAT, the lot?

William Kelly

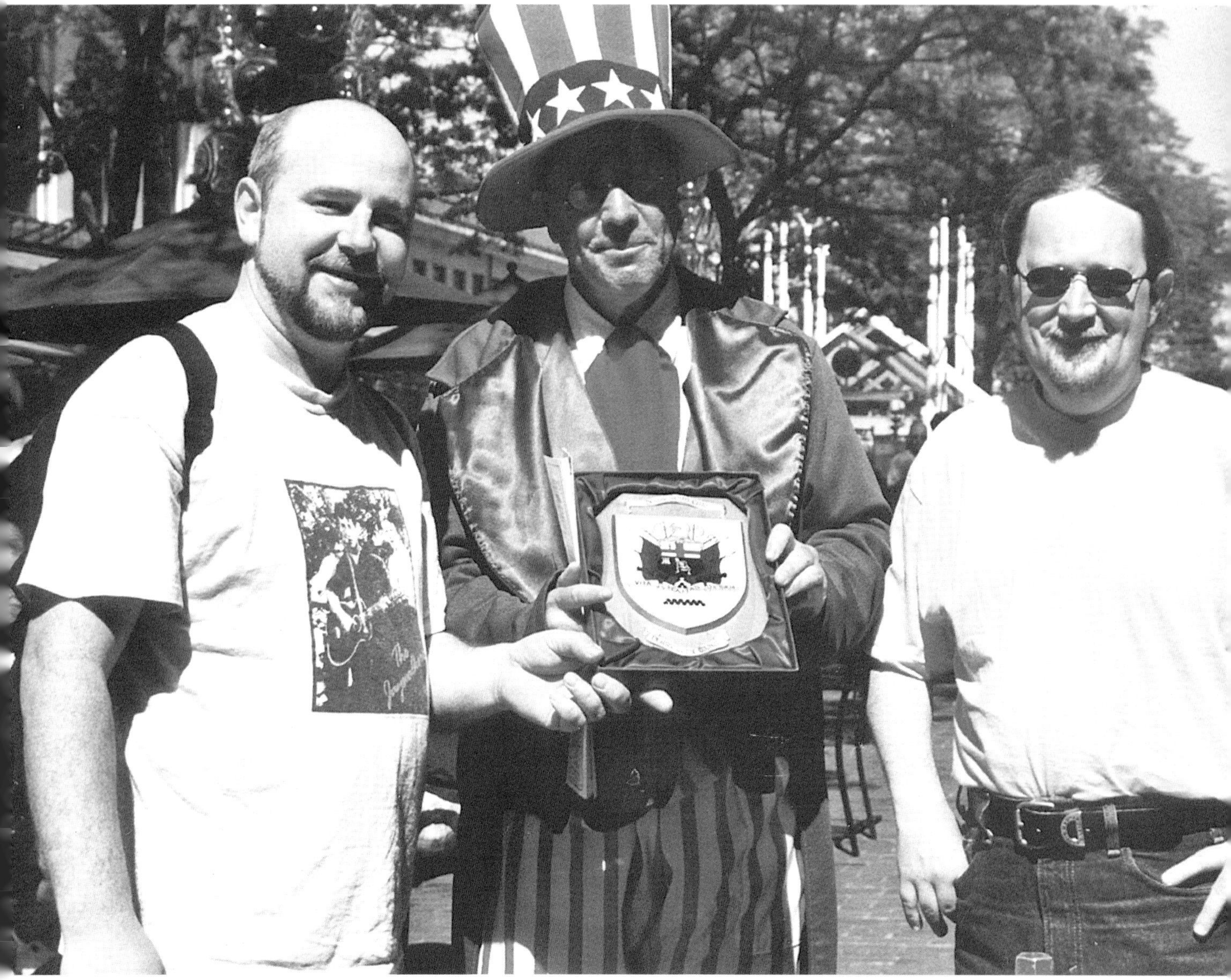

Searching for the President
(We all make mistakes!)